بسم الله الرحمن الرحيم

IMĀM ABŪ ḤANĪFA'S

Al-Fiqh al-Akbar

Explained

لا إله إلا الله محمد رسول الله

IMĀM ABŪ ḤANĪFA'S

Al-Fiqh al-Akbar Explained

by Abu 'l-Muntahā al-Maghnīsāwī
with Selections from ʿAlī al-Qārī's Commentary,
including Abū Ḥanīfa's *Kitāb al-Waṣiyya*

Compiled and Translated with an Introduction by
ABDUR-RAHMAN IBN YUSUF MANGERA

White Thread
PRESS

First Edition November 2007
Reprint January 2014, September 2016, February 2020, January 2021

ISBN 978-1-933764-03-0

Published by
White Thread Press
WT Press Limited
London, UK
www.whitethreadpress.com

Distributed in the UK by
Azhar Academy Ltd. London
www.azharacademy.com

Library of Congress Cataloging-in-Publication Data

Maghnīsāwī, Aḥmad ibn Muḥammad, d. 1591 or 2.
Imām Abū Ḥanīfa's *al-Fiqh al-akbar explained* / by Abū al-Muntahā al-Maghnīsāwī; with selections from ʿAlī al-Qārī's Commentary, including Abū Ḥanīfa's *Kitāb al-Waṣiyya;* compiled and translated with introduction by Abdur-Rahman ibn Yusuf.
p. cm.
Includes bibliographical references and index.
ISBN-13: 978-1-933764-03-0 (hardcover: alk. paper)
1. Abū Ḥanīfah, d. 767 or 8. *Fiqh al-akbar.* 2. Islamic law–Early works to 1800. 3. Islam–Doctrines–Early works to 1800. 4. Hanafites–Early works to 1800. I. Abū Ḥanīfah, d. 767 or 8. *Fiqh al-akbar.* English. II. Abū Ḥanīfah, d. 767 or 8. *Waṣīyah.* English. III. Qārī al-Harawī, ʿAlī ibn Sulṭān Muḥammad, d. 1605 or 6. *Minaḥ al-rawḍ al-azhar fi sharḥ al-Fiqh al-akbar.* English. Selections. IV. Ibn Yusuf, Abdur-Rahman, 1974- V. Title.
KBP300.A282A3436 2007
340.5>9–dc22

2007021094

British Library Cataloguing in Publication Data. A catalogue record for this book is also available from the British Library.

♾ Printed and bound in Turkey on acid-free paper. The paper used in this book meets the minimum requirement of ANSI/NISO Z39.48-1992 (R 1997) (Permanence of Paper). The binding material has been chosen for strength and durability.

Book design and typography by ARM

For

Shaykh Adib Kallas

Shaykh Naushad Ahmad

Shaykh Tahir Wadi

TRANSLITERATION KEY

ء (أ إ)	' (A slight catch in the breath. It is also used to indicate where the *hamza* has been dropped from the beginning of a word.)
ا	a, ā
ب	b
ت	t
ث	th (Should be pronounced as the *th* in *thin* or *thirst.*)
ج	j
ح	ḥ (Tensely breathed *h* sound.)
خ	kh (Pronounced like the *ch* in Scottish *loch* with the mouth hollowed to produce a full sound.)
د	d
ذ	dh (Should be pronounced as the *th* in *this* or *that.*)
ر	r
ز	z
س	s
ش	sh
ص	ṣ (A heavy *s* pronounced far back in the mouth with the mouth hollowed to produce a full sound.)
ض	ḍ (A heavy *d/dh* pronounced far back in the mouth with the mouth hollowed to produce a full sound.)
ط	ṭ (A heavy *t* pronounced far back in the mouth with the mouth hollowed to produce a full sound.)
ظ	ẓ (A heavy *dh* pronounced far back in the mouth with the mouth hollowed to produce a full sound.)
ع	ʿ, ʿa, ʿi, ʿu (Pronounced from the throat.)
غ	gh (Pronounced like a throaty French *r* with the mouth hollowed to produce a full sound.)
ف	f
ق	q (A guttural *q* sound with the mouth hollowed to produce a full sound.)
ك	k
ل	l
م	m
ن	n
و	w, ū, u.
ه	h
ي	y, ī, i

ﷺ	*Ṣalla 'Llāhu ʿalayhi wa sallam*—used following the mention of the Messenger Muḥammad, translated as, "May Allāh bless him and give him peace."
عليه السلام	*ʿAlayhi 'l-sallam*—used following the mention of a prophet or messenger of Allāh, translated as, "May the peace of Allāh be upon him."
رضي الله عنه	*Raḍiya 'Llāhu ʿanhu*—used following the mention of a Companion of the Messenger ﷺ, translated as, "May Allāh be pleased with him."
رضي الله عنهم	*Raḍiya 'Llāhu ʿanhum*—used following the mention of more than one Companion of the Messenger (and also after a female Companion in this work for lack of an appropriate glyph), translated as, "May Allāh be pleased with them."

CONTENTS

Translator's Introduction

In the name of Allāh, Most Gracious, Most Merciful.

All praise is to Allāh, who is one in His essence, unique in His characteristics, possessor of all attributes of perfection, and exalted above all attributes of imperfection. All praise is to Allāh, the One and Only, the Eternal and Absolute, who begets not nor is begotten, who is as He has always been, and there is none like unto Him.

Blessings and salutations on the best of Allāh's creation, the most sublime in character, our Master Muḥammad, the seal of those who have passed and the guide to the straight path—and upon his pure and chaste family, and his Companions, and those who have followed the Ahl al-Sunna wa 'l-Jamāʿa (The People of Sunna and the Community) with excellence until the Day of Judgment.

The treatise *Al-Fiqh al-Akbar* (The Greater Knowledge) has for centuries been accepted as a reliable work on Islamic beliefs. As one of the earliest works written on the subject and as one of the surviving works of the Great Imām of jurisprudence and theology, Abū Ḥanīfa Nuʿmān ibn Thābit al-Kūfī (d. 150/767),[1] the text has been widely studied around the Muslim world for centuries. A number of commentaries have been written on this concise work by renowned scholars of Islam such as Mullā ʿAlī al-Qārī and Abu 'l-Muntahā al-Maghnīsāwī, and it is quoted and referred to frequently in the works of scholars. One can quickly grasp the breadth of Imām Abū Ḥanīfa's understanding of Islamic beliefs from a statement made by the esteemed Egyptian jurist and theologian, Imām Abū Jaʿfar al-Ṭaḥāwī,[2] at the beginning

1 When two dates are mentioned in this way, the first represents the Hijrī date and the second the Gregorian.

2 Imām Aḥmad ibn Muḥammad ibn Salāma ibn Salama ibn ʿAbd al-Malik, Abū Jaʿfar al-Azdī al-Miṣrī al-Ṭaḥāwī al-Ḥanafī. He initially studied Shāfiʿī law under his uncle Muzanī, who was a

of his universally recognized treatise, *Al-ʿAqīda:*[3] "This is an exposition of the beliefs of the Ahl al-Sunna wa 'l-Jamāʿa according to the jurists of the Muslim umma (community), Abū Ḥanīfa, Abū Yūsuf,[4] and Muḥammad (may Allāh have mercy on them)."

The suitability of this work's title, *Al-Fiqh al-Akbar,* is noteworthy. *Fiqh* means "understanding," "knowledge," or "intelligence." The knowledge and understanding of a particular subject is also called *fiqh,* as in *fiqh al-lugha,* "the science of language." The term *fiqh* by itself is commonly used by scholars of Islam to refer to "jurisprudence" or "the science of the law." The title of this text—*Al-Fiqh al-Akbar,* roughly translated as "The Greater Intelligence, Understanding, or Insight"—points to the noble subjects addressed in this book, which are divine oneness (*tawḥīd*) in particular and Islamic doctrine (*ʿaqīda*) in general. Because of the sublime aim of *ʿaqīda* over all other subjects—to gain insight about the Creator of the universe and to discover what one owes to Allāh and what one receives from Him—it seems most appropriate to translate the title of this book as "The Greater Science" or "The Greater Knowledge," which is very likely the reason for the author's choice of title.

ISLAMIC BELIEFS

ʿIlm al-tawḥīd, the science of divine oneness, is one of the most important and noble sciences. Not only does it refine one's understanding of the Creator, His messengers, and His communication with creation, but it also enables one to gain insight into the reality and purpose of this world and into the eschatological matters of the Hereafter. These are in fact the three major themes of any work on Islamic beliefs: (1) the divine being and attributes (*ilāhiyyāt*), (2) the functions of prophethood (*nubuwwāt*), and (3) eschatology and that which

student of Imām Shāfiʿī. He then took up the Ḥanafī school and became a great Ḥanafī scholar. Some of his most important works are *Sharḥ Maʿāni 'l-Āthār, Sharḥ Mushkil al-Āthār,* and his famous treatise on *ʿaqīda.* He passed away in 321/933. See *Siyar Aʿlām al-Nubalāʾ* 15:17.

3 The actual name of this work is *Bayān al-Sunna wa 'l-Jamāʿa* (Exposition of the Beliefs of the Sunna and the Community).

4 Yaʿqūb ibn Ibrāhīm Abū Yūsuf al-Anṣārī of Kūfa, the imām, *mujtahid,* judge of judges, and ḥadīth master. A disciple of Abū Ḥanīfa, he remained in his company for seventeen years and became a jurist under his tutelage. He was one of the most noble and knowledgeable students of the Imām and passed away in 182/798.

comes after death (*mughayyabāt*). In the face of the present-day onslaught of varied ideologies and beliefs, and the promotion of unfettered freedom of thought, it is essential for all Muslims, the youth in particular, to have a firm grasp on their beliefs. The basic understanding one absorbs by being brought up in a Muslim home is scarcely adequate. There is ample textual proof to the necessity of learning Islamic doctrine. In the Qur'ān it states, "Know, therefore, that there is no god but Allāh" (47:19), and the Messenger of Allāh ﷺ said, "Say, 'I believe in Allāh,' and thereafter stand firm" (*Muslim*). Studying philosophy without prior grounding in Islamic theology is disconcerting and can make one question his or her faith. Those with exposure to confused renditions of metaphysics and other recondite disciplines sometimes find it very difficult to accept the Islamic beliefs of which they were hitherto unaware. They are compelled, then, to assess these beliefs in light of the ideas that they have subconsciously or knowingly adopted. For some, this path leads to immense intellectual and emotional confusion and trauma which takes years to overcome. Others are engulfed by their predicament and become staunch proponents of "reform" and "progressivism" in the religion. Certain extreme cases—Allāh forbid—end in outright apostasy. Only sincere believers who are blessed by Allāh with the light of true knowledge and recourse to Him are saved.

Another benefit of studying one's *ʿaqīda,* beyond this very basic level, is attaining a real and true appreciation of one's beliefs and a deeper understanding of them, both of which lead to the elimination of doubts. Further study also curtails unnecessary and unconstructive debates regarding the nature of divinity. Where is Allāh? How Powerful is He and how much control does He have? Does Allāh evolve? What is Allāh and what is He not? What constitutes true belief? Are deeds important or is just calling oneself a Muslim sufficient for one's salvation? Are prophets capable of sin? What is our perspective on the Companions? Are there other creations of Allāh beyond what we can see? What comes after death? Is there such a thing as eternity? Questions like these can easily be answered by studying more advanced books on Islamic doctrine, such as *Al-Fiqh al-Akbar* or *ʿAqīda Ṭaḥāwiyya,* under the tutelage of reliable scholars. However, the true benefit of this learning lies beyond any intellectual satisfaction that one gains in this world; there is a higher purpose. The scholars, while explaining the first rules (*mabādiʾ*) of this science, state that its objective is to attain, by the mercy and grace of Allāh, success in the Hereafter, the good pleasure of the All-merciful, and entry into the gardens of eternal bliss.

Brief Sketch of the Origins of Islamic Theology

The earlier generations had little need for a codified form of theology. Most of the time, Sūrat al-Ikhlāṣ[5] would suffice. Moreover, during the lifetime of Allāh's Messenger ﷺ, in particular, whenever a question of faith or belief arose, he was there to answer it. There was no need then to formally systematize *ʿaqīda,* just as there was no need to do so for *fiqh, tafsīr,* and other religious sciences. Nearly the same was the condition of the era of the Companions and that of the Followers, the blessed period known as that of the pious predecessors (*salaf ṣāliḥīn*).[6] Nevertheless, although Islamic belief and practice were for the most part unshakable during this period, faint tremors ominously signaled the quake that would soon rumble, then rock, the umma. Seeing the danger posed to sacred Islamic knowledge by deviant individuals, ambitious politicians, and an increasingly troubled populace, scholars from each successive generation, in response to the exigencies of their respective times, compiled and systematized Islamic norms, ideas, and beliefs, and meticulously crafted the disciplines we recognize today.

The origin of rigorous theological study can be traced back to as early as the caliphate of ʿUthmān ﷺ. During his time, various alien ideas took root, with varying durability, in Muslim society and found an eager audience. During the ʿAbbāsid period, starting around the middle of the second century AH, the introduction of Hellenistic philosophy into Muslim lands led to heated discord. The newly formed Muʿtazila managed to attain great favor with the ruling class, winning several caliphs over to their beliefs. They used their powerful political purchase to question and reinterpret many fundamentals of Islam and force conformity to their beliefs, or at least cow any would-be dissenters into silence. Those who had the courage to object were mercilessly persecuted, most notably Imām Aḥmad ibn Ḥanbal[7] (may Allāh have mercy

5 Qur'ān 112:1–4.

6 *Salaf* or *salaf ṣāliḥīn* can be translated as "righteous predecessors" or "righteous ancestors." In Islamic terminology, it generally refers to the first three generations of Muslims: the Companions (*ṣaḥāba*), the Followers (*tābiʿīn*), and Followers of the Followers (*atbāʿ al-tābiʿīn*) regarding whom the Messenger of Allāh ﷺ said, "The people of my generation are the best, then those who follow them, and then those who follow them" (*Bukhārī*). Some have said that the appellation refers to all the generations up to the fifth century AH. The *khalaf* (successors) are then those who came after these three generations, or it refers in some cases to those who came after 500 AH (see Bājūrī, *Tuḥfat al-Murīd ʿalā Jawharat al-Tawḥīd* 55).

7 Abū ʿAbdillāh Aḥmad ibn Muḥammad ibn Ḥanbal ibn Hilāl ibn Asad al-Dhuhlī al-Shaybānī al-Marwazī (then al-Baghdādī) was born in 164/780. About him, Dhahabī says, "The true shaykh

on him), who was cruelly put to the lash for refusing to accept false doctrines concerning the Qur'ān. It was out of this turbulent setting that the orthodox theological schools of Abu 'l-Ḥasan al-Ashʿarī and Abū Manṣūr al-Māturīdī emerged.

Many of the differences one finds in Islamic doctrine and scholastic theology (*kalām*) literature are primarily between the Ashʿarīs and Māturīdīs and the Muʿtazila and, on a lesser scale, the Khawārij, Jabriyya, Murji'a, and a few other groups. The differences that some point to between the Ashʿarīs and the Māturīdīs are not theologically significant and have clear historical reasons, which we shall touch on below. It is more appropriate to view them as two approaches to the same theology and treat them as one. Indeed, the scholars do just that, referring to both groups collectively as Ashʿarīs when contrasting them with other sects. Both groups have always been mutually tolerant and never labelled the other innovative or heretical. It is only when their doctrine is set against the Muʿtazilī and other doctrines that we see major theological divergence. An exhaustive study of each of these groups, and of others, and the effects their interplay had on Muslim government and society has been charted in the venerable tomes of history and theology. It is far beyond our purpose here to give even a synopsis of these works, but to gain a proper context in which to place *Al-Fiqh al-Akbar,* it is fitting to give a brief overview of the major theological groups whose origins date back to the author Imām Abū Ḥanīfa's time.

The Ashʿarīs

The eponymous founder of the Ashʿarī school was the "Imām of the Theologians," ʿAlī ibn Ismāʿīl ibn Abī Bishr al-Ashʿarī al-Yamānī al-Baṣrī (*Siyar Aʿlām al-Nubalā'* 15:88). A descendant of the famous Companion Abū Mūsā al-Ashʿarī, he was born in Baṣra in the year 260/873 and died in 324/935.

Imām Ashʿarī was born at a time when several bickering sects were busying themselves with leveling charges of heresy and unbelief at other Muslims. Of these, the Muʿtazila emerged as the strongest by far and earned the most adherents, especially once they started to garner support from the caliphate.

---

of Islam and leader of the Muslims in his time, the ḥadīth master and proof of the religion." He had memorized one million ḥadīths by heart, was a great theologian, and was the founder of the Ḥanbalī school of *fiqh*. He died in 241/855 in Baghdad (see Dhahabī, *Tadhkirat al-Ḥuffāẓ* 2:431; *Siyar Aʿlām al-Nubalā'* 11:187).

Abu 'l-Ḥasan al-Ashʿarī himself began as a Muʿtazilī. Growing up as the step-son and student of the famous Muʿtazilī teacher Abū ʿAlī al-Jubbā'ī (d. 303/915), he became firmly grounded in their ideology and proficient in their methods of argumentation. He was a skilled debater to boot. All these qualities made him the ideal candidate to be the Muʿtazilīs' star scholar, a post he held for many years. However, at the age of forty, he shocked all by severing himself from them and publicly renounced their beliefs. He then set out to defend the true beliefs of the Ahl al-Sunna wa 'l-Jamāʿa held by the great jurists and ḥadīth scholars of the time.

Much has been related regarding Imām Ashʿarī's conversion to orthodoxy. The great ḥadīth master and historian Ibn ʿAsākir relates from Ismāʿīl ibn Abī Muḥammad ibn Isḥāq al-Ashʿarī (may Allāh have mercy on him):

> Ashʿarī was our shaykh and imām, the one in whom we placed our reliance. He persisted on the ideology of the Muʿtazila for forty years. Then he isolated himself in his house for fifteen days. When he came out, he went to the Grand Masjid, ascended the pulpit, and said, "O people, I retreated from you for this period because, in my study of the evidences [of certain theological matters], they seemed to me to be on par with each other, and the truth over the false or the false over the truth was not discernible to me. I thus sought guidance from Allāh, Most Blessed, Most High, and He guided me to the beliefs that I have recorded in this book of mine. I am now divested of all that I believed, just as I am divested of this garment of mine." He took off the garment he was wearing and cast it aside, and he passed the books on to the people. Among them were *Al-Lumaʿ* (The Sparks). He then said, "Henceforth, I shall endeavor to refute the doctrines of the Muʿtazila and lay bare their mistakes and weaknesses."[8] When the scholars of ḥadīth and jurisprudence read these books, they adopted their contents and embraced them wholeheartedly, so much that their school of thought came to be attributed to him.

Another incident, related by Qārī, Taftāzānī, and others, may have also contributed to his conversion. They relate that Shaykh Abu 'l-Ḥasan al-Ashʿarī once asked his teacher Abū ʿAlī al-Jubbā'ī, "What is your opinion regarding three brothers, one of whom dies obedient, another disobedient,

---

8 See *Tabyīn Kadhib al-Muftarī fī mā Nusiba ila 'l-Imām Abi 'l-Ḥasan al-Ashʿarī* (Showing the Untruth of the Liars, Concerning What Has Been Ascribed to Imām Abu 'l-Ḥasan al-Ashʿarī).

and the third as a child?" He replied, "The first will be rewarded, the second punished with Hellfire, and the third will neither be punished nor rewarded." Ashʿarī asked, "If the third one says, 'O Lord, why did you give me death at a young age and not leave me to grow up so I could be obedient to you and thus enter Paradise?'" Jubbā'ī replied that Allāh would say, "I knew that if you had grown up you would have disobeyed and thus entered the Hellfire, so it was better for you to have died young." So Ashʿarī said, "If the second one says, 'My Lord, why did you not let me [too] die young so I would not have disobeyed and entered Hellfire?' What will the Lord say then?" Jubbā'ī was confounded.[9] Ashʿarī abandoned the Muʿtazila doctrine and took to refuting it and establishing what had been transmitted from the Sunna and confirmed by the *jamāʿa,* or the community, of Companions and pious predecessors. Therefore, he and his followers were called Ahl al-Sunna wa 'l-Jamāʿa or "the People of the Sunna and the Community"[10] (*Minaḥ al-Rawḍ al-Azhar* 220, *Sharḥ al-ʿAqā'id al-Nasafiyya* 55).

The Māturīdīs

Muḥammad ibn Muḥammad ibn Maḥmūd, Abū Manṣūr al-Māturīdī, the

9 The opinion of Jubbā'ī and the Muʿtazila essentially exaggerates the justice of Allāh. They argue that reason dictates the righteous and wicked to Allāh and obligates Him to declare it as such; moreover, they also require that Allāh always act in the best interests of people or in a manner that is to their greatest advantage. In view of this, Jubbā'ī, when asked, was unable to resolve the problem presented by Ashʿarī and this led to Ashʿarī leaving the Muʿtazila sect (see *Tuḥfat al-Murīd* 66).

10 Najm al-Ghazzī (d. 1061/1650) says in *Ḥusn al-Tanabbuh fi 'l-Tashabbuh,* "The way of the Ahl al-Sunna wa 'l-Jamāʿa is what the Prophet of Allāh ﷺ and his noble Companions followed. And it is that which is followed by the vast majority of the Muslims throughout all ages. They are "the Group," which will emerge victorious in [upholding] the truth; in effect, they represent the saved sect from among the seventy-three groups. It is reported by the authors of the *Sunans* (and Tirmidhī declares it authentic [*ṣaḥīḥ*]) from Abū Hurayra ؓ that the Messenger of Allāh ﷺ said, "The Jews dispersed into seventy-one groups, and the Christians into seventy-two groups, and my umma will divide into seventy-three groups." This ḥadīth has been transmitted through numerous other chains, among which is the report narrated by ʿAbdullāh ibn ʿAmr in which he ﷺ said, "All of them will be in the Fire except for one group." They asked, "Who are they, O Messenger of Allāh?" He replied, "That which I and my Companions follow" (Tirmidhī judges this acceptable [*ḥasan*]). Among them is also the report of Muʿāwiya ؓ in which the Messenger ﷺ said, "Seventy-two will be in the Fire and one will be in Paradise and that is 'the Group'" (*Abū Dāwūd* and others). A similar tradition is the report of Ibn ʿAbbās ؓ in which he ﷺ said, "All of them will be in the Fire except for one." So it was asked, "What is the one?" He ﷺ held his hand and said, "The Group: so hold fast to the rope of Allāh all together and do not become disunited" (*Ibn Māja* et al.). (Maydānī, *Sharḥ al-ʿAqīda al-Ṭaḥāwiyya* 44).

"Imām of the Theologians," was the eponymous founder of the other major Sunnī school of theology. He was born in Māturīd, a district of Samarqand, in present-day Uzbekistan.[11] Aside from being one of the imāms of the fundamentals of *dīn,* he was a prominent jurist of the Ḥanafī school, having studied under Nuṣayr ibn Yaḥyā al-Balkhī, and was the author of numerous works in *fiqh, uṣūl, tafsīr,* and *kalām* (*Al-Fawā'id al-Bahiyya* 195).[12] He passed away in 333/944. Abū Zahra (d. 1396/1976) says in his *Al-Madhāhib al-Islāmiyya,*

> Abū Manṣūr al-Māturīdī and Abu 'l-Ḥasan al-Ashʿarī were contemporaries, and both were striving in the same cause. The difference was that Imām Ashʿarī was geographically closer to the camps of the opponent [the Muʿtazila]. Baṣra had been the birthplace of the Muʿtazilī ideology and the place from where it grew and spread, and it was also one of the main fronts in the ideological war between the Muʿtazila and the scholars of ḥadīth and jurisprudence (*fiqh*). Though Abū Manṣūr al-Māturīdī was far from this battlefield, its echoes had reached the lands where he lived, and hence, there were Muʿtazila in Transoxiana mimicking the Muʿtazila of Iraq. It was Māturīdī who stood up to combat them."[13]

What we learn from the biographies of the two Imāms is that their goal was one: to defend the orthodox beliefs of the Ahl al-Sunna wa 'l-Jamāʿa against the onslaught of innovators, especially the Muʿtazila. Though their objectives were the same, certain elements of their methodologies inevitably diverged,

---

11 This area was previously known as Transoxiana or "the Land beyond the River" (*Mā Warā' al-Nahr*), that is, beyond the Oxus River (the Greek name for the Amu Darya); essentially, it refers to areas in Central Asia corresponding with modern-day Uzbekistan, Tajikistan, and southwest Kazakhstan.

12 Among his works are *Kitāb Ta'wīlāt al-Qur'ān* (Book on the Interpretations of the Qur'ān), *Kitāb al-Maqālāt, Kitāb al-Tawḥīd, Ma'ākhidh al-Sharā'iʿ,* and *Kitāb al-Jadal* in *uṣūl al-fiqh, Bayān Wahm al-Muʿtazila* (Exposition of the Errors of the Muʿtazila), *Radd al-Uṣūl al-Khamsa,* a refutation of Abū Muḥammad al-Bāhilī's exposition of the Five Principles of the Muʿtazila, *Radd al-Imāma,* a refutation of the Rāfiḍī concept of *imāma, Al-Radd ʿalā Uṣūl al-Qarāmiṭa,* and *Radd Tahdhīb al-Jadal, Radd Waʿīd al-Fussāq,* and *Kitāb Radd Awa'il al-Adilla,* all three in the refutation of Kaʿbī (see Kawtharī's introduction to Bayāḍī's *Ishārat al-Marām* 7). His other teachers include Abū Naṣr Aḥmad ibn ʿAbbās al-ʿIyāḍī and Abū Bakr Aḥmad ibn Isḥāq ibn Ṣāliḥ al-Jūzajānī.

13 Shaykh Murtaḍā al-Zabīdī says, "From among our scholars, Ibn al-Bayāḍī reported that [we cannot assume that] Māturīdī was a follower of Ashʿarī just because Ashʿarī is thought to be the first to expound on the doctrine of the Ahl al-Sunna wa 'l-Jamāʿa. Māturīdī was expounding the doctrine of [the Ahl al-Sunna from] Abū Ḥanīfa and his companions well before Ashʿarī expounded that of the Ahl al-Sunna. Therefore, as mentioned in *Al-Tabṣira al-Nasafiyya,* there was not a generation devoid of a group upholding the *dīn* [from the time of the Imām to Māturīdī and thereafter] (*Itḥāf al-Sāda al-Muttaqīn* 2:5).

commensurate with the unique circumstances of each Imām's locality. Some scholars sum up their differences as follows: Ashʿarī did not give much preference to reason in the presence of sacred texts,[14] even if they were transmitted by lone narrators (*khabar āḥād*) rather than through uninterrupted transmission (*tawātur*),[15] while Māturīdī would attempt to reconcile between reason and the transmitted text (*manqūl*), as long as it was possible to do so without too much difficulty or without sacrificing fairness. This slight difference in methodology did not produce any substantial discrepancy in their theological precepts, but indeed served only to make the existing theological discourse all the richer. The differences were on ancillary matters that had no bearing on agreed-upon fundamentals, and most could be reduced to mere differences in phraseology. These two schools are thus both classified as orthodox schools of Islamic theology and of the Ahl al-Sunna wa 'l-Jamāʿa, with the Māturīdīs coming under the general heading of "Ashʿarīs" when contrasted with the Muʿtazila, Khawārij, and other innovators.[16]

It should be interesting to note that most of the followers of the Ḥanafī school of jurisprudence have historically been followers of the Māturīdī school of theology. However, one third of them, along with three-quarters of the Shāfiʿīs, all of the Mālikīs, and some Ḥanbalīs, adhere to the Ashʿarī school. A few Ḥanafīs, Ḥanbalīs, and Shāfiʿīs subscribed to the Muʿtazilī school, and aside from another group of Ḥanbalīs, who remained on the school of the predecessors (*salaf*) in the practice of *tafwīḍ* (consigning the knowledge of the details of ambiguous [*mutashābihāt*] sacred texts to Allāh),

14 This does not mean that Ashʿarī shared the position of some of the ḥadīth scholars of his time who were completely opposed to the use of reason in Islamic doctrine and restricted themselves to the texts of the Qur'ān, Sunna, and to consensus (*ijmāʿ*) (see *Itḥāf al-Sāda al-Muttaqīn* 2:6); this group actually opposed him for employing certain rational proofs in his debates with the sectarians. In general, Ashʿarī was less inclined than Māturīdī to reconcile between reason and transmitted texts as can be surmised from the Ashʿarī opinions on the status of people to whom the message of Allāh has not reached, and the issue of reason being able to determine good and evil (see "Understanding Good and Evil Through Reason" and note 196 below). Kawtharī considers the Māturīdīs to be a middle path between the Muʿtazila and the Ashʿarīs (*Muqaddimāt al-Imām al-Kawtharī* 51).

15 Narrations transmitted by such a large number of people in each generation that it is impossible for them to have conspired to tell a lie. This level of transmission renders them undisputable texts.

16 See *Muqaddimāt al-Imām al-Kawtharī*, ʿAbd al-Salām Shannār's introduction to Bājūrī's commentary on *Umm al-Barāhīn*, Shahrastānī's *Al-Milal wa 'l-Niḥal*, and Taftāzānī's introduction to Nasafī's *ʿAqā'id*.

many others adopted the Ḥashawiyya ideology[17] (*Muqaddimāt al-Imām al-Kawtharī* 48).

The Muʿtazila

Isolationists or Dissenters. The doctrine of the Muʿtazila originated in Baṣra in the early second century, when Wāṣil ibn ʿAṭā' (d. 131/748) left the circle of Ḥasan al-Baṣrī after a theological dispute regarding *al-manzila bayn al-manzilatayn*[18] and whether a person guilty of enormities remains a believer. Ḥasan al-Baṣrī said, "ʿAṭā' has dissented from us," and thereafter, he and his followers were called the Dissenters, or Muʿtazila.[19] The Muʿtazila (also called Muʿtazilites) named themselves *Ahl al-Tawḥīd wa 'l-ʿAdl* (The People of Divine Oneness and Justice), claiming that their theology grounded the Islamic belief system in reason. Muʿtazilī tenets focused on the Five Principles: (1) *tawḥīd* (divine oneness), (2) *ʿadl* (divine justice), (3) *waʿd wa waʿīd* (promise and threat), (4) *al-manzila bayn al-manzilatayn* (the rank in between two ranks), and (5) *amr bi 'l-maʿrūf wa 'l-nahy ʿan al-munkar* (enjoining good and forbidding evil).

The founders and leaders of this sect included Abū ʿAlī Muḥammad ibn ʿAbd al-Wahhāb al-Jubbā'ī, ʿAmr ibn ʿUbayd, Bishr ibn Saʿīd, Ibrāhīm ibn al-Naẓẓām, Yashama ibn al-Muʿtamir, Abu 'l-Hudhayl al-ʿAllāf, and Abū Bakr ʿAbd al-Raḥmān ibn Kaysān al-Aṣamm. Over time, the Muʿtazila split into more than twenty subgroups, such as the Wāṣiliyya, Hudhaliyya, and

---

17 Ḥashawiyya. Stuffers or Crammers. A sect who attribute human qualities to Allāh and are thus anthropomorphists (*mujassima*). They say that Allāh has literally (*ḥaqīqatan*) settled Himself on the Throne (but not necessarily as the average human being may comprehend). They are named *ḥashawiyya* (stuffers) because they introduced or stuffed many strange concepts into the Messenger's ḥadīths ﷺ from Israelite sources. Some have said that the difference between the Ḥashawiyya and the *mujassima* (anthropomorphists) is that the Ḥashawiyya (especially the later ones) did not explicitly reveal their anthropomorphism in unequivocal terms as did the *mujassima*. Hence, they can be considered Crypto-Anthropomorphists. See also *Itḥāf al-Sāda al-Muttaqīn* 2:11.

18 That is, those who are guilty of enormities and die without repentance are not considered believers or unbelievers, but rather, they are in an intermediate position between the two. They claim that such people will occupy a place in Hellfire although they will face a less severe punishment than that of pure unbelievers.

19 There are also other opinions regarding the origin of the name Muʿtazila. Shaykh Zāhid al-Kawtharī quotes from Abu 'l-Ḥusayn al-Ṭarā'ifī al-Dimashqī (d. 377/987) that "the origin of the Muʿtazila came from some of the supporters of ʿAlī ﵁. When Ḥasan ﵁ transferred the office of caliphate to Muʿāwiya ﵁, this group withdrew from the public and confined themselves to their masjids and to worship." See Kawtharī's introduction to *Tabyīn Kadhib al-Muftarī*.

Naẓẓāmiyya, each named after their respective founders, and some of them even considered the other subgroups to be unbelievers. However, they shared opposition to the Ahl al-Sunna wa 'l-Jamāʿa in several core beliefs, one of which was their negation of the attributes (*ṣifāt al-maʿānī*). Unlike the Ahl al-Sunna wa 'l-Jamāʿa, they claimed that Allāh knows, wills, and sees through His essence, not through the attributes of knowledge, will, and sight. Furthermore, they denied the beatific vision by the dwellers of Paradise. They believed that Allāh creates His speech in a body and that the Qur'ān is therefore created; that reason can dictate the righteous and wicked to Allāh and obligate him to declare it as such; that it is obligatory on Allāh to punish the sinner and reward the obedient; that the servant is the creator of his willful actions; and that unbelief and disobedience are not created by Allāh (hence, they are also Qadariyya).[20] Nevertheless, it must be remembered that although such beliefs are corrupt and invalid, orthodox Muslim scholars did not necessarily charge the Muʿtazila with apostasy, nor did they regard it permissible to label them unbelievers because of their views. However, they did render them the status of innovators and transgressors.[21]

The Qadariyya

Libertarians. These were the proponents of absolute free will, or libertarianism. The ideology of the Qadariyya (sometimes called Qadarites) is fundamentally shared by the Shīʿa[22] and the Muʿtazila, both of whom deny that Allāh creates

20 These beliefs are explained in the commentary of *Al-Fiqh al-Akbar* below.

21 For more details, see section "Reconciling the Conflicting Opinions Regarding the *Takfīr* of the People of the *Qibla*" below.

22 Hence, Seyyed Hossein Nasr writes in his introduction to Sayyid Muḥammad Ḥusayn Ṭabāṭabā'ī's *Shi'ite Islam* (*Shīʿah dar Islām*), "Intelligence can judge the justness or unjustness of an act and this judgment is not completely suspended in favor of a pure voluntarism on the part of God. Hence, there is a greater emphasis upon intelligence (*ʿaql*) in Shi'ite theology and a greater emphasis upon will (*irāda*) in Sunnī *kalām,* or theology, at least in the predominate Asharite school. The secret of the greater affinity of Shi'ite theology for the "intellectual sciences" (*al-ʿulūm al-ʿaqliyya*) lies in part in this manner of viewing Divine Justice" (*Shi'ite Islam* 11). The Sunnī focus on the will of Allāh and their disavowal of the human intelligence as the ultimate determiner of what is just and unjust, emanates from the Qur'ānic teachings that "Allāh does what He pleases" (14:27), that "He will not be questioned as to what He does" (21:23), and that His actions are not subject to human scrutiny and classification, since "You might dislike something when it is good for you, and you might like something when it is bad for you. Allāh knows, and you know not" (2:216). While the Shi'ite view may seem attractive and in accordance with the prevalent Christian belief, the philosophy and doctrine of the Ahl al-Sunna wa 'l-Jamāʿa are to subject intelligence to revelation, especially since it is a greater error to define the nature of Allāh

evil but rather ascribe to man the ability to create evil. Maʿbad ibn Khālid al-Juhanī (d. 80/699) was the first to speak in denial of *qadar* (predestination).

The Khawārij

Separatists or Seceders. The Khawārij (or Kharijites) were the first sect to split from mainstream Islam. After the arbitration[23] between ʿAlī and Muʿāwiya ﷺ, a small number of pietists separated from them and withdrew to the village of Ḥarūrā' under the leadership of ʿAbdullāh ibn Wahb al-Rāsibī and were joined near Nahrawān by a larger group. This was the group responsible for the assassination of ʿAlī ﷺ and the failed attempts to assassinate Muʿāwiya and ʿAmr ibn al-ʿĀṣ ﷺ. Even more extreme than the Muʿtazila, they held actions to be an integral part of faith and thus considered anyone guilty of an enormity to be an unbeliever.

There were some other theological sects that emerged which did not have as much influence as the Muʿtazila, but nonetheless added to the fierce sectarianism that characterized the period.

The Jabriyya

Fatalists. The belief of the Jabriyya (or Jabrites) is diametrically opposed to that of the Qadariyya. They had a fatalistic outlook and believed that man has no free will in his actions; that man is under compulsion, or *jabr,* just as a feather is at the mercy of the winds; and that he has no choice even in his intentional actions. A subgroup of the Jabriyya are the Jahmiyya.

The Jahmiyya

They were followers of Jahm ibn Ṣafwān al-Samarqandī (d. 128/745) and considered pure fatalists (*Jabriyya*). Jahm expressed his heretical beliefs in

---

by mere human reason than to have a person entertain the false notion that Allāh gives life to "evil." Moreover, according to this erroneous logic, it follows that He would be unjust in doing so. The Qur'ān teaches that Allāh "is never unjust to [His] servants" (8:51). When this verse is read along with the aforementioned verses, one can see that the doctrine of the Ahl al-Sunna wa 'l-Jamāʿa is more in agreement with the Qur'ānic teachings.

23 Following the murder of ʿUthmān, ʿAlī ﷺ was made the successor; however, due to certain differences of opinion regarding how to treat the murderers of ʿUthmān, a battle ensued between ʿAlī and Muʿāwiya ﷺ at Ṣiffīn. The battle was indecisive, and the two parties agreed to an arbitration. See *Itmām al-Wafā' fī Sīrat al-Khulafā'* 256–261.

Tirmidh (present-day Uzbekistan) and was executed by the Umayyad governor of Balkh and Jūzajān, Salm ibn Aḥwaz al-Māzinī, in Marw (present-day Turkmenistan). Like the Muʿtazila, he rejected the eternal divine attributes, but he also held other heretical beliefs. For example, he was one of the first to say the Qur'ān was created, having learned this idea from his Damascene teacher Jaʿd ibn Dirham (d. 124/742). Another belief attributed to him is that Paradise and Hell are transient. A number of beliefs are sometimes falsely ascribed to him, according to Imām al-Kawtharī, and people sometimes hurl the name Jahmiyya as an insulting epithet upon any disagreeable opponent.[24] Certain beliefs held by Jahm ibn Ṣafwān do take one out of Islam into unbelief, as do some of those held by the Karrāmiyya.

The Karrāmiyya

Their name and beliefs are traced to Abū ʿAbdillāh Muḥammad ibn Karrām (d. 255/868). About them, Shahrastānī[25] writes, "They believed that many contingent things exist in the essence of Allāh. For example, they believe that the informing of past and future events exists in His essence just as the books revealed to the messengers exist in His essence [rather than being through His attributes].[26] They are anthropomorphists (*mujassima*), for Muḥammad ibn Karrām declared that his god (as Allāh is transcendent above what he ascribes to Him) rests on the Throne; that He is "above," as in the physical direction; that He is substantive; and that there are [physical] movement, displacement, and descension for Him, among other irrational ideas. Some Karrāmiyya also claimed that Allāh is a body (*jism*). The Karrāmiyya divided over time into twelve sects (*Al-Milal wa 'l-Niḥal* 1:108–109).

---

24 *Al-Milal wa 'l-Niḥal* 1:86–88; *Muqaddimāt al-Kawtharī,* "Introduction to *Tabyīn Kadhib al-Muftarī,*" 43.

25 Muḥammad ibn ʿAbd al-Karīm ibn Aḥmad Abu 'l-Fatḥ al-Shahrastānī was a philosopher of Islam, an Imām of *kalām* in the school of Ashʿarī, a historian, and a heresiographer. He was born in Shahrastān between Nīshāpur and Khawārizm and moved to Baghdad in 510/1116, where he stayed for thirty years before returning to his hometown. He authored *Kitāb al-Milal wa 'l-Niḥal* (The Book of Sects and Creeds) among other works. Ibn al-Samʿānī reports that he was accused of having Ismāʿīlī leanings and others say he was sympathetic to the philosophers. He passed away in 548/1153 (*Lisān al-Mīzān* 2:427, *Al-Wāfī bi 'l-Wafayāt* 1:409, *Al-Aʿlām* 6:215).

26 By considering these things to exist in the essence of Allāh, the Karrāmiyya are rendering His essence a locus for created things, whereas time, place, and change are qualities that apply only to created things. In reality, He creates things through His attributes, while the things created are the effects of His attributes.

The Murji'a

Postponers, Deferrers, or Antinomians. They were a group of innovators who claimed that disobedience does not harm one, but that Allāh forgives all sins as long as one has faith, thus going to the opposite extreme of the Khawārij. Because of their belief, they frequently neglected their religious rites.

Although these sects may no longer exist today as formal groups, some of their beliefs have continued and are heard being advocated by contemporary figures who style themselves as reformers. All praise is due to Allāh, then, who has preserved His faith and created in it the power to continually cleanse itself of innovations and spurious reformations. The Messenger of Allāh ﷺ said, "This sacred knowledge will be borne by the reliable authorities of each successive generation, who will [preserve it and] remove from it the alterations of the excessive, the interpolations of the corrupt, and the false interpretations of the ignorant" (*Bayhaqī,* Khaṭīb al-Baghdādī, *Sharaf Aṣḥāb al-Ḥadīth*).

AL-FIQH AL-AKBAR

The Authorship of Al-Fiqh al-Akbar

There is some difference of opinion regarding the attribution of *Al-Fiqh al-Akbar* to Abū Ḥanīfa. The nineteenth-century Indian scholar and biographer, ʿAllāma Shiblī Nuʿmānī (d. 1368/1949), writes that no extant book could be rightly attributed to Imām Abū Ḥanīfa (*Sīrat al-Nuʿmān* 84). The Dutch Orientalist A. J. Wensinck makes a similar statement: "The *Fiqh Akbar (II),* it is true, opens in the singular, probably because by doing so, it seeks to uphold the fiction of Abū Ḥanīfa's authorship; but later the singular is dropped in favor of the plural" (*The Muslim Creed* 102). On the other hand, the famous seventeenth-century Ottoman scholar Ḥājī Khalīfa (or Kātib Çelebi, *Kashf al-Ẓunūn* 5:162) as well as other renowned biographers such as Ziriklī (*Al-Aʿlām* 234) and Kaḥḥāla (*Muʿjam al-Muʾallifīn* 103) consider it to be the work of the Imām.[27] The commentators of *Al-Fiqh al-Akbar* are also in agreement

27 Similarly, Carl Brockelmann and Fuat Sezgin have mentioned *Al-Fiqh al-Akbar* among Imām Abū Ḥanīfa's works. See *Geschichte der Arabischen Litterature* 1:177; *G.A.L. Supplement* 1:285; and *Tārīkh al-Turāth al-ʿArabī* (*Geschichte des Arabischen Schrifttums*) vol. 1, pt. 3, p. 37.

that the text was indeed that of the noble Imām himself. The Ottoman scholar Maghnīsāwī writes, "The treatise *Al-Fiqh al-Akbar,* which the Great Imām authored, is a reliable and accepted work" (*Sharḥ al-Fiqh al-Akbar* 2). ʿAlī al-Qārī, the ḥadīth scholar, theologian, and jurist, writes in his commentary, "The Great Imām, the Magnanimous, the Great Honorable Exemplar of Mankind, Abū Ḥanīfa of Kūfa (may Allāh have mercy on him) states in his work called *Al-Fiqh al-Akbar* . . ." (*Minaḥ al-Rawḍ al-Azhar* 43).[28]

Furthermore, the indexer and bookseller of the fourth century, Ibn al-Nadīm, states in his *Kitāb al-Fihrist,* which was compiled in 377/987: "His [Abū Ḥanīfa's] works are the books *Al-Fiqh al-Akbar, Al-Risāla* (The Epistle) to [ʿUthmān] al-Battī, and *Al-ʿĀlim wa 'l-Mutaʿallim* (The Scholar and the Pupil)" (156). This fourth century record is sufficient to invalidate the opinion of Wensinck, who writes that "after the first half of the tenth century AD [fourth CE], in which the *Fiqh Akbar (II)* probably originated, several doctors composed creeds of a more or less varying structure."

Imām ʿAbd al-Qāhir al-Baghdādī (d. 429/1037) writes, "The first of the theologians from among the jurists and leaders of the schools were Abū Ḥanīfa and Shāfiʿī,[29] for indeed Abū Ḥanīfa composed a treatise in the rebuttal of the Qadariyya called *Al-Fiqh al-Akbar.*" Imām Abū Muẓaffar al-Isfirāyīnī states in his *Al-Tabṣīr fī 'l-Dīn,* "Abū Ḥanīfa's *Al-ʿĀlim wa 'l-Mutaʿallim* contains conclusive proofs against the people of heresy and innovation, and the book *Al-Fiqh al-Akbar* that has been related to us by a reliable authority through a transmission from Nuṣayr ibn Yaḥyā from Abū Ḥanīfa . . . ." Shaykh Wahbī Ghāwjī, after quoting Isfirāyīnī's statement, says, "I saw an excellent manuscript of *Al-Fiqh al-Akbar* in the library of Shaykh al-Islām ʿĀrif Ḥikmat (collection 226) in the illuminated city of Madīna (may there be a thousand blessings and peace upon its inhabitants), which was from the transmission of ʿAlī ibn Aḥmad al-Fārisī from Nuṣayr ibn Yaḥyā from Abū Muqātil from ʿIṣām ibn

28 This attribution is also verified by Ibn Abi 'l-ʿIzz al-Ḥanafī at the outset of his *Sharḥ al-ʿAqīda al-Ṭaḥāwiyya* where he says, "The science of the foundations of the faith is the noblest of sciences, since the nobility of a science is by what is known through it, and this is the "greater knowledge" (*al-fiqh al-akbar*) relatively speaking to the science of the branches [of the faith]. This is why Imām Abū Ḥanīfa (may Allāh have mercy on him) called his statements and compilation of the fundamentals of faith, *Al-Fiqh al-Akbar* . . ." (69).

29 The scholar of his time, defender of ḥadīth, imām and jurist of the umma, founder of the Shāfiʿī school of *fiqh,* Abū ʿAbdillāh Muḥammad ibn Idrīs al-Shāfiʿī al-Qurashī. He died in 204/819 in Cairo.

Yūsuf from Ḥammād, the son of Abū Ḥanīfa. This confirms the attribution of *Al-Fiqh al-Akbar* to the Imām (may Allāh have mercy on him)" (*Al-Taʿlīq al-Muyassar* 12–13).

An Interesting Explanation

Mawlānā Muḥammad Sarfrāz Khān Ṣafdar[30] provides an interesting explanation for the confusion behind the attribution of *Al-Fiqh al-Akbar* to the Imām. He writes that those who claim that there are no works of Imām Abū Ḥanīfa in existence today are in sheer delusion, and that Ibn al-Nadīm has attributed the book to the Imām. He then states:

> ʿAllāma Ṭāsh Kubrīzāda[31] writes that Imām Abū Ḥanīfa has discussed most aspects of the science of *kalām* in his books *Al-Fiqh al-Akbar* and *Al-ʿĀlim wa 'l-Mutaʿallim.* As for the assertion that these two works are not authored by Imām Abū Ḥanīfa but by Abū Ḥanīfa al-Bukhārī,[32] this is a mere fabrication of the Muʿtazila, who were under the false impression that Imām Abū Ḥanīfa was one of their supporters. ʿAllāma Ḥāfiẓ al-Dīn al-Bazzāzī[33] writes in his book *Manāqib Abī Ḥanīfa* that he personally saw the two books, *Al-Fiqh al-Akbar* and *Al-ʿĀlim wa 'l-Mutaʿallim,* written in the handwriting of Shams al-Dīn al-Kardarī al-Barātiqīnī al-ʿImādī,[34] who in turn stated that they were authored by the Imām. A large group of scholars have also affirmed Imām Abū Ḥanīfa as being the author of these two

30 Muḥammad Sarfrāz Khān Ṣafdar ibn Nūr Aḥmad Khān ibn Gul Aḥmad Khān was born in 1332/1914 in the Hazāra district in present-day Pakistan. His teachers include Mawlānā Ḥusayn Aḥmad Madanī, Iʿzāz ʿAlī, Muḥammad Ibrāhīm Balyāwī, and Muftī Muḥammad Shafīʿ. He is a ḥadīth scholar, a specialist in many Islamic sciences, a prolific writer with many works to his name, and has been teaching *Ṣaḥīḥ al-Bukhārī* for a number of years (*Akābir ʿUlamā'e Deoband* 510–511).

31 Muḥammad ibn Aḥmad ibn Muṣṭafā, Ṭāsh Kubrīzāda al-Rūmī al-Ḥanafī, the historian, exegete, and biographer, was the author of *Tuḥfat al-ʿUlūm* and *Miftāḥ al-Saʿāda wa Miṣbāḥ al-Siyāda*. He was born in 959/1552 and died in 1030/1621 (*Muʿjam al-Mu'allifīn* 9:21).

32 This is most likely a reference to Abū Jaʿfar Muḥammad ibn ʿAbdillāh ibn Muḥammad al-Hindawānī al-Balkhī al-Ḥanafī, called Abū Ḥanīfa al-Ṣaghīr (the Younger) for his complete mastery of jurisprudence. He studied under Abū Bakr ibn Muḥammad ibn Abī Saʿīd and passed away in 362/972 at the age of 62 in Bukhārā (*Tāj al-Tarājim* 22).

33 Muḥammad ibn Muḥammad Ḥāfiẓ al-Dīn ibn Nāṣir al-Dīn al-ʿImādī al-Kardarī al-Bazzāzī al-Ḥanafī (d. 816/1413 or 827/1424), author of *Jāmiʿ al-Fatāwā* and other works (*Al-Ḍaw' al-Lāmiʿ* 4:499, *Muʿjam al-Mu'allifīn* 3:177).

34 Shams al-Dīn or Shams al-A'imma Abu 'l-Waḥda Muḥammad ibn ʿAbd al-Sattār ibn Muḥammad al-ʿImādī al-Kardarī al-Barātiqīnī, called the "Teacher of the Imāms," was proficient in the Ḥanafī school and its principles. He died in Bukhārā in 642/1244 (*Al-Wāfī bi 'l-Wafayāt* 1:399, *Tāj al-Tarājim* 22).

works, among them Imām Fakhr al-Islām al-Bazdawī,[35] in whose book *Al-Uṣūl* this agreement is mentioned. Shaykh ʿAbd al-ʿAzīz al-Bukhārī[36] also affirms their authorship in his commentary of *Al-Uṣūl*" (*Maqāme Abū Ḥanīfa* 108).

The claim of the Muʿtazila that *Al-Fiqh al-Akbar* was authored by Abū Ḥanīfa al-Bukhārī was triggered by those sections of the treatise that contain rebuttals of the Muʿtazilī doctrine. This was very damaging to them, since they considered Abū Ḥanīfa to be a Muʿtazilī; hence, they falsely attributed the texts to Muḥammad ibn Yūsuf al-Bukhārī, who was also known as Abū Ḥanīfa.

Two Versions of Al-Fiqh al-Akbar

An intriguing twist to this issue is that there are actually two works known as *Al-Fiqh al-Akbar* attributed to the Great Imām. The two are referred to by orientalists as *Fiqh Akbar (I)* and *Fiqh Akbar (II)*—the commentary of Maghnīsāwī and ʿAlī al-Qārī being of *Fiqh Akbar (II)* and Abu 'l-Layth al-Samarqandī's commentary (incorrectly published as Abū Manṣūr al-Māturīdī's commentary) being of *Fiqh Akbar (I)*. Wensinck states, "It is a strange fact that neither in Arabic literature nor in the European catalogues of Arabic manuscripts is any discrimination made between the two" (*The Muslim Creed* 103).

Al-Fiqh al-Absaṭ

Wensinck says regarding *Fiqh Akbar (I)*:

> We possess, however, another document, which contains valuable indications, namely, the *Fiqh Absat.* It rests on the answers given by Abu Hanifa to questions regarding dogmatics put to him by his pupil Abu Muti al-Balkhi. So as far as I can see, this pamphlet, a unique copy of which is preserved in Cairo, is genuine. Here we find, as a matter of fact, all the articles of *Fiqh Akbar (I),* with the exception of the art. 7. This makes it probable that the editor and commentator of *Fiqh Akbar*

35 ʿAlī ibn Muḥammad ʿAbd al-Karīm ibn Mūsā al-Bazdawī, the great imām known as Fakhr al-Islām (Pride of Islam). He was born around 400 and was the author of many works, including *Al-Mabsūṭ, Sharḥ al-Jāmiʿ al-Kabīr, Sharḥ al-Jāmiʿ al-Ṣaghīr,* and *Al-Uṣūl.* He is the brother of Ṣadr al-Islām al-Bazdawī and the student of ʿUmar al-Nasafī. He died in 482/1089 and was buried in Samarqand (*Al-Fawāʾid al-Bahiyya* 124).

36 ʿAbd al-ʿAzīz ibn Aḥmad ibn Muḥammad, ʿAlāʾ al-Dīn al-Bukhārī al-Ḥanafī, the jurist and scholar of *uṣūl* from the inhabitants of Bukhārā. He authored the famous two-volume commentary on Bazdawī's *Uṣūl* called *Kashf al-Asrār,* and *Sharḥ Muntakhab al-Ḥusāmī.* He died in 730/1330 (*Al-Aʿlām* 4:13).

> *(1)* has borrowed the text on which he commented from the *Fiqh Absat.* So the *Fiqh Akbar (1),* though not composed by Abu Hanifa, is proved to be derived from genuine utterances of the master, with the possible exception of art. 7 (*The Muslim Creed* 123).

What Wensinck overlooks here is that what he refers to as *Fiqh Akbar (1)* is in fact *Al-Fiqh al-Absaṭ.* There are actually two works of Abū Ḥanīfa known as *Al-Fiqh al-Akbar.* One is the popular narration of the Imām's son Ḥammād; it has attracted more commentaries, as those of Maghnīsāwī and Qārī, and is always referred to as *Al-Fiqh al-Akbar.* The other narration is that of Abū Muṭīᶜ Ḥakam ibn ᶜAbdillāh al-Balkhī, which is cast as a dialogue. It is longer and is referred to as *Al-Fiqh al-Absaṭ* (The Extensive Knowledge) to differentiate it from *Al-Fiqh al-Akbar.* There are also various editions of *Al-Fiqh al-Absaṭ,* which may explain Wensinck's error. A quick glance at these editions reveals discrepancies and inconsistencies in the text.

Conclusion

The evidence above, taken together—especially Ibn al-Nadīm's listing (4th/10th century) and the manuscript in ᶜĀrif Ḥikmat (Madīna) containing the chain back to Ḥammād, son of Abū Ḥanīfa—demonstrates the authorship of the Imām. Thanks to modern computer and printing technology, in recent years the world has seen the publication of many rare manuscripts. Therefore, the ready availability of Abū Ḥanīfa's words does not seem as farfetched today as it may have seemed a hundred years ago to Shiblī Nuᶜmānī. Were one still to insist that the Great Imām did not author them, it is at least more difficult to deny that their contents reflect his teachings. Earl Edgar Elder states in his introduction to *A Commentary on The Creed of Islam:*[37] "*Al-Fiqh al-Akbar (1)* which, even though it is wrongly attributed to Abū Ḥanīfa (d. 150), reflects his teaching" (xvii). In his commentary on *Iḥyā ᶜUlūm al-Dīn, Itḥāf al-Sāda al-Muttaqīn,* Murtaḍā al-Zabīdī discusses the various opinions surrounding the authorship of the five books attributed to Abū Ḥanīfa:

> It has come to be taken for granted (*wa min al-maᶜlūm*), based on the aforementioned, that the authorship of these books belongs to the Imām, but the accurate opinion is that the discussions [on Islamic creed] treated in these books are in

37 This is Elder's translation of Taftāzānī's commentary on Nasafī's *ᶜAqā'id.*

> fact from the dictations of the Imām to his students Ḥammād, Abū Yūsuf, Abū Muṭīʿ al-Ḥakam ibn ʿAbdillāh al-Balkhī, and Abū Muqātil Ḥafṣ ibn Muslim al-Samarqandī. Some of these students compiled the discussions and a group of specialists, such as Ismāʿīl ibn Ḥammād (the grandson of the Imām), Muḥammad ibn Muqātil al-Rāzī, Muḥammad ibn Samāʿa, Nuṣayr ibn Yaḥyā al-Balkhī, Shaddād ibn al-Ḥakam, and others, transmitted them from these scholars, until they reached Abū Manṣūr al-Māturīdī through reliable chains of transmission. Therefore, whoever ascribes them to the Imām has done so correctly because those discussions were his dictations. Whoever has attributed them to Abū Muṭīʿ al-Balkhī, or to a contemporary, or someone who lived after him, has also done so correctly, because the works were compiled by them. Another example of this [type of compilation] is the *Musnad* attributed to Imām Shāfiʿī, which is actually the rendering of Abū ʿAmr Muḥammad ibn Jaʿfar ibn Muḥammad ibn Maṭar al-Naysābūrī, Abu 'l-ʿAbbās al-Aṣamm, from the principles laid down by Imām Shāfiʿī. We now mention for you those who transmitted these books and relied upon them. One of them is Fakhr al-Islām al-Bazdawī, who quoted a portion of *Al-Fiqh al-Akbar, Al-ʿĀlim wa 'l-Mutaʿallim,* and *Al-Risāla* at the beginning of his *Uṣūl.* . . . Portions of the five books, *Al-Fiqh al-Akbar, Al-ʿĀlim wa 'l-Mutaʿallim, Al-Fiqh al-Absaṭ, Al-Risāla,* and *Al-Waṣiyya,* have been quoted in approximately thirty books by various Imāms [of the Ḥanafī school], and this much is sufficient [to substantiate] that the great scholars have completely accepted these works. And Allāh knows best." (*Itḥāf al-Sāda al-Muttaqīn* 2:14)

The Transmission Chains of the Five Books and Their Manuscripts

Shaykh Zāhid al-Kawtharī writes that the Imām's five books are the main sources used by the Ḥanafī Māturīdī scholars for understanding the correct Islamic doctrine of the Messenger of Allāh ﷺ, his illustrious Companions, and the People of the Sunna who followed them. He continues, explaining that Abū Manṣūr al-Māturīdī and Imām Abū Jaʿfar al-Ṭaḥāwī both based their works on Abū Ḥanīfa's books. Manuscripts of the books exist in the Fatih Nation Library (Fatih Millet Kütüphanesi) in Istanbul and the National Library of Egypt (in Cairo). They have all been previously published as a collection, and *Al-Waṣiyya* was published with its commentary many times. Likewise, Ḥammād's narration of *Al-Fiqh al-Akbar* and its commentaries are in print. A commentary of Abū Muṭīʿ's version of *Al-Fiqh al-Akbar* (*Al-Fiqh al-Absaṭ*) was also published in India and Egypt, but the publishers have incorrectly attributed it to Abū Manṣūr al-Māturīdī. The inaccuracy of this attribution is clearly demonstrated by the presence of quotes from later authorities in the text. The commentary belongs to Abu 'l-Layth al-Samarqandī (d. 373/983), a fact confirmed by many manuscripts in the National Library of Egypt (collections 343 and 393, and *ʿIlm al-Kalām* 195).

Kawtharī then provides the chains for these books in the introduction to his edited collection. He says that *Al-ʿĀlim wa 'l-Mutaʿallim* is transmitted by Abū Muqātil Ḥafṣ ibn Salam al-Samarqandī from Abū Ḥanīfa, *Al-Risāla* (The Epistle) sent to ʿUthmān ibn Muslim al-Battī is transmitted by Abū Yūsuf from Abū Ḥanīfa, *Al-Fiqh al-Absaṭ* is by Abū Muṭīʿ al-Ḥakam ibn ʿAbdillāh al-Balkhī from Abū Ḥanīfa, *Al-Fiqh al-Akbar* is by Ḥammād from his father Abū Ḥanīfa, and *Al-Waṣiyya* (The Testament) is also transmitted by Abū Yūsuf from Abū Ḥanīfa. Regarding Ḥammād's narration of *Al-Fiqh al-Akbar,* which is what concerns us here, Kawtharī quotes the chain found in a handwritten manuscript in the Library of Shaykh al-Islām ʿĀrif Ḥikmat in the noble city of Madīna. In it, Shaykh Ibrāhīm al-Kūrānī cites his chain to ʿAlī ibn Aḥmad al-Fārisī from Nuṣayr ibn Yaḥyā from Ibn Muqātil (Muḥammad ibn Muqātil al-Rāzī) from ʿIṣām ibn Yūsuf from Ḥammād[38] from his father Abū Ḥanīfa

38 Since, some attempts have been made at discrediting the narrators of *Al-Fiqh al-Akbar,* it is important to point out the true status and truthfulness of these scholars. *Ḥammād ibn Abī Ḥanīfa:* Ḥammād being the son of the Imām was no doubt well versed in the opinions and ideology of his father. During his father's lifetime, he had reached the level where he began issuing *fatwās* (*Al-Jawāhir al-Muḍī'a*). Imām Dhahabī states at the end of the biography of Imām Abū Ḥanīfa, "And his son the jurist, Ḥammād ibn Abī Ḥanīfa was a man of great knowledge, piety, uprightness, and complete abstinence" (*Siyar Aʿlām al-Nubalā'* 6:403). Ibn Khallikān also described him as *ṣāliḥ* (righteous) and [endowed with] *khayr* (good) (*Lisān al-Mīzān* 3:267). ʿAbdullāh ibn al-Mubārak, known for transmitting only from reliable sources, has taken ḥadīths from him (*Lisān al-Mīzān* 3:267). *ʿIṣām ibn Yūsuf:* Ibn Ḥibbān mentions him among his list of reliable narrators (*thiqāt*) and Khalīlī regarded him as *ṣadūq* (very honest) (*Lisān al-Mīzān* 5:436). Imām Dhahabī has mentioned that he and his brother were considered the greatest scholars of Balkh (*Tārīkh al-Islām,* "Events of the years 211–220 AH," p. 296); it is further said that the scholars of Balkh had extremely strong links with Abū Ḥanīfa as is evident from the book *Mashā'ikh Balkh min al-Ḥanafiyya* (The Ḥanafī scholars of Balkh). *Muḥammad ibn Muqātil:* He was a student of Imām Muḥammad al-Shaybānī. Several juridical rulings are transmitted from him, and these rulings have been extensively quoted in the books of Ḥanafī jurisprudence. Imām Dhahabī says, "He was from among the great jurists" (*Tārīkh al-Islām,* "Events of the years 241–250 AH," p. 472). *Nuṣayr ibn Yaḥyā:* He is recorded as being "from the jurists and ḥadīth scholars of Balkh" (*Mashā'ikh Balkh min al-Ḥanafiyya* 53), "from among the great jurists and pioneers of Balkh" (67), and "a scholar, ascetic, and specialist" (159). Aside from this, it is also important to keep in mind that *Al-Fiqh al-Akbar* and the points contained therein have enjoyed widespread acceptance through the successive generations of Ḥanafī scholars and others all the way from the beginning as Zabīdī in his *Itḥāf* (2:13–14 [see also quote above, p. 28]) and Bayāḍī in his *Ishārat al-Marām* (22-23) have detailed.

(may Allāh be pleased with them all). He says that there are two manuscripts in this library, and they are the oldest and most reliable extant manuscripts. He goes on to mention some of the discrepancies found between the various manuscripts, which we will discuss in other parts of this book.[39]

Imām Abū Ḥanīfa's Methodology in Al-Fiqh al-Akbar

Al-Fiqh al-Akbar is a clear and concise text. It is not too difficult for a person with sufficient command of Arabic and an elementary understanding of the Islamic creed to understand. The work begins by mentioning the foundational articles of faith, and goes on to discuss the eternal essence (*dhāt*) of Allāh Most High, His names and attributes, and the Qur'ān as His eternal speech. Thereafter, it elaborates on how one acquires true faith (*īmān*) or enters into a state of unbelief (*kufr*) after coming into this world. The subject of prophets and messengers is also taken up in some detail, followed by a discussion on the four rightly-guided caliphs and other Companions, and what the attitude of believers should be toward them. In refuting the Muʿtazila, Khawārij, and others, the text proves that the believer does not leave Islam by committing sins. A discussion of the miracles bestowed by Allāh Most High on His various servants is presented, followed by an in-depth analysis of *īmān* (true faith) and *islām* (submission) and the extent to which a person's faith increases and decreases. Other issues raised in the text include the generosity and justice of Allāh in dealing with His servants; eschatological issues, such as the questioning in the grave; the Ascension (*miʿrāj*) of the Messenger ﷺ; as well as Gog and Magog and other awaited signs of the Last Day. Although the Imām follows a particular order in the text, he sometimes repeats certain points already mentioned for emphasis; for instance, because of the Qur'ān's weighty importance, he asserts several times that the eternal speech of Allāh is unlike the created words of human beings.

Commentaries on Al-Fiqh al-Akbar

Among the many commentaries on *Al-Fiqh al-Akbar,* the commentary of Abu 'l-Muntahā al-Maghnīsāwī stands out as the most concise. Despite its brevity, it is comprehensive and sufficiently explicates the points propounded by Abū Ḥanīfa. This commentary avoids lengthy and intricate discussions on

39 See introduction to the five books published by Al-Maktaba al-Azhariyya li 'l-Turāth.

the more subtle points of Islamic theology and belief and suffices with lucid, comprehensible, and short explanations of the text. These qualities make it an ideal choice for an English translation.

The method of commentary is classical, wherein the commentary is interwoven with the text, glossing words and sentences and commenting on whole sections. Sometimes a word is sufficient, while other times, a sentence or even a paragraph or two is offered as an explanation. As Maghnīsāwī mentions in the beginning of his commentary, his intention was only to compile helpful statements from reliable books regarding the points mentioned in *Al-Fiqh al-Akbar,* along with excerpts from the Qur'ān and ḥadīths. Occasionally, he presents morphological breakdowns for words and parses sentences. These are difficult to render and usually unhelpful to the English-speaking reader, so most of them have been omitted in this translation. It also bears mentioning that Maghnīsāwī, a Ḥanafī Māturīdī scholar, does not diverge with any of the views of Imām Abū Ḥanīfa mentioned in *Al-Fiqh al-Akbar.*

Maghnīsāwī begins his commentary with a short sermon, a prayer for protection from erroneous beliefs (a tradition of many righteous scholars), and quotes a statement by Imām ʿAlī al-Bazdawī on the various types of knowledge. He then formally begins his explanation of *Al-Fiqh al-Akbar.* At the end of his commentary, he closes with another prayer to Allāh to guide everyone onto the straight path.

In contrast, Mullā ʿAlī al-Qārī's commentary of *Al-Fiqh al-Akbar* is much more detailed and incorporates Abū Ḥanīfa's *Al-Waṣiyya* in it as well. The commentary is a treasure for those seeking a thorough elucidation of the tenets of faith according to the Māturīdī school, as well as an understanding of the differences between the theological schools and sects. This commentary is quite extensive and beyond the scope of this translation; hence, only the relevant discussions that are not covered by Maghnīsāwī have been culled for inclusion in this translation. Aside from these, numerous other commentaries were written on *Al-Fiqh al-Akbar.* Details of these commentaries have been provided in a separate section at the end of this introduction.

This Translation of Al-Fiqh al-Akbar and its Commentary

I was fortunate to come upon Maghnīsāwī's commentary of *Al-Fiqh al-Akbar* in the library of Madrasah Zakariyyah, Johannesburg, South Africa, when searching for a topic for my B.A. honors thesis at Rand Afrikaans University (now University of Johannesburg). This commentary seemed to be appropriate for my purpose, and deserving of further research and eventual translation into the English language. The late Professor Abdur-Rahman Doi agreed to this project.[40]

At the time of producing this work, no English translation of the text of *Al-Fiqh al-Akbar* or of a commentary on it were available to me. However, some time after completing the translation, I found a reference to A. J. Wensinck's translation of *Al-Fiqh al-Akbar* in Elder's *A Commentary on The Creed of Islam* (xxvii). I later found the translation as part of *The Muslim Creed* by Wensinck. Still later, I came across another translation of the text by Hamid Algar. However, in comparison, all three translations are very different from each other. As for Maghnīsāwī's commentary of *Al-Fiqh al-Akbar,* I am not aware of any other translation in English.

For the initial translation, I used the edition of Maghnīsāwī's commentary on *Al-Fiqh al-Akbar* published by Qadīmī Kutub Khāna, Karachi, Pakistan. This is actually a reproduction from an edition published by Majlis Dā'irat al-Maᶜārif al-Niẓāmiyya of Hyderabad Deccan, India. At the time, this was the only edition of Maghnīsāwī's commentary to which I had access. When necessary, I consulted other editions of *Al-Fiqh al-Akbar* that were included in editions of Qārī's commentary.

After completing my thesis, I had the good fortune to study *Minaḥ al-Rawḍ al-Azhar,* the larger commentary by Mullā ᶜAlī al-Qārī, with Shaykh Adīb Kallās of Damascus, Syria. I am deeply indebted to him, for he graced me with the opportunity to attend several classes he was teaching in *ᶜaqīda* and, despite his busy schedule, went through ᶜAlī al-Qārī's entire commentary with me during the short time I had in Syria. He also honored me with an *ijāza,* or teaching authorization, in this book. He possessed deep insight into doctrinal issues and made them easily comprehensible to me, explaining them with simple, yet remarkably articulate words, often using nothing more than everyday examples. I was able to improve and enhance this work greatly

40 The professor was a fatherly figure to his students, and we benefited much from his experiences at the University of Ife, Nigeria and the International Islamic University in Kuala Lumpur, Malaysia, and from his knowledge of and association with prominent orientalists like A. J. Arberry at Cambridge, UK during his doctoral studies. He passed away a year after I had completed the translation for the thesis. May Allāh bless him, illuminate his grave, and shower him with His mercy.

by sitting in his company. May Allāh grant him a long life and reward him abundantly in this world and the next.

After the work was submitted as a thesis, it sat unpublished for nearly a decade. During this time, I received numerous requests and much encouragement—and a bit of earnest, but kindly, importuning—to publish it. For despite the importance of this subject matter to theological discussions currently prevalent within the Muslim community, there was and remains a scarcity of books on it published in English, especially translations of classical texts and their commentaries. Over the years, I have been fortunate to come across and study many editions of *Al-Fiqh al-Akbar* and its various commentaries, along with other books on Islamic theology, which have helped me prepare this translation for publication.

All praise is to Allāh Most High. After much addition to the original translation, this edition is now before you. It includes numerous notes selected with care from ʿAlī al-Qārī's commentary, the entire *Kitāb al-Waṣiyya* of Imām Abū Ḥanīfa, and notes from other sources. For the parts taken from ʿAlī al-Qārī's commentary, *Minaḥ al-Rawḍ al-Azhar,* I have used the edition of the Albanian Ḥanafī scholar Shaykh Wahbī Sulaymān Ghāwjī al-Albānī, published by Dār al-Bashā'ir al-Islāmiyya, Beirut, which he based on the 1956 Cairo edition of Maṭbaʿa Muṣṭafā al-Bābī al-Ḥalabī and a manuscript from the Ẓāhiriyya Library in Damascus. I have also been extremely fortunate to have obtained electronic copies of several hand-written manuscripts of *Al-Fiqh al-Akbar, Kitāb al-Waṣiyya, Minaḥ al-Rawḍ al-Azhar,* and Maghnīsāwī's commentary from the libraries of Al-Azhar University in Cairo and the University of Tokyo (see pp. 38–39 for samples and bibliography for complete list). These have proved invaluable in cross-referencing and verifying the texts of the published editions and clarifying the discrepancies found in them. I have also verified the entire published edition of Maghnīsāwī's commentary used for this translation with a copy of the oldest manuscript in my possession, *MS. 2401* from Tokyo, written in 1059/1649. Upon comparison, it is clear that the published edition, upon which this translation is based, is far superior to all the manuscript copies I had in my hands; the editors may very well have had access to a more accurate manuscript. One exception to this is a confusing paragraph, which crept in from Qārī's commentary and contains many errors. Of the nine manuscripts of Maghnīsāwī I was able to consult, none of them included this paragraph. This point has been highlighted in the footnotes, along with a few portions of the *Al-Fiqh al-Akbar* text that is surrounded by some confusion.

Format Used in This Manual

The layout of this edition presents the voweled Arabic text of *Al-Fiqh al-Akbar,* followed immediately by its translation in English. Punctuation and vowelling of the Arabic text has been added by the translator, as classical texts generally do not contain either. Thereafter, the translation of the text is presented again in maroon with Maghnīsāwī's running commentary in black. Every effort has been expended to render the translation of the text and commentary intelligible. Where an explanatory note or phrase interrupts the text of *Al-Fiqh al-Akbar* in mid-sentence, if grammatically possible, it is accommodated into the sentence; otherwise, a solidus (/) is used to separate them. When the text is then resumed, it is introduced by a click symbol (|) and thus set off from the preceding portion. Notes from ʿAlī al-Qārī's commentary are then added as independent paragraphs wherever elaboration of the text was necessary; sometimes these glosses are direct translations and other times, a summary or paraphrase is provided along with the page references in parentheses to help distinguish it from Maghnīsāwī's commentary. The translated text of *Kitāb al-Waṣiyya* is broken up and added into the relevant sections with Qārī's commentary where it has not been quoted already by Maghnīsāwī.

As mentioned earlier, notes on morphology and grammatical structure have been omitted in this English translation, since the intended meaning is usually conveyed in English. English equivalents to Arabic terms have been used and when appropriate, transcriptions of Arabic terms are enclosed in parentheses, e.g., Necessarily Existent (*wājib al-wujūd*) and possibly existent (*mumkin al-wujūd*). In rare cases, they are presented the other way around. All other comments, explanatory words, and sentences are enclosed in square brackets within the translated text for smoother reading. Longer glosses are placed as footnotes. The translations of the Qur'ānic verses and ḥadīths are also provided with their proper references. Some of the references pertaining to Qārī's commentary were supplied by Qārī himself, though the rest are provided by the editor, Shaykh Ghāwjī. Those pertaining to Maghnīsāwī's commentary have been supplied by the translator, as they were absent in the original. If a ḥadīth is in *Ṣaḥīḥ al-Bukhārī* or *Muslim* or both, then only reference from those works are given, though the narration may be transmitted by other authorities as well. When not found in any of these two collections, other authorities are cited, namely, the four *Sunan* collections (*Sunan Abī Dāwūd, Tirmidhī, Nasā'ī,* and *Ibn Māja*) and the *Muwaṭṭā* of Imām Mālik, the *Musnad* of Imām Aḥmad, the *Sunan* of Dāramī, and a few others. A few of the ḥadīths could not be found by the translator. For easier reading, most of these references have been included in parentheses in the main text, though some of the lengthier ones were added as footnotes. All footnotes are the translator's except when otherwise referenced.

The translator is also responsible for organizing the text into sections and placing suitable titles above each, without any change to the original sequence in *Al-Fiqh al-Akbar.* Likewise, subtitles have been interspersed through Qārī's commentary to introduce the approaching discussion. Biographies of Imām Abū Ḥanīfa (with a special focus on his status as a theologian), Maghnīsāwī, and Qārī have been added after this introduction. Biographical notes on most of the scholars mentioned throughout the work have also been included, the majority of which are from the editors' footnotes of Qārī's commentary, though others were taken from the major biographical dictionaries. Moreover, a detailed bibliography of the published and unpublished sources consulted for this translation has been added.

I would like to say here that none of this would have been possible without the guiding advice and encouragement of my parents and teachers, and the support of my wife and children. I am grateful to all those who helped in the preparation of this work, especially Ḥāfiẓ Amir Toft for editing the translation of Maghnīsāwī's commentary and the introduction; my students Eemann Tomeh, Boumediene Hamzi, and Ustādha Shamira Chothia and Ustādha Nadia Mhatey for helping select and type up the notes from Qārī's commentary after each of our classes on it; Muftī Ahmad Bagia for providing obscure biographical data on some of the authorities mentioned in the text and details on the various commentaries of *Al-Fiqh al-Akbar;* Muftī Husain Kadodia for providing me electronic copies of all the manuscripts that have helped me enhance this work; Irfana Hashmi for thoroughly editing the entire text; Shaykh Abdullah Ali and Professor Aron Zysow for providing many insightful comments, revisions, and suggestions; Brooke Santos for editing and indexing; and Mawlānā Ismail Nakhuda, Shaykh Faraz Rabbani, Shaykh Mohammed H Abasoomer, and all others for their assistance and encouragement.

May the blessings and salutations of Allāh be upon His beloved Messenger ﷺ, who conveyed this beautiful religion to us, and may He have mercy upon all my teachers reaching back to Imām Abū Ḥanīfa all the way to the Companions ﷺ. May Allāh forgive me, my parents, my teachers, and all those who assisted in this publication. May Allāh bless this endeavor and grant it an excellent acceptance by Him. May Allāh make this a source of light in front of me, above me, on my sides, and all around me on the day when there will be no light except His Light and no reward except His, Most Exalted is He.

ABDUR-RAHMAN IBN YUSUF MANGERA
Jumādā Ūlā 1, 1428 | May 18, 2007

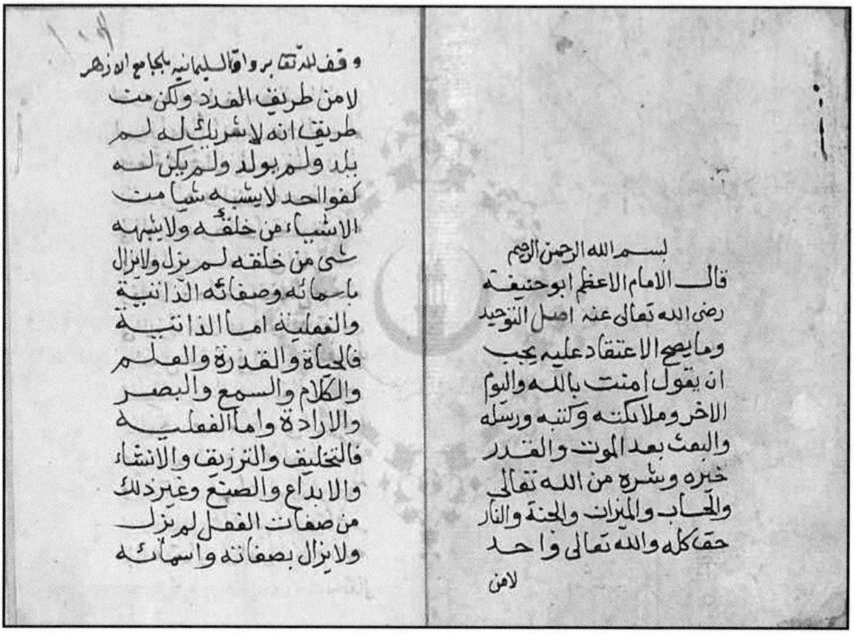

وقف لله تعالى برواق السليمانية بالجامع الازهر
لا من طريق العدد ولكن من
طريق انه لا شريك له لم
يلد ولم يولد ولم يكن له
كفوا احد لا يشبه شيئا من
الاشياء من خلقه ولا يشبهه
شيء من خلقه لم يزل ولا يزال
باسمائه وصفاته الذاتية
والفعلية اما الذاتية
فالحياة والقدرة والعلم
والكلام والسمع والبصر
والارادة واما الفعلية
فالتخليق والترزيق والانشاء
والابداع والصنع وغير ذلك
من صفات الفعل لم يزل
ولا يزال بصفاته واسمائه

بسم الله الرحمن الرحيم
قال الامام الاعظم ابو حنيفة
رضى الله تعالى عنه اصل التوحيد
وما يصح الاعتقاد عليه يجب
ان يقول امنت بالله واليوم
الاخر وملائكته وكتبه ورسله
والبعث بعد الموت والقدر
خيره وشره من الله تعالى
والحساب والميزان والجنة والنار
حق كله والله تعالى واحد
لا من

Opening spread of Abū Ḥanīfa's *Al-Fiqh al-Akbar* (*MS. 2756*)

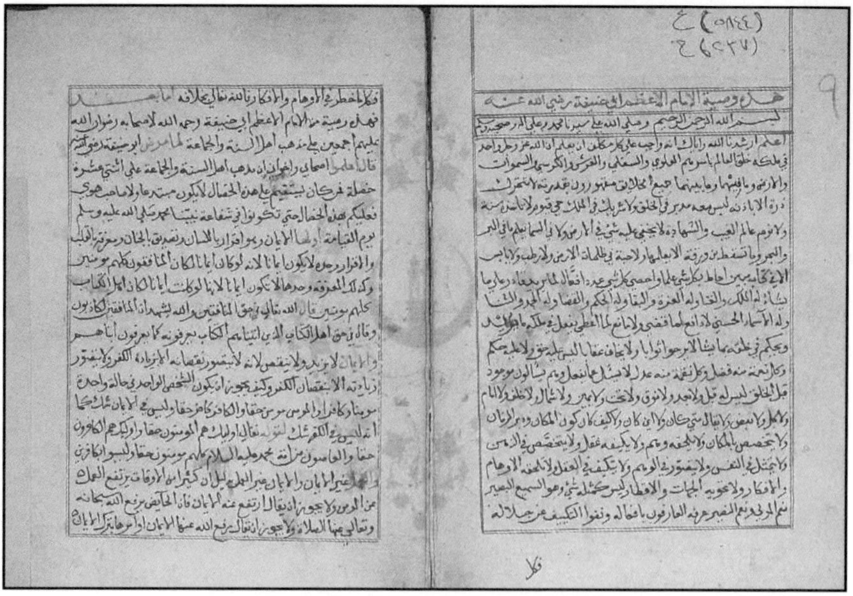

Opening spread of Abū Ḥanīfa's *Kitāb al-Waṣiyya* (*MS. 5844*)

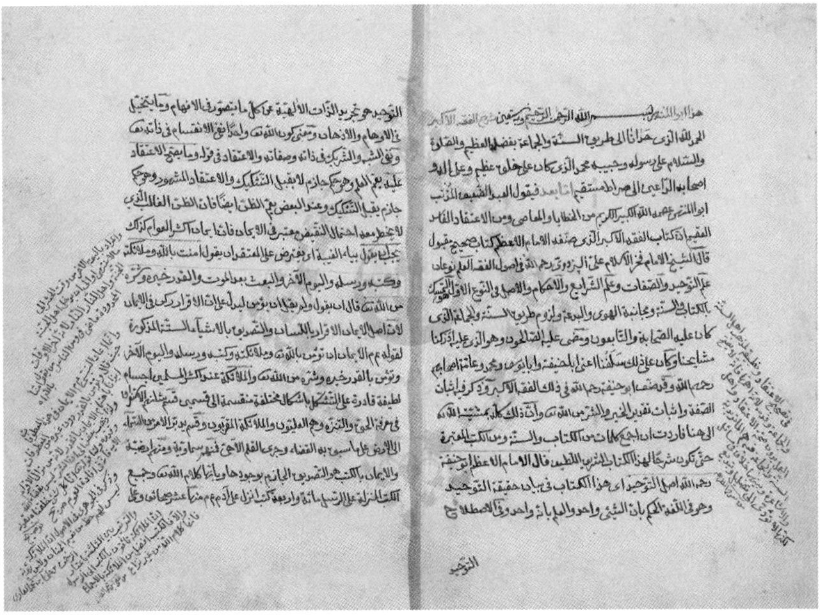

Opening spread of Maghnīsāwī's Commentary (*MS. 42996*)

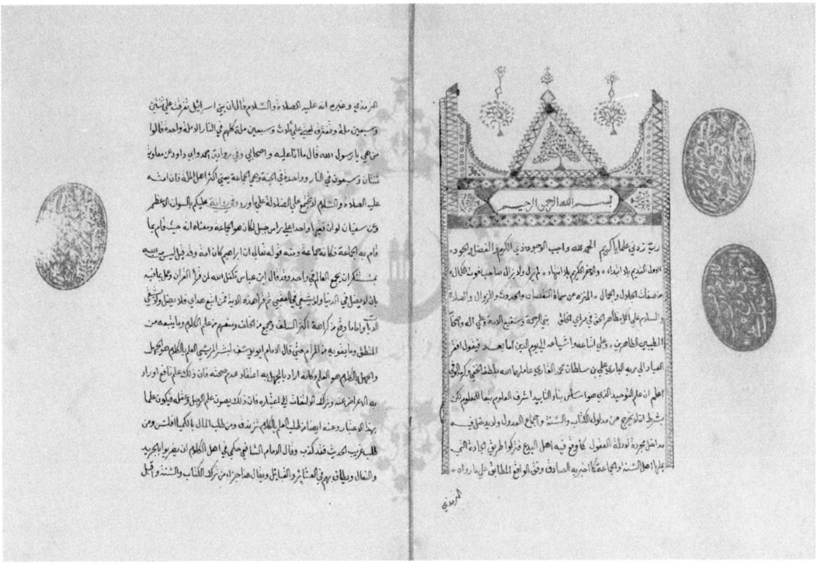

Opening spread of ʿAlī al-Qārī's Commentary (*MS. 17924*)

سبحان الله

Biographies

Abū Ḥanīfa Nuʿmān ibn Thābit

Nuʿmān ibn Thābit ibn Zūṭā ibn Mahan, the Greatest Imām (Imām Aʿẓam) who is better known by his agnomen (*kunya*) of Abū Ḥanīfa, was born in Kūfa, which had during this period become well-known as a center of learning. The legacy of the Companions ʿAbdullāh ibn Masʿūd (d. 32/652) and ʿAlī (d. 40/660) ؓ, both great scholars of the Qur'ān and the Sunna, took root and learning flourished in Kūfa. For it was there that Ibn Masʿūd was sent by the second caliph, ʿUmar ؓ, to teach and deliver legal rulings.

The famous historian Khaṭīb al-Baghdādī states that Imām Abū Ḥanīfa was born in the year 80/699. His father Thābit called upon caliph ʿAlī ibn Abī Ṭālib ؓ to pray for him and his family. Ismāʿīl ibn Ḥammād (the Imām's grandson) said, "I believe that his prayer bore fruit" (*Tārīkh Baghdād* 15:448). Imām Abū Ḥanīfa belonged to the pious generation who followed the illustrious Companions; they were designated as the Followers (*tābiʿūn*). The Imām had the good fortune of seeing some Companions of the Messenger of Allāh ﷺ such as Anas ibn Mālik, (d. 93/711), the personal attendant of the Holy Prophet, Sahl ibn Saʿd (d. 91/709), and Abu 'l-Ṭufayl ʿĀmir ibn Wāthila (d. 100/718).

Imām Abū Ḥanīfa was first brought up as a trader like his forefathers, but he soon started taking a deep interest in education. During this period, Islamic knowledge was being disseminated at the feet of renowned jurists such as Imām Awzāʿī in Syria, Ḥammād in Baṣra, Sufyān al-Thawrī in Kūfa, Mālik ibn Anas in Madīna, and Layth in Egypt (*Tadhkirat al-Ḥuffāẓ* 1:175).

One day, when Imām Abū Ḥanīfa was passing by the house of Imām Shaʿbī, a learned scholar of Kūfa, Shaʿbī mistook him for one of his students and asked, "Where are you going, young man?" Imām Abū Ḥanīfa named a merchant whom he was going to see. "I meant to ask," said Shaʿbī, "Whose classes do you attend?" "Nobody's, Sir," replied Imām Abū Ḥanīfa. Shaʿbī remarked, "I see signs of intelligence in you. You ought to sit in the company of learned men." This encouragement sparked a new light in the heart of Abū Ḥanīfa for studying *fiqh* (Islamic jurisprudence) and theology. He embarked on his studies and became a great Imām in the various fields of Islamic learning.

His first areas of concentration were the foundations of faith (*uṣūl al-dīn*) and debating with the people of deviance. He visited Baṣra more than twenty-seven times to debate and remove doubts raised by the deviant sects regarding aspects of the Sharīʿa. Among the many he debated and silenced were Jahm ibn Ṣafwān (the leader of the Jahmiyya sect), the Muʿtazila and Khawārij who surrendered to his proofs, and the extreme Shīʿa, who likewise accepted [the truth of his claims].[41]

Muwaffaq relates in *Al-Manāqib* that Abū Ḥafṣ al-Ṣaghīr said, "Abū Ḥanīfa studied *kalām* and debated people until he became proficient in it." He also relates from Zaranjarī that "Abū Ḥanīfa would lead a class (*ḥalaqa*) in *kalām*," before studying under Ḥammād. He also relates through Ḥārithī that Abū Ḥanīfa said, "I was possessed of skill in theological debate, and a period of time passed [like this]. . . . The people of argumentation and debate were [mostly] in Baṣra, for which I entered Baṣra more than twenty times. Sometimes I would stay for a year, sometimes less and other times more. I would debate the various groups of the Khawārij: the Ibāḍiyya, Ṣufriyya, and the groups of the Ḥashawiyya." Then he related how he turned to studying jurisprudence (*fiqh*) (*Muqaddimāt al-Imām al-Kawtharī* 175).

ʿAllāma Muḥammad al-Murtaḍā al-Zabīdī quotes from Muḥammad ibn Muḥammad al-Kardarī's *Manāqib al-Imām al-Aʿẓam* that Khālid ibn Zayd al-ʿAmurī said, "Abū Ḥanīfa, Abū Yūsuf, Muḥammad, Zufar, and Ḥammād son of Abū Ḥanīfa would debate people on theological issues, i.e., they would overcome their opponents for they were the imāms of the science [of theology]. It is related from Abū ʿAbdillāh al-Ṣaymarī that Imām Abū Ḥanīfa was the theologian of this umma in his time, and its jurist regarding the lawful and the unlawful (*Itḥāf al-Sāda al-Muttaqīn* 2:14).

The Imām's books on *ʿaqīda* are *Al-Fiqh al-Akbar* (The Greater Knowledge), *Al-Fiqh al-Absaṭ* (The Extensive Science), *Kitāb al-Waṣiyya* (The Testament),

41 *Al-Taʿlīq al-Muyassar* 7 from *Manāqib al-Bazzāzī* 1:121.

Kitāb al-ʿĀlim wa 'l-Mutaʿallim (The Scholar and the Student), and *Risāla Abī Ḥanīfa ilā ʿUthmān al-Battī, ʿĀlim Ahl al-Baṣra* (Abū Ḥanīfa's Epistle to the Scholar of the People of Baṣra, ʿUthmān al-Battī).

Imām ʿAbd al-Qāhir al-Baghdādī al-Shāfiʿī (d. 429/1037) writes in his *Uṣūl al-Dīn,* "The first of the theologians from among the jurists and leaders of the schools were Abū Ḥanīfa and Shāfiʿī, for Abū Ḥanīfa had composed a treatise on the rebuttal of the Qadarites called *Al-Fiqh al-Akbar"* (308). Abū Muẓaffar al-Isfirāyīnī al-Shāfiʿī states in his *Al-Tabṣīr fī 'l-Dīn,* "The book *Al-ʿĀlim wa 'l-Mutaʿallim* of Abū Ḥanīfa contains conclusive proofs against the people of heresy and innovation . . . and whoever peruses the book *Al-Fiqh al-Akbar* that has been related to us by a reliable authority through a reliable transmission (Nuṣayr ibn Yaḥyā from Abū Ḥanīfa) and what Abū Ḥanīfa compiled in *Al-Waṣiyya* that he wrote to Abū ʿAmr ʿUthmān al-Battī and rebutted in it the innovators, and those which Shāfiʿī wrote, will not find any kind of difference in their opinions; anything that is related against what we have mentioned of their opinions is indeed falsehood fabricated by an innovator to promote his innovation." ʿAllāma Kawtharī, after quoting this passage, writes that this is proof of the unity in doctrine of the Imāms, and then says, "In the light of his books, his students and their students after them endeavored to distinguish the truth in matters of belief without ambiguity or confusion according to the beliefs of the Prophet ﷺ and his Companions ۞. They thus spread sound belief along with their jurisprudence in all parts of the world in a praiseworthy manner appropriate to this important service (*Muqaddimāt al-Imām al-Kawtharī* 177).

The above quotes indicate the importance and concern Abū Ḥanīfa and his companions had for *ʿilm al-kalām* (Islamic theology), such that Abū Jaʿfar al-Ṭaḥāwī (may Allāh have mercy on him) titled his *ʿAqīda* "Exposition of the Beliefs of the Jurists of the Faith, Abū Ḥanīfa, Abū Yūsuf, and Muḥammad (may Allāh have mercy on them)," and then compiled the agreed upon beliefs of the predecessors (*salaf*) as though they were shared by all.

After *kalām,* Abū Ḥanīfa turned his focus on jurisprudence. The inspiration for this scholarly shift is related by Zufar from the Great Imām himself. He said,

> I studied *kalām* so deeply that I reached a status where people would gesture with their fingers in my direction [in awe]. We used to sit close to the class of Ḥammād

> ibn Abī Sulaymān, when once a woman approached me and asked, "A man has a wife who he intends to divorce according to the *sunna;* how does he do it?" I told her to go and ask Ḥammād and then come back and inform me. She went to Ḥammād and asked him. Ḥammād told her, "He should issue a single divorce to her while she is not menstruating and refrain from having intercourse with her. Then he should leave her until she completes three menstrual cycles. As soon as she takes her ritual bath [at the completion of the third] she will be [out of wedlock] and ready for remarriage." She came back and informed me and I said, "I have no need for theology," and picked up my sandals and went and sat in Ḥammād's class. I used to listen to his [Ḥammād's] explication of the various rulings and would memorize them, and then Ḥammād would repeat them the next day and I would be able to recall them accurately and his other students would err, until Ḥammād announced, "Nobody should sit at the head of the circle in front of me other than Abū Ḥanīfa."

After attending the lectures of Ḥammād in jurisprudence, the Imām also began his study of ḥadīth. Some of the scholars from whom he learned this science were Salama ibn Kuhayl, Shaʿbī, ʿAwn ibn ʿAbdillāh, Aʿmash, Qatāda, Shuʿba, and many other famous scholars who had studied ḥadīth under the Companions (*ṣaḥāba*). Ibn Maʿīn has been reported as saying, "I would never place anyone above Wakīʿ [ibn al-Jarrāḥ]. He would issue his legal rulings (*fatāwā*) according to the opinion of Abū Ḥanīfa and would memorize all the ḥadīths from him. He had heard a great deal of ḥadīths from Abū Ḥanīfa (*Iʿlā' al-Sunan* 19:315).

Imām Abū Ḥanīfa's fame as a great scholar and news of his intellectual gifts and originality spread far and wide. But along with his fame, came increased criticism of his use of analogical deductions (*qiyās*) seemingly at the expense of the Qur'ān and Sunna as proof texts. The following narrative elucidates this further. On his second visit to Madīna, he met Imām Bāqir, the great grandson of the Messenger ﷺ. When introduced to him, Imām Bāqir addressed him thus: "So it is you who contradicts the ḥadīth of my grandfather on the basis of juristic analogy." Imām Abū Ḥanīfa replied: "I seek refuge in Allāh. Who dare contradict the ḥadīth of the Messenger ﷺ?" "After you sit down Sir, I shall explain my position." The conversation that ensued between the two great men quickly dispelled the myth that the Great Imām was ruling in contradiction to the Qur'ān and Sunna of the Messenger ﷺ.

Imām Abū Ḥanīfa asked Imām Bāqir, "Who is the weaker, the man or the woman?" Imām Bāqir replied, "Woman." Abū Ḥanīfa then asked, "Which of them is entitled to the larger share in the inheritance?" Imām Bāqir replied, "The man." Abū Ḥanīfa said, "If I had been making mere deductions through analogy, I should have said that the woman should get the larger share, because on the face of it, the weaker one is entitled to more consideration. But I have not said so. To take up another subject, which do you think is the higher duty, prayer (*ṣalāt*) or fasting?" Imām Bāqir said, *"Ṣalāt."* Abū Ḥanīfa said, "That being the case, it should be permissible for a woman during her menstruation to postpone her prayers and not her fasts. But the ruling I give is that she must postpone her fasting and not her prayers [which she is excused from making up at all, following in the footsteps of the Messenger of Allāh ﷺ]." Imām Bāqir was so impressed by this dialogue and the firmness of Imām Abū Ḥanīfa's faith and his love for the Prophet ﷺ that he immediately got up and kissed his forehead (A. R. Doi, *Sharīʿah: The Islamic Law* 94).

The rulings of Imām Abū Ḥanīfa reach up to seventy thousand, as can be gleaned from the laws (*masāʾil*) which have been discussed by Imām Muḥammad al-Shaybānī and other disciples of Imām Abū Ḥanīfa. These legal rulings and the Imām's discussion of them are grounded in ḥadīths. The Imām was very learned and skilled in the science of ḥadīth, as many scholars of his time, such as Aʿmash and ʿAbdullāh ibn al-Mubārak, have testified. Though he incorporated his knowledge and understanding of ḥadīths in his derivation of legal rulings, he would not necessarily narrate each and every single ḥadīth considered before ruling. That is why most of his ḥadīths did not come to us as ḥadīths, but came as jurisprudential judgments, directly based upon the ḥadīths of the Holy Prophet ﷺ.

His students included ʿAbdullāh ibn al-Mubārak, the famous ascetic and imām of ḥadīth who used to declare, "If Allāh had not benefited me through the teachings of Abū Ḥanīfa and Sufyān al-Thawrī, I would have been like any other person" (Suyūṭī, *Tabyīḍ al-Ṣaḥīfa* 1:617).

Although his merits and scholarship were recognized by his teacher, Ḥammād, due to his sincere regard for him, Imām Abū Ḥanīfa refrained from establishing a school of his own even when he was older. When Ḥammād died in 120/737, Abū Ḥanīfa was offered his chair, which he accepted, though reluctantly. Around this time, Imām Abū Ḥanīfa had a dream where he was digging up the Messenger of Allāh's ﷺ grave. He was very frightened and wanted to give up the position as a result of this dream. The great scholar Ibn Sīrīn comforted him and interpreted the dream as an indication that he was to revive the dead branches of learning in Islam. It was then that Imām Abū Ḥanīfa settled down to teach. He became so famous that everywhere he traveled, people gathered around him for interviews, discussions, and debates. His students came from all over the Muslim World. He was visited by large numbers of people who listened to his religious discourses, so much so that he began to be suspected of complicity in every upheaval that took place in that country (*Sharīʿah: The Islamic Law* 98).

It was in the month of Rajab 150/767, that the Great Imām passed away from the poison that was administered to him by prison guards under the command of the ʿAbbāsid Caliph Manṣūr. His funeral prayer was performed six times, and each time, fifty thousand people took part. Even after his burial, people kept coming from afar for approximately twenty days and performing the funeral prayers on him. In 459/1101, a mausoleum was built on his grave by a Seljuk ruler. The same ruler also built a large *madrasa* near his grave in the memory of this great Imām who had so profoundly inspired later generations. The area of Baghdad where his grave is situated is known today as Al-Aʿẓamiyya after him.

ABU ʾL-MUNTAHĀ AL-MAGHNĪSĀWĪ

His full name is Aḥmad ibn Muḥammad, Abu ʾl-Muntahā Shihāb al-Dīn. He was born in Magnisia (Maghnīsā),[42] a town in present-day western Turkey (*Al-Aʿlām* 1:234). Very little is known about the life of this great scholar. His date of birth, among other aspects of his life, also seems to be unknown. It is likely that he was born in the very early part of the eleventh century, given that his death was either in 1090/1679 (*Muʿjam al-Muʾallifīn* 2:159; *Kashf al-Ẓunūn* 5:162) or in 1000/1592 (*Al-Aʿlām* 1:234). It is clear however, that he lived around the turn of the first millennium.

Some sources state that he completed his commentary of *Al-Fiqh al-Akbar* in 989 AH or a year earlier. If this is the case, then it is most likely that the opinion of the Ottoman biographer Muḥammad Ṭāhir Barūsehlī that his death

42 This is the ancient name of Manisa in Turkey. See *Webster's New World Geographical Dictionary.*

was in 1000 AH is more accurate, and, accordingly, he was born in the early tenth century. This means a difference of ninety years between the two dates of death, and a period of a hundred and one years between the completion of the commentary and his death date given by the others. Ziriklī prefers the opinion of Barūsehlī and disregards that of Ḥājī Khalīfa (*Al-Aʿlām* 1:234).

ʿAllāma Maghnīsāwī was an accomplished jurist of the Ḥanafī school and a master in the science of Qur'ān Recitation (*muqri'*). Aside from his commentary on *Al-Fiqh al-Akbar,* he authored many books, including *Iẓhār al-Maʿānī fī Sharḥ Ḥazr al-Amānī* (The Explanation of the Meanings: An Exposition of the Assessment of Aspirations), a commentary of Shāṭabī's *Qaṣīda* in *qirā'a* (Qur'ānic recitation) in Turkish, and the *Qaṣīda Nūniyya* on Islamic theology (*Osmanlı Müellifleri* 228). With the exception of his commentary on Shāṭabī's *Qaṣīda,* all his other works were in Arabic.

MULLĀ ʿALĪ AL-QĀRĪ

ʿAlī ibn Sulṭān Muḥammad al-Qārī, more popularly known as Mullā ʿAlī al-Qārī, was an ascetic, ḥadīth scholar, jurist, theologian, and author of what has been hailed as the most comprehensive Arabic commentary on the *Mishkāt al-Maṣābīḥ,* entitled *Mirqāt al-Mafātīḥ.* He is also famous for his commentary on *Al-Fiqh al-Akbar,* called *Minaḥ al-Rawḍ al-Azhar* (Gifts of the Blooming Gardens). Qārī was born in Herat, Afghanistan, where he received his primary years of Islamic education. Thereafter, he traveled to Makka, where he studied under numerous scholars, including Shaykh Aḥmad ibn Ḥajar al-Haytamī al-Makkī and Quṭb al-Dīn al-Ḥanafī. He was called *Al-Qārī,* "The Reciter," because of his mastery of the science of Qur'ānic recitation. Mullā ʿAlī al-Qārī remained in Makka, where he taught until his death in 1014/1606. His written works include a two-volume commentary on Qāḍī ʿIyāḍ's *Al-Shifā'* (The Cure); a two-volume commentary on Imām Ghazālī's abridgment of the *Iḥyā' ʿUlūm al-Dīn* (The Revival of the Religious Sciences), entitled *ʿAyn al-ʿIlm wa Zayn al-Ḥilm* (The Spring of Knowledge and the Adornment of Understanding); and a book of prophetic invocations, *Al-Ḥizb al-Aʿẓam* (The Supreme Daily *Dhikr*).

OTHER COMMENTARIES ON *AL-FIQH AL-AKBAR*

We have already discussed the commentary of Samarqandī on *Al-Fiqh al-Absaṭ* (inaccurately attributed to Abū Manṣūr al-Māturīdī) and the commentaries of Mullā ʿAlī al-Qārī and Abu 'l-Muntahā al-Maghnīsāwī in the introduction. Shiblī Nuʿmānī mentions a few other commentaries written on *Al-Fiqh al-Akbar* (see *Imām Abū Ḥanīfa: Life and Works* 79). The following are the names and details of some other commentaries that exist in manuscript form in various libraries around the world, most of which have never been published.[43] It is not known whether they are based on Ḥammād's narration of *Al-Fiqh al-Akbar* or Abū Muṭīʿ's narration *Al-Fiqh al-Absaṭ*.

Al-Qawl al-Faṣl Sharḥ al-Fiqh al-Akbar by Muḥammad ibn Bahā' al-Dīn ibn Luṭfullāh al-Raḥmāwī al-Bālīksarī al-Qusṭunṭīnī al-Qayṣarī al-Rūmī al-Bayrāmī al-Ḥanafī (Muḥy al-Dīn ibn Bahā' al-Dīn) better known as Bahā' al-Dīn Zāda (d. 952–956/1539–1549). (Ṭāsh Kubrīzāda, *Al-Shaqā'iq al-Nuʿmāniyya* 2:166–167, *Fihris al-Azhariyya* 3:238, *Fihris al-Asadiyya* 5:172, *Kashf al-Ẓunūn* 1:863, 2:1034, 2:1287, 2:2022, Ghazzī, *Al-Kawākib al-Sā'ira* 2:28–29) This commentary on Ḥammād's version is published in Istanbul and is widely available.

Sharḥ al-Fiqh al-Akbar li 'l-Imām Abī Ḥanīfa by Murād ibn ʿUthmān ibn ʿAlī ibn Qāsim, Abū ʿAlī al-ʿAmurī al-Mūṣilī al-ʿIrāqī al-Ḥanafī (d. 1092/1681). (Muḥammad Khānjīzāda, *Tadhyīl Kashf al-Ẓunūn* [manuscript] 1:284, Entries 3102, 3103, Rashīd Effendi, *Fihris* 6, *Muʿjam al-Mu'allifīn* 12:213, Baghdādī, *Hadiyyat al-ʿĀrifīn* 2:242)

Sharḥ al-Fiqh al-Akbar li 'l-Imām Abī Ḥanīfa by Sayyid Nūrullāh ibn Muḥammad Rafīʿ ibn ʿAbd al-Raḥīm, Nūr al-Dīn al-Shērwānī al-Rūmī al-Barūsawī al-Ḥanafī (d. 1065/1655). (*Osmanlı Müellifleri* 2:43, *Al-Fihris al-Shāmil* 9:2483, *Hadiyyat al-ʿĀrifīn* 2:499)

Al-Ḍaw' al-Akthar fī Sharḥ al-Fiqh al-Akbar (*Īḍāḥ al-Maknūn* 2:74). Author unknown.

---

43 Details on these commentaries have been generously provided by Shaykh Ahmad Ibn Muhammad Bagia of the UK (may Allāh reward him).

ʿAqd al-Jawhar Naẓm Nathr al-Fiqh al-Akbar by Abu 'l-Baqā' al-Aḥmadī (d. 918/1512). (*Kashf al-Ẓunūn* 2:1287)

Sharḥ al-Fiqh al-Akbar li 'l-Imām Abī Ḥanīfa by Sayyid Muḥammad ibn Yūsuf ibn ʿAlī Muḥammad ibn Yūsuf ibn ʿAlī ibn Muḥammad ibn Yūsuf ibn Ḥusayn ibn Muḥammad ibn ʿAlī ibn Hamza ibn Dāwūd ibn Abi 'l-Ḥasan Zayd, Abu 'l-Fatḥ Ṣadr al-Dīn al-Jundī al-Ḥusaynī al-Dihlawī then al-Kulbarkawī al-Hindī al-Ḥanafī more well known as Keysūdarāz. (Dihlawī, *Akhbār al-Akhyār* 80–86, 97, *Tārīkh Farishta* 2:746–749, Raḥmān ʿAlī, *Tadhkira ʿUlamā' al-Hind* 86, Jamīl Aḥmad, *Ḥarakat al-Ta'līf* 71, Lāhōrī, *Khizānat al-Aṣfiyā'* 1:344–346, Āzād Bilgāmī, *Subḥat al-Marjān* 29, Shawkat ʿAlī Khān, *Fihris Tōnk* 3:29–29, ʿAbd al-Ḥayy al-Ḥasanī, *Nuzhat al-Khawāṭir* 3:118–121)

Al-Durr al-Azhar fī Sharḥ al-Fiqh al-Akbar by ʿAbd al-Qādir ibn Muḥammad ibn Idrīs ibn Muḥammad Maḥmūd ibn Muḥammad Kalīm al-ʿUmrī al-Silhetī al-Bengālī al-Ḥanafī (d. 13th century). (Ṭabāṭabā'ī, *Siyar al-Muta'akhkhirīn* 98, Ṣāliḥiyya, *Al-Muʿjam al-Shāmil* 2:233) This commentary has been published by Majlis Dā'irat al-Maʿārif, Hyderabad (1298/1880), Maṭbaʿat al-Taqaddum (1323/1905), and Maṭbaʿat al-Maymaniyya (1327/1909) Cairo, and Delhi (1307/1890).

Sharḥ al-Fiqh al-Akbar by Sayyid Afḍal ibn Amīn ibn Ibrāhīm ibn Khūnd Mīr al-Ḥusaynī al-Rājbandarwī al-Arkātī al-Rifāʿī al-Hindī al-Ḥanafī more well known as Shaykh Sayyid Afḍal Rājbandarwī (d. 1193/1779). (*Nuzhat al-Khawāṭir* 6:698)

Sharḥ al-Fiqh al-Akbar by ʿAbd al-Aʿlā ibn ʿAbd al-ʿAlī ibn Niẓām al-Dīn ibn Quṭb al-Dīn al-Shahīd ibn ʿAbd al-Ḥalīm al-Anṣārī al-Sihālwī al-Bārabankawī al-Farangī Maḥallī al-Lakhnawī al-Hindī (d. 1207/1792–1793). (*Ḥarakat al-Taʾlīf* 326, *Nuzhat al-Khawāṭir* 7:997)

Sharḥ al-Fiqh al-Akbar by Isḥāq al-Rūmī more well known as Isḥāq al-Ṭabīb (d. 949/1543). (Ibn ʿImād, *Shadharāt al-Dhahab* 8:281, Ṭāsh Kubrīzāda, *Al-Shaqā'iq al-Nuʿmāniyya* 2:166–167, Ghazzī, *Al-Kawākib al-Sā'ira* 2:122)

Sharḥ al-Fiqh al-Akbar by ʿAlī ibn Murād ibn ʿUthmān ibn ʿAlī, Nūr al-Dīn Abu 'l-Faḍl al-ʿUmarī al-Mawṣilī al-Ḥanafī (d. 1147/1737). (*Hadiyyat al-ʿĀrifīn* 1:766)

Al-Qawl al-Muyassar ʿala 'l-Fiqh al-Akbar by ʿAzā ibn ʿAlī ibn ʿAbdillāh ibn Muḥammad ʿĪsā ibn ʿAbdillāh al-Maymanī al-Ḥadīdī al-Yamānī al-Ḥanafī (d. 1369/1949). (*Tashnīf al-Asmāʿ* 380)

Sharḥ al-Fiqh al-Akbar by Abu 'l-Najā ibn Khalaf ibn Muḥammad ibn Muḥammad ibn ʿAlī al-Fawwī al-Miṣrī al-Ḥanafī then al-Shāfiʿī (d. 849/1445). (*Al-Ḍaw' al-Lāmiʿ* 6:11, 143–145)

Al-Miṣbāḥ al-Azhar Sharḥ al-Fiqh al-Akbar by Sulaymān ibn Raṣad al-Zayyātī al-Miṣrī al-Azharī al-Shādhilī al-Ḥanafī (d. 1347/1928). (*Fihris al-Azhariyya* 8:462)

Al-Irshād fī Sharḥ al-Fiqh al-Akbar li 'l-Imām Abī Ḥanīfa by Muḥammad ibn Muḥammad ibn Muḥammad ibn Maḥmūd ibn Aḥmad, Akmal al-Dīn ibn Shams al-Dīn ibn Jamāl al-Dīn Abū ʿAbdillāh al-Bābartī al-Rūmī then al-Miṣrī (al-Dimashqī) al-Ḥanafī (d. 786/1384). (*Kashf al-Ẓunūn* 1:69). Manuscripts of this commentary are preserved by [IDC Publishers of the Netherlands,] Al-Azhariyya Cairo and in Palestine under the title *Al-Ḥikma al-Nabawiyya fī Sharḥ Al-Fiqh al-Akbar li 'l-Imām Abī Ḥanīfa,* and in [the University of Birmingham,] Selly Oak, under the title *Mukhtaṣar al-Ḥikma fī Sharḥ al-Fiqh al-Akbar.*

Tuḥfat al-Nabī fī Sharḥ wa Tarjamat al-Fiqh al-Akbar, an Ottoman Turkish translation and commentary by Muṣṭafā ibn Muḥammad ibn Muṣṭafā al-Murādī al-Kūzalḥiṣārī al-Rūmī al-Khulūṣī al-Naqshbandī al-Ḥanafī (d. 1215/1800). (*Hadiyyat al-ʿĀrifīn* 2:454, *Fihris al-Azhariyya* 2:145)

Naẓm al-Fiqh al-Akbar li 'l-Imām Abī Ḥanīfa by Ibrāhīm ibn Ḥusām al-Dīn al-Kirmiyānī al-Rūmī al-Ḥanafī known as Sayyidī Sharīfī (d. 1016/1608). (*Kashf al-Ẓunūn* 2:1287)

Al-Ḥikmat al-Nabawiyya fī Sharḥ al-Fiqh al-Akbar by Isḥāq ibn Muḥammad ibn Ismāʿīl ibn Ibrāhīm ibn Zayd, Abu 'l-Qāsim al-Samarqandī al-Ḥanafī, more well known as Ḥakīm Isḥāq (d. 342/953 or 345/956). He also wrote a shorter commentary called *Mukhtaṣar al-Ḥikmat al-Nabawiyya fī Sharḥ al-Fiqh al-Akbar* (Qurashī, *Al-Jawāhir al-Muḍīʾa* 1:371–372, *Kashf al-Ẓunūn* 2:1287, Mashūkhī, *Fihris Maktaba ʿĀrif Ḥikmat* 155–156, Ibn al-Athīr, *Al-Lubāb* 3:241–242). Another commentary is mentioned in *Īḍāḥ al-Maknūn* called *Al-Sharīʿa al-Muṣṭafawiyya wa 'l-Sunna al-Muḥammadiyya lā bi 'l-ʿAqli* [*bal bi*] *'l-Riwāya fī Sharḥ al-Fiqh al-Akbar* (*Īḍāḥ al-Maknūn* 2:48). The author's name is not mentioned but it is likely that it is the one by Ḥakīm Isḥāq.

Sharḥ al-Fiqh al-Akbar by Ilyās ibn Ibrāhīm al-Sīnūbī (or Sīnābī) then al-Barūsawī al-Rūmī al-Ḥanafī (891/1486). (*Kashf al-Ẓunūn* 1:854) Manuscripts of this commentary are preserved [in the Library of the University of Leiden and] in Riyāḍ.

There is nothing like unto Him (Qur'ān 42:11)

❁

Behold! In the creation of the heavens and the earth; in the alternation of the night and the day; in the sailing of the ships through the ocean for the profit of mankind; in the rain that Allāh sends down from the skies, and the life that He gives therewith to an earth that is dead; in the beasts of all kinds that He scatters through the earth; in the change of the winds, and the clouds compelled between heaven and earth; (here) indeed are signs for a people that are wise (Qur'ān 2:164).

الحمد لله رب العالمين

IMĀM ABŪ ḤANĪFA'S

Al-Fiqh al-Akbar

Explained

by Abu 'l-Muntahā al-Maghnīsāwī
with Selections from ʿAlī al-Qārī's Commentary,
Including Abū Ḥanīfa's *Kitāb al-Waṣiyya*

الله أكبر

Prologue

THE SCHOLARS' APPROACH TO *ʿILM AL-KALĀM*

Summarized from ʿAlī al-Qārī's Introduction

The Dispersion of the Umma

The Messenger of Allāh ﷺ said, "Verily, the Banī Isrāʾīl broke up into seventy-two factions, and my umma will break up into seventy-three, all of whom will be in the Fire except one." The Companions asked, "Who are they, Messenger of Allāh?" He replied, "Those who are on my way and that of my Companions" (*Tirmidhī*)[44]

---

44 Shaykh Khalīl Aḥmad Sahāranpūrī (d. 1346/1927) writes regarding this ḥadīth in his commentary on *Sunan Abī Dāwūd, Badhl al-Majhūd:* "Blameworthy conflict is that which takes place regarding the fundamentals of religion (*uṣūl al-dīn*). As for the differences of the umma regarding its branches (*furūʿ*), they are not considered blameworthy, but stem from the mercy of Allāh, Most Pure. You can observe that the groups who differ in the branches of religion are united in its fundamentals, and do not accuse one another of deviancy. As for those who are opposed to one another in the fundamentals, they accuse one another of deviancy and unbelief. The specific number [mentioned in the ḥadīth] should be interpreted as indicating plurality in general. If differences in fundamentals and the branches are both considered, their number would go into the hundreds. However, if only the differences in the fundamentals are considered, it is possible that the number indicated [in the ḥadīth] is more definitive [or representative of a real number]. Moreover, if all the sub-factions of these various sects were to be enumerated [in this regard], they would not exceed this number by a lot (i.e., seventy-three).... It is thus best to say that this number will certainly be reached [by the end of time] and the total cannot be less than it, but there is no problem if it exceeds this number" (*Al-Taʿlīq al-Muyassar* 28). Whenever any statement is made by a person, there is a particular criterion in the mind of the speaker. Sometimes, the criteria, framework, or benchmark may be revealed by the speaker and sometimes, as in the case of the ḥadīth above, it may not be. It is difficult to ascertain what benchmark was in the mind of the Messenger of Allāh ﷺ when he made this remark. For instance, what is the exact size of a group for it to be considered one of the seventy-two sects, what is the number of its adherents, and the intensity of their deviance? Will they all come within a certain time period or is this applicable until the end of time? How strong will their influence be? Clearly, the Messenger ﷺ certainly had a criteria in

The Scholars' Approach to ʿIlm al-Kalām

Much has been related regarding the disapproval of the majority of the *salaf* and a number of the *khalaf* (successors) of *ʿilm al-kalām* (polemical theology)[45] and their prohibition of it and any science related to it, such as logic (*manṭiq*), etc. So much that Abū Yūsuf (may Allāh have mercy on him) said to Bishr al-Marīsī,[46] "Knowledge of *kalām* is ignorance, and ignorance of *kalām* is knowledge." It is possible that by ignorance of it, he meant the "belief" that it is incorrect, as this ignorance would be considered beneficial knowledge, or he was deterring one from it and stating that one should not pay attention to it, as this is what will protect a person's knowledge and intellect, and in this way it will be considered knowledge. It is also related from him that "those who seek knowledge of *kalām* will lose their religion, and those who seek wealth through alchemy will become poor, and those who look for obscure and strange (*gharīb*) ḥadīths will fall into falsehood."

Imām Shāfiʿī (may Allāh have mercy on him) said, "My ruling regarding people of *kalām* is that they be beaten with sticks and sandals and paraded among the clans and tribes and it should be said, 'This is the recompense of those who abandon the Qur'ān and Sunna and turn their attention to the *kalām* of the innovators.'" He also said, "A servant's meeting Allāh with any sin other than shirk is better than his meeting Allāh with *kalām*."[47] [29]

---

mind, since he gave details on the saved sect (*firqa nājiya*), which gives us some corresponding insight into the deviant heretic groups. Many heresiographers like Baghdādī, Shahrastānī, Jīlī, and Ibn ʿAbd al-Barr have studied and counted the various sects and their subgroups that have appeared in the history of Islam, such as the Muʿtazila, Khawārij, Shīʿa, Ḥashawiyya, etc.; they have come up with different results based on their size, influence, or endurance, among other things. See Badre ʿĀlam Mīrathī, *Tarjumān al-Sunna* 1:63–65.

45 The disapproval here is toward "polemical" or "speculative" theology rather than Islamic theology proper [Theo (God) Ology (Study)], i.e., the study of Islamic beliefs (*ʿaqīda*) or *tawḥīd*. Whereas the latter is designed to defend the proper beliefs of Islam from heresy and to bring the populous back to the original foundational and fundamental creed, the former points to hairsplitting debates on doctrine. Both can be referred to as *ʿilm al-kalām*.

46 Bishr ibn Ghiyāth, Abū ʿAbd al-Raḥmān al-Marīsī al-ʿAdawī, a jurist and Muʿtazilī theologian who studied *fiqh* with Abū Yūsuf; he was the head of the Marīsiyya sect. About him, Dhahabī says, "[He was] a misguided innovator from whom it is not permissible to relate, and although he did not meet Jahm ibn Ṣafwān, he adopted his idea of the createdness of the Qur'ān and preached it (*Siyar Aʿlām al-Nubalā'* 10:199–202).

47 Ibn ʿAsākir al-Dimashqī (d. 571/1175) clarifies that Shāfiʿī's condemnation of *kalām* was more directed at the open debates about *qadar* (predestination) and other sectarian polemics. See *Tabyīn Kadhib al-Muftarī* 335-340.

Imām Ghazālī[48] sheds some light on this issue in his *Iḥyā' ʿUlūm al-Dīn* and explains that there are two extreme positions when viewing *ʿilm al-kalām:* (1) those who hold it to be an innovation and unlawful, and that a servant's meeting Allāh with any sin other than shirk is better than him meeting Allāh with *kalām,* and (2) those who classify it as obligatory knowledge, either individual or communal, going so far as to say that it is the most superior form of worship and the most complete way of reaching nearness to Allāh Most High, because it is used to establish the Oneness of Allāh and defend His noble religion.

Ghazālī's opinion is that there is both harm and benefit in it, depending on the circumstance. The harms of *kalām* are due to what occurs in the heart of the one studying it. It may lead one to doubts, reconsideration of one's beliefs, and loss of firm conviction. This is what occurs at the beginning of taking this path. Another harm is that it may deepen the conviction of the innovator in his errant belief because of his need to defend himself against those who wish to prove him wrong. On the other hand, Ghazālī mentions that it is also thought that *kalām* can unveil certain realities and allow one to gain a greater understanding of the truth of one's position. However, he explains, "In *kalām,* there is not much realization of this honorable objective, and perhaps stumbling and misguidance are more likely than any unveiling and understanding." He then says that if you had heard this explanation from a *muḥaddith* (ḥadīth scholars who were averse to any form of *kalām*) or *ḥashawī* (crypto-anthropomorphist), then you may say that "the ignorant are the enemies of what they are unaware of," so hear this from one experienced in *kalām* after reaching the extreme limits of the theologians and the depths of other sciences beyond that, one [who has] established that the path to the realities of knowing [Allāh] are blocked from this way. Yes, *kalām* is not completely devoid of revealing, clarifying, or defining certain aspects, but this is rare. [30–32]

The abhorrence of these scholars of the study of *kalām* came about for a number of reasons. The first reason is that it diverts one's energies away from the study of the fundamentals of Islam and causes one to become occupied with that which is not beneficial in advancing the objectives of faith. The

48 The reviver of the fifth century and the proof of Islam, Abū Ḥāmid Muḥammad ibn Muḥammad ibn Aḥmad al-Ṭūsī al-Ghazālī, was a great Shāfiʿī scholar and author of numerous works in *fiqh,* philosophy, theology, and spirituality. He died in 505/1111.

second is that their debate and arguing, even for the truth, frequently leads to ill-mannered disputation.

Third, it leads to doubt and vacillation in one's beliefs. Thus a person can become devoid of faith after having been a true believer. The great Imām Aḥmad ibn Ḥanbal condemned Ḥārith ibn Asad al-Muḥāsibī[49] for writing a rebuttal of the innovators, despite his piety and asceticism. He said, "Woe be to you! Do you not first relate their innovations and then rebut them? Through your writing do you not cause people to study their innovation and ponder over their misleading arguments, which leads the readers to study them deeply, formulate opinions, and lead to confusion?" It states in *Kitāb al-Khulāṣa,*[50] "Studying *kalām,* delving deeply into it, and debating beyond what is necessary is prohibited, just as the study of astronomy in order to ascertain the times of prayer and the *qibla* direction is not blameworthy, but going beyond that is unlawful [e.g., astrology]."

In short, just as true belief and its evidences inspire true faith and complete conviction in religious people, corrupt beliefs negatively affect the heart and harden it, taking it away from the presence of the Lord, blackening the heart, and weakening one's faith. In fact, it is the strongest source for sealing an evil end to one's life. We ask Allāh for forgiveness and safety. Have you not seen that when Satan desires to steal the faith of a servant in his Lord, he does not do so except by placing in his heart a false belief?

Fourth, it leads to immersion in the study of *kalām* to the exclusion of the study of the laws of Islam that are derived from the Qur'ān and Sunna and the consensus (*ijmāʿ*) of the umma. Some will study *kalām* for thirty years to become theologians but will be ignorant of important rulings related to purification, prayer, and fasting. Fifth, the result of *kalām* and argumentation is confusion in the interim, and misguidance and doubt in the future, as Ibn Rushd the Grandson (Averroës),[51] one of the most brilliant Muslim philoso-

---

49 He was Abū ʿAbdillāh Ḥārith ibn Asad al-Muḥāsibī al-Baghdādī, the famous ascetic. He died in 243/857 (*Ṣifat al-Ṣafwa* 2:270).

50 This is *Khulāṣat al-Fatāwā* of Ṭāhir ibn Aḥmad ibn ʿAbd al-Rashīd ibn al-Ḥasan, Iftikhār al-Dīn al-Bukhārī al-Ḥanafī. He was born in Bukhārā and authored *Khizānat al-Fatāwā, Khizānat al-Wāqiʿāt, and Al-Niṣāb* and died in Sarakhs in 542/1147 (*Hadiyyat al-ʿĀrifīn* 1:224, *Muʿjam al-Mu'allifīn* 5:32).

51 The philosopher Abu 'l-Walīd Muḥammad ibn Aḥmad ibn Muḥammad ibn Rushd al-Andalusī; known as Averroës in the West; he was born in Cordoba, where his father and grandfather had both been judges and his grandfather was also the *imām* of the Mosque of Cordoba. He wrote *Bidāyat al-Mujtahid,* among many other books in various subjects, and died in 595/1195. He is

phers, said in his *Tahāfut al-Tahāfut* (Incoherence of the Incoherence). [Many had chosen the path of *kalām* only to regret it later in life,] such as Āmidī,[52] Shahrastānī, Khuwanjī,[53] Rāzī,[54] and one of his greatest students, Khusrūshāhī.[55] Likewise, Ghazālī, who reached a state of confusion and undecidedness in matters of *kalām,* turned to the ḥadīths of Allāh's Messenger ﷺ and died with a copy of *Ṣaḥīḥ al-Bukhārī* on his chest. Abu 'l-Maʿālī al-Juwaynī,[56] upon his death bed, lamented, "I have delved into a deep ocean and I left the people of Islam and their knowledge, and I entered what was prohibited to me. Now if my Lord does not accept me with His mercy, then woe to the son of Juwaynī. Here I am, dying upon the beliefs of my mother," or he said, "of the old women of Nīshāpūr."

Sixth, speaking purely from one's opinion and intellect in matters of Islamic jurisprudence (*fiqh*) and Sharīʿa (Sacred Law) is an innovation and misguidance. It is considered even more reprehensible to do so with respect to the science of divine oneness and attributes. Lastly, it leads to paying careful attention to the speech of the philosophers and their foolish followers who rejected the verses sent down from the heavens and became engrossed with the ignorant, whom they considered scholars of deep understanding.

---

called al-Ḥafīd (the Grandson) to distinguish him from his grandfather Abu 'l-Walīd Muḥammad ibn Aḥmad (d. 520/1126).

52 Abu 'l-Ḥasan ʿAlī ibn Muḥammad ibn Sālim al-Taghlibī, the jurist and *uṣūl* scholar given the title Sayf al-Dīn. He initially adhered to the Ḥanbalī school, after which he became a proponent of the Shāfiʿī school and studied in Baghdad and the Levant. Later, he moved to Cairo and studied there, and then went to Hama and Damascus. He died in Damascus in 631/1233. Among his excellent works is *Al-Iḥkām fī Uṣūl al-Aḥkām.*

53 Muḥammad ibn Nāmāwar ibn ʿAbd al-Malik, Abū ʿAbdillāh al-Khuwanjī was of Persian origin. He moved to Egypt where he took a post as a judge. He died in 646/1248.

54 The ḥadīth master and biographer Dhahabī writes about Rāzī, "The erudite learned scholar of a variety of subjects Fakhr al-Dīn Muḥammad ibn ʿUmar ibn al-Ḥusayn al-Qurashī al-Bakrī al-Ṭabaristānī, the exegete, the great one from among the geniuses, the wise, and the authors. He was born in 544/1149, and his writings became popular throughout the lands of the East and West. He had a profound intellect. Some issues are found in his writing that are away from the Sunna. May Allāh forgive him for that, for he died on the praiseworthy path, and Allāh takes care of the hearts." He died in Herat in 606/1209 (see *Siyar Aʿlām al-Nubalā'* 21:500–501).

55 ʿAbd al-Ḥamīd ibn ʿĪsā al-Khusrūshāhī (Khusrūshāh is a village by Marw, present-day Turkmenistan) al-Tabrīzī al-Shāfiʿī was a theologian who studied under Fakhr al-Dīn al-Rāzī. Then he went to the Levant after the death of his teacher, where he taught. He later moved to Karak (in Jordan) and stayed by Malik Nāṣir Dāwūd. He passed away in Damascus in 652/1254, leaving behind many written works.

56 ʿAbd al-Malik ibn ʿAbdillāh ibn Yūsuf ibn Muḥammad, Abu 'l-Maʿālī al-Juwaynī al-Naysābūrī, Shaykh of the Shāfiʿīs, the Imām of the Two Sanctuaries (Imām al-Ḥaramayn). Author of numerous works in both the fundamental and derived sciences, he passed away in 478/1085.

In conclusion, what was brought by the Prophet ﷺ is complete, sufficient, and satisfactory. It was the path of the predecessors and their followers among the Imāms of *ijtihād,* the greatest scholars of exegesis and ḥadīth, and the foremost pillars of *taṣawwuf.* [32–42]

MAGHNĪSĀWĪ'S INTRODUCTION

All praises are for Allāh, who guided us toward the path of the Ahl al-Sunna wa 'l-Jamāʿa through His tremendous generosity. And blessing and peace be upon His beloved Messenger, Muḥammad, who possessed sublime character, and upon his family and Companions, who called to the Straight Path.

To proceed: The weak and sinful servant Abū 'l-Muntahā (may Allāh, the Almighty and Gracious, protect him from errors and sins, and from defective and errant belief) states:

The treatise *Al-Fiqh al-Akbar,* which the Great Imām composed, is an accepted and reliable treatise. The Imām and Pride of Islam, Shaykh ʿAlī al-Bazdawī states in [his book], *Uṣūl al-Fiqh* (The Principles of Jurisprudence): "Knowledge is of two kinds: knowledge of divine oneness (*tawḥīd*) and attributes (*ṣifāt*), and knowledge of jurisprudence, sacred laws, and legal ordinances. The principle governing the former is to hold fast to the Qur'ān and Sunna, refrain from following whim and innovation, and remain steadfast on the path of the Ahl al-Sunna wa 'l-Jamāʿa, whereupon strode the Companions (*ṣaḥāba*), Followers (*tābiʿūn*), and the pious predecessors. It is the path upon which we found our learned scholars (*mashā'ikh*), and upon it were our predecessors, Abū Ḥanīfa, Abū Yūsuf, and Muḥammad, and all of their colleagues (may Allāh have mercy on them). Abū Ḥanīfa (may Allāh have mercy on him) composed *Al-Fiqh al-Akbar* on the subject [of the science of divine oneness and attributes] and discussed therein the establishment of the attributes [of Allāh], that good and evil destiny is from Him Most High, and that it is all through the will of Allāh."

Therefore, I intended to compile statements from the Qur'ān and Sunna, and from other reliable works, that would stand as a commentary for this distinguished and refined treatise.

THE FUNDAMENTALS OF DIVINE ONENESS AND TRUE FAITH

أَصْلُ التَّوْحِيْدِ وَمَا يَصِحُّ الْإِعْتِقَادُ عَلَيْهِ يَجِبُ أَن يَّقُوْلَ: آمَنْتُ بِاللهِ، وَمَلَائِكَتِهِ، وَكُتُبِهِ، وَرُسُلِهِ، وَالْبَعْثِ بَعْدَ الْمَوْتِ، وَالْقَدَرِ خَيْرِهِ وَشَرِّهِ مِنَ اللهِ تَعَالٰى، وَالْحِسَابِ، وَالْمِيْزَانِ، وَالْجَنَّةِ، وَالنَّارِ، وَذٰلِكَ كُلُّهُ حَقٌّ.

[This treatise is on] the fundamentals of divine oneness and [tenets] upon which it is correct to base [one's] belief. It is obligatory [for a person] to state: I believe in Allāh, His angels, His scriptures, His messengers, resurrection after death, that destiny, good and evil, is from Allāh Most High, the Reckoning, the Scale, Paradise, and Hellfire; and that they are all true.

❁

The Greatest Imām (Imām Aʿẓam), Abū Ḥanīfa (may Allāh have mercy on him) states: The fundamentals of divine oneness meaning that "this treatise is an explanation of the reality of divine oneness." Literally, *tawḥīd* (divine oneness) means to declare something to be one and to know it is one. Technically, it means to rid the divine essence (*al-dhāt al-ilāhiyya*) of all that is conceived by the intellect and all delusional imaginations and fancies of the mind. The meaning of "Allāh being one" is to negate the divisibility of His essence and to negate any similarity or partner in His essence and attributes. The word *iʿtiqād* (belief) in the author's statement and [tenets] upon which it is correct to base [one's] belief encompasses knowledge (*ʿilm*), that is, a definite judgment that does not allow for doubt; it also encompasses the common meaning of belief (*iʿtiqād*), that is, a definite judgment that does allow for doubt. According to some scholars, *iʿtiqād* encompasses opinion (*ẓann*), just as it encompasses the common meaning of belief, because preponderant opinion (*al-ẓann al-ghālib*) in which there is no possibility of an antithesis (*naqīḍ*) is accepted in faith, since this characterizes the faith of most lay persons.

[Qārī] "And [tenets] upon which it is correct to base [one's] belief": This is the meaning of Abū Ḥanīfa's statement, "*Fiqh* is for each soul to recognize what is due to it and for what it is responsible." It is worth noting that the Imām avoided expounding proofs for the existence of Allāh Most High, because such a reality is undeniable, based on what can be clearly witnessed. Allāh says, "Their messengers said, 'Is there any doubt in Allāh, the Maker of the heavens and earth?'" (Qur'ān 14:10) and "And if you ask them who has created the heavens and the earth, they will surely say 'Allāh'" (31:25). So it is that the True Reality (Allāh) is established in the primordial nature (*fiṭra*) of mankind as indicated by the words of Allāh Most High: "The primordial nature in which Allāh created mankind" (30:30). One need only look at all the wonders of creation to realize that all of its order, uniqueness, and perfection can only be the creation of the One Wise Creator.[57] [49–51]

All of the prophets (upon them be peace) were sent to firmly establish divine oneness, and their unanimous call was "There is no god but Allāh" (*lā ilāha illa 'Llāh*); and they were not ordered to call people to saying "Allāh is existent," but they sought to eradicate worship of any being other than Allāh Most High as a response to the imagination and whimsical fantasies of people in this regard. [Such foolishness is demonstrated] in the following verses: "But those who take for protectors other than Allāh (say), 'We only serve them in order that they may bring us nearer to Allāh'" (Qur'ān 39:3) and "These are our intercessors with Allāh" (10:18). It is also true that establishing the oneness of Allāh serves to establish with greater firmness the matter of Allāh's existence. [50]

Allāh says, "Behold! In the creation of the heavens and the earth; in the alternation of the night and the day; in the sailing of the ships through the

---

57 These statements establish one of the characteristic features of Māturīdī thought, namely that one does not need divine revelation to establish the existence of the Creator. In other words, one who does not receive any revelations from Allāh Most High will still be expected to conclude on his own that He exists and will be held accountable for this belief. However, such a person would not be expected to uphold the religious laws or the Sharīʿa. The Ashʿarīs differ in that they say it is not required of people who have not received divine revelation to believe in a Creator. Rather, divine revelation is required for accountability in both expressing belief and upholding the religious laws (see "Understanding Good and Evil Through Reason" below for more details).

ocean for the profit of mankind; in the rain that Allāh sends down from the skies, and the life that He gives therewith to an earth that is dead; in the beasts of all kinds that He scatters through the earth; in the change of the winds, and the clouds compelled between heaven and earth; (here) indeed are signs for a people that are wise (2:164).

Therefore, anyone who observes the wondrous creation of Allāh mentioned above and what Allāh mentions in the following verses: "We created Man from a quintessence (of clay), then We placed him as (a drop of) sperm in a place of rest, firmly fixed, then We made the sperm into a clot of congealed blood, then of that clot We made a (fetus) lump, then We made out of that lump bones and clothed the bones with flesh, then We developed out of it another creature. So blessed be Allāh, the best to create!" (23:12–14) and "Soon will We show them Our signs in the (furthest) regions (of the earth), and in their own souls, until it becomes manifest to them that this is the Truth. Is it not enough that your Lord witnesses all things?" (41:53), [if anyone reflects on these words, he] will be compelled to conclude that all matter of creation with its elaborate systems cannot be devoid of a Creator who brought them out of nothingness, or of a Wise Administrator who created in them a variety of inherent qualities. [51]

The above should be sufficient for those of insight (*uli 'l-abṣār*), and thus, we have abstained from presenting the logical arguments for the existence of Allāh Most High that experts present. However, these can be summarized as a whole [by the statement]: the universe is originated (*ḥādith*); it came out of nothingness, and was thus in need of an Eternal Creator who preceded it to bring it into existence. This can only be Allāh Most High, who says, "Allāh is the Creator of all things, and He is the Guardian and Disposer of all affairs" (39:62) and "Your Guardian-Lord is Allāh, who created the heavens and the earth in six days" (7:54). Therefore, whosoever believes that the universe is preeternal (*qadīm*) is an unbeliever [because such belief negates the existence of a Creator or negates Allāh being its Creator]. [52]

Thus after establishing the source of all existent things being the Necessarily Existent (*wājib al-wujūd*),[58] we establish that the Necessarily Existent

58 In many of the later Ashʿarī *ʿaqīda* texts "existence" or "being" is divided into three categories: (1) Necessarily existent (*wājib al-wujūd*), which defines the existence of Allāh Most High. Allāh Most High exists independently through Himself, and His existence is necessary for the existence of all other things. None of His creation share in His existence. (2) Contingently or possibly existent

will never cease to be, because that which is established in preeternity is also everlasting and eternal. Therefore, preeternality without beginning (*qidam*) and everlastingness without end (*baqā'*) are classified as part of His negating attributes (*ṣifāt salbiyya*).[59] Some have classified the two attributes from among the establishing attributes (*nuʿūt thubūtiyya*),[60] since they establish the permanence of Allāh Most High as His preeternality negates his non-existence at any time in the past, and his everlastingness negates His non-existence at any time in the future.[61] [53]

It is obligatory [for a person] to state: I believe in Allāh/ The author uses the words "to state" and not simply "to believe" in order to indicate that affirmation (*iqrār*) is an integral part of true faith (*īmān*), because the integral parts of true faith are affirmation and conviction (*taṣdīq*) in the six articles mentioned [above], based on the statement of Allāh's Messenger ﷺ: "True faith is that you believe in Allāh, His angels, His scriptures, His messengers, the Last Day, and that you believe in destiny, the good and bad of it" (*Muslim,* "al-Īmān," 9).

[Qārī] In the Imām's statement, there is indication that verbal confession (*iqrār*) has legal weight, notwithstanding the difference of opinion of whether confession is a condition (*sharṭ*) of faith for the laws of Islam to apply to the person [in this world] or whether it is an integral pillar (*shaṭr*) of faith [such that its absence leads to the loss of faith]. The opinion of Imām Māturīdī, the most correct opinion according to Imām Ashʿarī, and what is related from

---

(*mumkin* or *jā'iz al-wujūd*), which defines the existence of created beings that may or may not exist, since their existence is not necessary. Allāh Most High determines their existence through His will, power, and knowledge, and if He so wills, they remain nonexistent. (3) Impossible existence (*mustaḥīl* or *mumtaniʿ al-wujūd*), which defines the impossible being, such as the existence of a partner in the essence of Allāh, His attributes, or actions, which is impossible both according to revelation and the intellect (see also *Sharḥ al-Ṣāwī ʿala 'l-Jawhara* 105).

59 This is because they negate their opposites from Allāh. The negating attributes are five: preeternity (*qidam*), everlastingness (*baqā'*), oneness (*waḥdāniyya*), being different from everything else (*mukhālafat al-ḥawādith*), and self-subsistence (*qiyām bi 'l-nafs*). Thus, since preeternity is a necessary attribute for Allāh, to be originated (*ḥudūth*) is impossible. To be everlasting is necessary for Allāh, and thus His coming to an end (*fanā'*) is impossible. Likewise, His being one, completely different from all of creation, and being self-subsistent are all necessary, and thus His being more than one (*taʿaddud*), being similar to creation (*muwāfaqat al-makhlūqāt*), or being in need of anything (*ḥāja ilā shay'*) are all impossible (*Al-Taʿlīq al-Muyassar* 53).

60 That is, the personal attributes (*ṣifāt dhātiyya* or *nafsiyya*). See note 99 for further details.

61 This is the terminology utilized by the scholars of *tawḥīd*. (*Al-Taʿlīq al-Muyassar*).

Imām Abū Ḥanīfa on this issue [is that belief in the heart is sufficient between a servant and Allāh, and] verbal confession is necessary only for a person to be treated as a believer in this world.[62] The above opinion is supported by the verse "For such, He has written faith in their hearts" (Qur'ān 58:22). However, Bazdawī [and a few others] say, "Whoever accepts faith in his heart but leaves off confession with the tongue without excuse is not a believer." This is also the opinion adopted by the expert jurists.[63]

In Imām Abū Ḥanīfa's statement, there is also indication that using the testimonial formula "I bear witness" (*ashhadu*) is not a condition for the verbal confession of faith, as opposed to some Shāfiʿī scholars who deem adherence to the formula necessary. Rather, one can say "There is no god but Allāh" (*lā ilāha illa 'Llāh*) without the testification and mean by that that one believes in and is convinced of the existence of Allāh Most High in terms of His Oneness and His being unique in His attributes. [53–54]

His angels/ "Angels," according to the majority of believers, are subtle bodies capable of taking on different forms. They are of two kinds: those who are absorbed in the gnosis (*maʿrifa*) of the True One and declaring His transcendence; they are the lofty ones (*ʿilliyyūn*) and the intimate (*muqarrabūn*) angels. The other kind of angels are those who manage the affairs from the heavens to the earth, according to what has been predestined and what has been inscribed by the Divine Pen. Some of them are employed in the heavens and the others deployed to the earth.

His scriptures/ [Belief in the scriptures] means to have firm conviction in their existence and in their being the word of Allāh Most High. The total number of scriptures (*ṣuḥuf*) revealed to the messengers is one hundred and four. Ten were revealed to Ādam (Adam) عليه السلام, fifty to Shīth (Seth) عليه السلام, thirty to Idrīs (Enoch) عليه السلام, ten to Ibrāhīm (Abraham) عليه السلام, the Tawrāh (Torah) to Mūsā (Moses) عليه السلام, the Zabūr (Psalms) to Dāwūd (David) عليه السلام, the Injīl (Evangel) to ʿĪsā (Jesus) عليه السلام, and the Furqān (Criterion) to Muḥammad عليه السلام.

His messengers/ *Rasūl* (messenger) is one who is given a sacred law (Sharīʿa) and [according to one opinion] a scripture. Hence, *rasūl* is more specific than *nabī* (prophet or envoy), but according to some scholars, it is synonymous

62 And thus he is able to lead prayer, marry a Muslim, be prayed upon at his death, and be buried in the cemetery of the Muslims, among other things.

63 See "Verbal Affirmation (*Iqrār*): An Integral or Condition?" below for a complete discussion.

with *nabī.* Belief in every prophet is essential, whether or not a scripture has been revealed to him.

[Qārī] The provided order of belief first in the angels, then in the scriptures, and then in the prophets is due to the fact that the angels brought the scriptures to the prophets. If they were to be ordered in terms of importance, it is clear that [belief in] the scriptures, being the word(s) of Allāh Most High, would precede [belief in] the angels.

Regarding the prophets, it is related in the *Musnad* of Imām Aḥmad that the Messenger of Allāh ﷺ was questioned regarding their number. He said, "One hundred and twenty-four thousand, among whom three hundred and thirteen were messengers, and the first of whom was Ādam and the last was Muḥammad ﷺ." Despite this, [many scholars say] it is best not to insist on a particular number, since the ḥadīth is a lone narration (*khabar wāḥid*), and to avoid including in their number those who were not of them and excluding those who were from among them. [55, 171]

resurrection after death/ This means that Allāh will resurrect the deceased from their graves by gathering their original body parts and returning the souls to them.

Resurrection and Transmigration (Tanāsukh)

[Qārī] To those who claim that belief in the resurrection is the same as belief in the transmigration of souls (*tanāsukh*),[64] they are not the same. Jalāl al-Dīn Rūmī said, "There is no belief system except that transmigration has some feature in it," in that they may seem to be one and the same. The truth of the matter is that transmigration is when a soul is moved into a completely new and separate body. Resurrection (*baʿth*), on the other hand, necessitates a piece of the original body to initiate the formation of the resurrected body.

64 *Tanāsukh.* Transmigration of the soul. This refers to the belief that after the end of one's life, the soul moves into another living form similar to reincarnation. It is often connected with a belief that the karma (or the actions) of the soul in one life (or, more generally, a series of past lives) determines the future existence. It is a belief found within Hindu traditions (such as Yoga, Vaishnavism, and Jainism), Greek philosophy, animism, theosophy, anthroposophy, Wicca, and other theological systems, including some traditions of Kabbalism and Christianity. Within Hinduism, transmigration is often equated with reincarnation (see also *Encyclopædia Britannica,* "Reincarnation").

It is related that this piece is to be the lowest portion of the backbone (*ʿajb al-dhanab*) or the coccyx. Furthermore, resurrection occurs in the Hereafter, whereas transmigration is claimed by its proponents to occur in this world. In addition, most believers in transmigration deny Paradise, Hellfire, and all the realities of the Hereafter, and this automatically classifies them as unbelievers. [56–57]

Resurrection of the Miscarried Embryo

[Qārī] As for the resurrection of the miscarried embryo, Abū Ḥanīfa's opinion is that if it had its soul blown into it [which occurs at about 120 days], then it will be resurrected; if not, then it will not. This is because resurrection is of both the soul and the body. [58]

that destiny, good and evil, is from Allāh Most High,[65] It is related that once Abū Bakr and ʿUmar ﷺ debated concerning the issue of destiny. Abū Bakr ﷺ asserted that good came from Allāh Most High and evil from one's self, and ʿUmar ﷺ attributed both to Allāh Most High. They took this matter to the Messenger of Allāh ﷺ who said, "Of all creation, the first to discuss destiny were Jibrīl (Gabriel) and Mīkā'īl. Jibrīl said the same as you said, ʿUmar, and Mīkā'īl said the same as you said, Abū Bakr. So they presented their case to [the angel] Isrāfīl who judged between them that all destiny, good or bad, is from Allāh." Thereafter, the Messenger of Allāh ﷺ said, "And this is my judgment between you," and then said, "Abū Bakr, if Allāh had willed no one to be disobedient, then he would not have created Iblīs (Satan) (may he be cursed)."[66] | the Reckoning, the Scale, Paradise, and Hellfire; and that they are all true. The Scale is defined as that with which the amounts of deeds will be determined; the mind is incapable of comprehending its form.[67]

---

65 In his commentary of *Ṣaḥīḥ Muslim,* Nawawī (d. 676/1277) says, "Know that the belief of the Ahl al-Sunna is affirmation of predestination (*qadar*)—that He Most Exalted destined all things in preeternity, and knew that they will occur at times known by Him" (*Al-Taʿlīq al-Muyassar* 59). See below for a more detailed discussion on *qadar.*

66 Related by Imām Abū ʿAbdillāh ibn Abī Ḥafṣ al-Kabīr in *Kitāb al-Radd ʿalā Ahl al-Ahwā'* through his chain from ʿAmr ibn Shuʿayb from his father from his grandfather (*MS. 4405*).

67 These issues are discussed in more detail below in the chapter "The Intercession and Some Other Eschatological Realities."

ALLĀH AND HIS ESSENTIAL AND ACTIVE ATTRIBUTES

وَاللهُ تَعَالٰى وَاحِدٌ، لَا مِنْ طَرِيْقِ الْعَدَدِ وَلٰكِنْ مِنْ طَرِيْقِ أَنَّهُ لَا شَرِيْكَ لَهُ، ﴿لَمْ يَلِدْ وَلَمْ يُوْلَدْ وَلَمْ يَكُن لَّهُ كُفُوًا أَحَدٌ﴾. لَا يُشْبِهُ شَيْئًا مِنَ الْأَشْيَاءِ مِنْ خَلْقِهِ وَلَا يُشْبِهُهُ شَيْءٌ مِنْ خَلْقِهِ، لَمْ يَزَلْ وَلَا يَزَالُ بِأَسْمَائِهِ وَصِفَاتِهِ الذَّاتِيَّةِ وَالْفِعْلِيَّةِ. أَمَّا الذَّاتِيَّةُ: فَالْحَيَاةُ وَالْقُدْرَةُ وَالْعِلْمُ وَالْكَلَامُ وَالسَّمْعُ وَالْبَصَرُ وَالْإِرَادَةُ. وَأَمَّا الْفِعْلِيَّةُ: فَالتَّخْلِيْقُ وَالتَّرْزِيْقُ وَالْإِنْشَاءُ وَالْإِبْدَاعُ وَالصُّنْعُ وَغَيْرُ ذٰلِكَ مِنْ صِفَاتِ الْفِعْلِ. لَمْ يَزَلْ وَلَا يَزَالُ بِأَسْمَائِهِ وَصِفَاتِهِ لَمْ يَحْدُثْ لَهُ اسْمٌ وَلَا صِفَةٌ. لَمْ يَزَلْ عَالِمًا بِعِلْمِهِ وَالْعِلْمُ صِفَةٌ فِي الْأَزَلِ، وَقَادِرًا بِقُدْرَتِهِ وَالْقُدْرَةُ صِفَةٌ فِي الْأَزَلِ، وَمُتَكَلِّمًا بِكَلَامِهِ وَالْكَلَامُ صِفَةٌ فِي الْأَزَلِ، وَخَالِقًا بِتَخْلِيْقِهِ وَالتَّخْلِيْقُ صِفَةٌ فِي الْأَزَلِ، وَفَاعِلًا بِفِعْلِهِ وَالْفِعْلُ صِفَةٌ فِي الْأَزَلِ. وَالْفَاعِلُ هُوَ اللهُ تَعَالٰى وَالْفِعْلُ صِفَةٌ فِي الْأَزَلِ، وَالْمَفْعُوْلُ مَخْلُوْقٌ وَفِعْلُ اللهِ تَعَالٰى غَيْرُ مَخْلُوْقٍ. وَصِفَاتُهُ فِي الْأَزَلِ غَيْرُ مُحْدَثَةٍ وَلَا مَخْلُوْقَةٍ، وَمَنْ قَالَ إِنَّهَا مَخْلُوْقَةٌ أَوْ مُحْدَثَةٌ أَوْ وَقَفَ أَوْ شَكَّ فِيْهِمَا فَهُوَ كَافِرٌ بِاللهِ تَعَالٰى.

Allāh Most High is One, not in terms of the number, but in that he has no partner. He neither begets nor is He begotten, and there is none co-equal or comparable unto Him. He is not like unto anything from among His creation and nothing from among His creation is like unto Him.

He was, is, and will forever be possessor of His names and of His essential and active attributes. As for His essential [attributes], they are life, power, knowledge, speech, hearing, seeing, and willing. And as for His active [attributes], they are creating, sustaining, bringing into being, originating, making, and others. He was and is ever possessed of His names and attributes; no name or attribute originated later for Him.

He has forever been the All-knowing with His knowledge, and knowledge was an attribute in preeternity; the All-powerful with His power, and power was an attribute in preeternity; the Speaker with His speech, and speech was an attribute in preeternity; the Creator with His creating, and creating was an attribute in preeternity; and the Doer with his doing, and doing was an attribute in preeternity.

The Doer is Allāh Most High, while doing was an attribute in preeternity. That which is done [i.e., product of His doing] is created, while His doing is uncreated. His attributes in preeternity are neither originated nor created [by another]. Whoever says that they are created or originated, or wavers or is doubtful, is an unbeliever in Allāh Most High.

Allāh Most High is One, not in terms of the number, but in that He has no partner. "One" is used sometimes to indicate half of two, this is the first [counting] number of the numerical system. That is the meaning of "one" in terms of the number one. Sometimes "one" is used to mean that an entity has no partner, no equal, and no peer in its essence or attributes [and that it is unique]. [According to this meaning], Allāh is "one" in that He has no partner, no equal, and no peer in His essence or attributes.

He neither begets, that is, He has no children, nor is He begotten from a mother and a father. This is a rebuttal of the Christian and Jewish belief that the Messiah (Masīḥ) عليه السلام and Ezra (ʿUzayr)[68] عليه السلام are the sons of Allāh Most

68 The Christian belief regarding Jesus عليه السلام is well known today, but the same cannot be said of the Jewish claim regarding ʿUzayr عليه السلام. Ibn Kathīr and Ibn Jarīr al-Ṭabarī relate from the scholar Suddī and others that the opinion of ʿUzayr being the son of God was held by a group of ignorant Jews who made this claim after an incident involving ʿUzayr عليه السلام. The ʿAmāliqa (Amalekites) overcame the Israelites, killed their scholars, and enslaved their elders. ʿUzayr was left weeping at the disappearance of knowledge from the Israelites. The Tawrāh was re-inspired to him, and he wrote it down for his people, but they remained skeptical of the Tawrāh he was reciting, until they regained their copies that they had hidden in the mountains and compared them with ʿUzayr's copy. When they found the two matching, some of their ignorant ones declared that he must be a son of God (Ibn Kathīr, *Tafsīr al-Qur'ān al-ʿAẓīm* 873–874). Ṭabarī and Qurṭubī also relate other opinions regarding this claim. One report states that it was Salām ibn Mishkam, Nuʿmān ibn Awfā, Wishāsh ibn Qays, and Mālik ibn al-Ṣayf who had come to the Messenger of Allāh ﷺ and made this claim. Qurṭubī also reports that Naqqāsh has said that no Jew is left now who believes that ʿUzayr was a son of God. See commentary of Sūrat al-Tawba, verse 30, in Ṭabarī's *Jāmiʿ al-Bayān fi Tafsīr al-Qur'ān* and Qurṭubī's *Al-Jāmiʿ li Aḥkām al-Qur'ān*. Even though this might not be a belief held by most Jews today, it was a belief during the time of the Messenger of Allāh ﷺ. And Allāh knows best.

High and of the philosophers' opinion regarding an intelligence (*ʿaql*)[69] being born from the Necessarily Existent (*wājib al-wujūd*) [Allāh]. Their opinions regarding these are baseless, because Allāh is the Self-Sufficient (Ṣamad); the Master, independent of everything, and upon whom everything other than Him is dependent. | and there is none co-equal or comparable unto Him. Nothing from among existence resembles Him. He is not a body (*jism*) that He could be measured, imagined, or divided; neither is He a substance (*jawhar*)[70] in which accidents [or abstract things] (*aʿrāḍ*)[71] subsist; nor is He an accident [or abstract thing] that can subsist in a substance.[72]

[Qārī] Allāh says, "If there were, in the heavens and the earth, other gods besides Allāh, they would both have become corrupted" (Qur'ān 21:22). To explain this, if there was a possibility of two gods, there would be a possibility of mutual hindrance (*tamānuʿ*) [and thus a problem with their effectiveness or absolute power]. For example, one of the gods could will a certain person to move, while the other wills that he remain motionless, both valid possibilities in and of themselves; likewise the association (*taʿalluq*) of will with each of them is also possible in and of itself, since there is no mutual opposition between the two [wills], but only a mutual opposition in the two things willed. Hence, either the two actions occur and the two opposites unite, or they do not occur, in which case one of the two gods is rendered powerless and not able to carry out his will. Powerlessness is a sign of being originated (*ḥudūth*) and of being possible (*imkān*) [as opposed to being necessary], for

69 This is referring to the first intelligence, i.e., the first effusion or emanation from God, the Necessary Being (*al-wājib al-wujūd*) or the First Principle (*al-mabda' al-awwal*) discussed by Muslim peripatetic philosophers like Fārābī and Ibn Sīnā. The issue of the intellects (*ʿuqūl*) was keenly discussed by Muslim peripatetics. Its origins is said to be from somewhat obscure and ambiguous statements of Aristotle in his last book of his treatise on the soul (*De Anima*). See *A Dictionary of Muslim Philosophy* 73–74.

70 *Jawhar* is a substance or atom. The unchanging physical essence of something. Taftāzānī says, "The *jawhar* is the thing that does not accept division, neither actually, nor in perception, nor by supposition. It is the part that is not further divided." It is also of importance to point out that the term substance (as originally defined within Greek philosophy) does not accurately correspond to the Islamic concept of substance or atom; there are some differences. For a full explanation, see *Sharḥ al-ʿAqā'id al-Nasafiyya* 76.

71 *ʿAraḍ* pl. *aʿrāḍ*. Accident. Something that must subsist in a substance (*jawhar*) and cannot subsist by itself; it refers to the perceptible qualities of an object such as its color, texture, size, and shape (e.g., the color red, love, or anger).

72 The section starting from "He is not a body (*jism*) . . ." until the end of the sentence is not found in any of the manuscripts.

in it is the defect of being in need of something. Therefore, [the possibility that both gods be in constant agreement does not negate this powerlessness] since plurality [also] necessitates the "possibility" of mutual hindrance [that one or the other could be rendered powerless from acting out his will, or that the two opposites unite], which [in turn] necessitates the impossible, and thus [the existence of multiple gods] is impossible.[73]

There is a difference of opinion among the scholars as to whether the above-mentioned verse from the Qur'ān is intended as a persuasive argument (*ḥujja iqnāʿiyya*) or as a definitive argument (*ḥujja qaṭʿiyya*). Taftāzānī says that it is a persuasive argument in that it appears at first to be definitive, but after deeper thought, it is not found to be convincing [because it does not necessarily negate all possible counter-arguments on the issue]. The connection (*mulāzama*) [between plurality and mutual hindrance] is usual as is appropriate to the case of statements that conform to rhetorical syllogism (*khiṭābiyyāt*). For mutual hindrance of one another and one overcoming the other are customary when there are multiple administrators;[74] this is indicated by the words of Allāh: "And some of them would assuredly have overcome others" (Qur'ān 23:91).[75] However, authorities such as Ghazālī, Ibn al-Humām,[76] and Bayḍāwī[77] were not satisfied by its classification as a persuasive argument and classified it as a definitive argument [that it leaves no room for counterarguments].[78] [61–62]

73 What this means is that though two gods could agree to not contradict each other, the mere possibility still exists that they might want to perform opposing acts. For instance, one may want a particular person to be moving and the other may want the same person to remain motionless. In such a case, either both will occur, which is impossible, or only one thing will occur, which means that one of the gods is rendered powerless from carrying out his will, and thus not very godly any more. Due to such a possibility, the plurality of gods is impossible, because God is All-powerful and not bound by restrictions or contingencies.

74 See Elder, *A Commentary on the Creed of Islam* 38.

75 Those who consider it persuasive do not contend that this is a weakness in the verse, but rather that there are certain logical proofs in the Qur'ān that are meant to be understood by the truly learned scholars only, and that there are others, such as this one, which employ rhetorical evidences that are made in normal speech for all lay people to understand.

76 Muḥammad ibn ʿAbd al-Wāḥid, Kamāl al-Dīn al-Sīwāsī al-Iskandarī, well known as Ibn al-Humām. He authored *Fatḥ al-Qadīr,* an eight volume commentary of Marghīnānī's *Al-Hidāya; Al-Taḥrīr,* on the principles of jurisprudence; and *Al-Musāyara*, on *ʿaqīda*. He died in 861/1456.

77 The Qāḍī ʿAbdullāh ibn ʿUmar ibn Muḥammad ʿAlī al-Bayḍāwī, author of the well-known commentary of the Qur'ān *Anwār al-Tanzīl wa Asrār al-Ta'wīl,* and *Bulūgh al-Sūl* on the principles of jurisprudence. Born in 575/1179, he died in 685/1286.

78 For more details, see Maydānī's commentary on the *Ṭaḥāwiyya* 89–51 and Zabīdī's *Itḥāf al-Sāda al-Muttaqīn* 2:207.

He is not like unto anything from among His creation for all creation belongs to Him.

[Qārī] His existence (*wujūd*) is His essence (*dhāt*), but His attributes (*ṣifāt*)[79] are neither His essence (*ʿayn dhātihī*) itself—in opposition to the statements of the philosophers—nor are they other than His essence (*ghayr dhātihī*) as the Muʿtazila have said,[80] nor are they originated (*ḥādith*) as the Karrāmiyya have said. This is in complete contrast to created beings, since their attributes are other than their essence according to everyone.[81] [63–64, 96]

---

79 The definition of the attributes of Allāh Most High are that they are particular qualities (*maʿānī*) associated with the essence of Allāh, which are preeternal by His being preeternal and are everlasting by His being everlasting. Imām Ṭaḥāwī says, "He is preeternal with His attributes before He created the universe. Bringing creation into existence did not add anything to His attributes that was not already there. As He was, together with His attributes, in preeternity, so He will remain with them throughout endless time. In other words, it was not after the act of creation that He could be described as "the Creator," nor was it by the act of origination that He could be described as "the Originator" (*Al-Taʿlīq al-Muyassar* 64).

80 This statement is slightly confusing. In essence, the Muʿtazila and the philosophers negated His attributes since they said Allāh is powerful and All-knowing through His essence and not through an attribute of power or knowledge. Taftāzānī says, "And thus it has been established that Allāh possesses the attributes of knowledge, power, life, and so on. This is unlike the view of the Muʿtazila who assert that He is knowing without possessing knowledge; He is powerful without possessing power, and so on. But their view is self-evidently impossible, for it is analogous to our saying, 'A thing is black but there is no blackness in it.' . . . The philosophers and the Muʿtazilites denied this and asserted that the attributes are the very essence itself. This means that His essence with respect to its connection with things known (*maʿlūmāt*) is described by the term "Knowing" and with respect to things over which He has power (*maqdūrāt*) is described by the term "Powerful," and so on (*A Commentary on the Creed of Islam* 49–50).

81 Thus, the correct belief according to the Ahl al-Sunna is that His attributes are neither His essence itself nor are they other than His essence. To elaborate, it has been established through the Qur'ān and Sunna that Allāh possesses many attributes (*ṣifāt*). However, if His attributes are said to be His very essence [as the Muʿtazila and philosophers claim], it results in His essence being devoid of attributes, since they would be one and the same as His essence, whereas they are understood to be two different things. The meaning of the "entity" or "essence" (*dhāt*) of Allāh is something completely different from His "attributes" (*ṣifāt*). On the other hand, saying that they are totally other than His essence is also problematic since this means they exist separately or are accidents (*aʿrāḍ*) and thus possible in their nature. This also means that they can exist or not exist as is the case in created beings, whereas the attributes of Allāh are eternal. So while people can lose their power, sight, or hearing, Allāh Most High cannot. Also, their being eternal and separate from Him would also mean that there exists a multiplicity of eternal beings (see *Al-Taʿlīq al-Muyassar* 63–64). A more simple way to understand this maybe through the following example about a human attribute. Upon entry of a knowledgeable person into a room we would not normally say, "knowledge entered the room." Instead we would either use the person's name or use an honorary title and say, "Shaykh so and so," or "Professor so and so" entered the room. Although we acknowledge the fact that the individual possesses the attribute of knowledge, the

and nothing from among His creation is like unto Him. No creation is like Him in its existence, because nothing is necessary in its essence (*wājib li dhātihī*) except Allāh, whereas everything other than Him is merely of possible existence; nor in knowledge, power, or any other attribute is there anything similar unto Him. This is clearly evident.

[Qārī] This statement is used to provide greater emphasis and explanation of the previous statement. It is derived from the verse, "There is nothing like Him" (Qur'ān 42:11) which can be more literally translated as, "There is not like His similitude anything," which means that nothing is similar to that which is similar to Him.[82] This phrase utilizes extreme lexical emphasis in order to magnify His uniqueness and difference from creation, Glorious and Mighty is He.[83] [64]

Know that Allāh Most High is One and without partner. He is preeternal (without beginning) and posteternal (without end). He was, is, and will forever be possessor of His names[84] and of His essential and active attributes.[85]

---

attribute is neither a completely independent entity separate from the person such that we would say, "Knowledge itself entered," nor is it intrinsically part of the person's essence such that we not acknowledge it but deny it. We must comprehend a special association between the two. The difference is that there is no doubt that the human attribute is acquired by the person and prone to loss in the future, whereas the attributes of Allāh have always been associated with Him and will remain that way for eternity.

82 This is a hypothetical premise, since there cannot be anything like Allāh and thus nothing like that assumed entity.

83 "There is nothing like unto him" (*Laysa ka mithlihī shay'*)—is part of a Qur'ānic verse that provides a universal rule on how to read and interpret the texts regarding Allāh Most High and His attributes; understanding the verse and its application is indispensable in this regard.

84 The difference between a name and an attribute is that a name (*ism.* pl. *asmā'*) is what indicates an essence by itself like the name "Allāh" or indicates the essence characterized by a particular attribute like "Powerful" (*qādir*) and "All-knowing" (*ʿālim*). An attribute (*ṣifa*), on the other hand, is that which indicates the quality (*maʿnā*) that is associated with the essence, like power (*qudra*) and knowledge (*ʿilm*). In other words, a name is what an entity is called or identified by and an attribute is the quality or characteristic it possesses. Allāh says, "The most beautiful names belong to Allāh: so call on Him by them" (Qur'ān 7:180) and "To Allāh applies the loftiest attributes" (16:60). See also *Tuḥfat al-murīd* 55 and *Sharḥ al-Ṣāwī ala 'l-Jawhara* 211.

85 Both the Māturīdīs and Ashʿarīs hold the essential attributes to be eternal. There is a difference of opinion regarding the active attributes which come under the collective attribute of *takwīn* (bringing into being). The Māturīdīs consider them to be eternal and the Ashʿarīs consider them to be created. The difference of opinion is said to be a semantic one. In reality, there are three components relating to each attribute. First is the attribute (*ṣifa*) itself; second is the association or the connection (*taʿalluq*) of the attribute to the effect; and third is the effect or result (*athar*) of

That is, none of His names or attributes originated later for Him. The difference between the essential and active attributes is that any attribute whose opposite can be attributed to Allāh Most High is an active attribute, e.g., the Creator [the opposite being the Giver of Death], and if its opposite cannot be attributed to Allāh Most High, then it is an essential attribute, e.g., life, glory, and knowledge. It is stated in *Al-Fatāwā al-Ẓahīriyya*[86] that if a person takes an oath on an attribute of Allāh Most High, the [nature of the] attribute must be considered: if it is an essential attribute, the oath will be valid; and if it is an active attribute, it will not be valid. Hence, if a person swears "by the glory of Allāh Most High" the oath is valid, because the opposite cannot be attributed to Allāh Most High. If a person swears "by the anger of Allāh Most High" or "by the displeasure of Allāh" the oath is not valid, because the opposite can be attributed to Allāh Most High, namely mercy.

As for His essential [attributes], they are life, for Allāh Most High is living with His life, which is an eternal attribute; power, for Allāh Most High is powerful over all things with His power, which is an eternal attribute; knowledge, for Allāh Most High is aware of all things existent. He is aware of the apparent and the hidden through His knowledge, which is an eternal attribute.

[Qārī] Knowledge (*ʿilm*) is an essential attribute, which when associated with things capable of being known (*maʿlūmāt*) exposes them. The knowledge of Allāh encompasses all things, and nothing so much as an atom from the heavens or earth remains outside His knowledge. He knows the apparent, the hidden, the parts, the wholes, the existent, the nonexistent, the possible, and the impossible. He knows what would result if the nonexistent were to come into existence. His knowledge is eternal and free from change. Allāh says, "Does He not know who created, and He is the Knower of the subtleties, the Aware?" (Qur'ān 67:14) and "With Him are the keys of the unseen, the

---

this association. Both schools hold the attributes of Allāh to be eternal and the other two components to be created. The reason for the difference then is that the Māturīdīs regard all attributes relating to *takwīn* as actual attributes. On the other hand, Ashʿarīs see *takwīn* as the associations of the attribute of power (*qudra*) and manifestation of the word *kun* ("be"), which they, in turn, consider necessary for the existence of any action, be it creating, providing sustenance, and so forth. However, associations, according to the Māturīdīs, are also created; hence, many scholars have considered this difference to be semantic only. See also *Al-Taʿlīq al-Muyassar* 66, and "The Use of the Word *"Kun"* for Creation" and "The Attribute *Takwīn"* below.

86 A collection of the formal legal opinions (*fatāwā*) of the judge and jurist Abū Bakr Ẓahīr al-Dīn Muḥammad ibn Aḥmad al-Bukhārī al-Ḥanafī (d. 619/1222).

treasures that none knows but He. He knows whatever there is on the earth and in the sea. Not a leaf falls but with His knowledge; there is not a grain in the darkness (or depths) of the earth, nor anything fresh or dry (green or withered), but is (inscribed) in a record clear" (6:59). [69–70]

speech, for Allāh Most High is the speaker with His speech, which is an eternal attribute. The speech of Allāh is unlike the speech of the creation, because they speak with organs and letters, and Allāh Most High speaks without organs or letters.

[Qārī] The speech of Allāh Most High is an eternal attribute, and it has no sounds, words, or letters. This is classified as His *kalām nafsī,* or internal speech, as opposed to *kalām lafẓī,* which is speech that is manifested in sounds, letters, or gestures. From a human vantage point, it resembles a thought which occurs within oneself before its articulation with the tongue. This is different from knowing something (*ʿilm*) since a person could articulate something completely in contradiction to what one knows. As for the actual words of the Qur'ān and other scriptures revealed by Allāh to mankind, these are understood to be an articulation of the divine archetype or the eternal speech of Allāh put into words and sounds in a manner that human beings can understand; and therefore [they also signify] His speech. However, they are not the internal divine speech referred to as an eternal attribute of Allāh, but a speech He created [to indicate His eternal speech]. [70]

When He speaks to His creation, it is with His eternal speech, the reflection of which is recorded as letters and words in the Preserved Tablet (*al-lawḥ al-maḥfūẓ*) [and in texts (*maṣāḥif*) for humans]. His speech is unlike the speech of created beings, as He says, "It is not fitting for a man that Allāh should speak to him except by revelation (*waḥy*)," i.e., by divine revelation in dreams, such as to the prophets, or by divine inspiration (*ilhām*),[87] such as to the friends of Allāh (*awliyā*), as the ḥadīth also states: "Verily Allāh speaks upon the tongue of ʿUmar ﷺ." Allāh continues by saying: "or from behind

87 Ḥujjat al-Islām [Ghazālī] says, "Knowledge gained [directly] without [contemplating] evidence is called *ilhām*. This can occur by witnessing the angel that is conveying the knowledge, an act specific to the prophets called *waḥy* (revelation), or without the witnessing of an angel, which is called *ilhām* and is specific to the friends of Allāh (*awliyā'*)." See Darwīsh's marginalia on *Sharḥ al-ʿAqā'id* 74.

a veil," such that one hears the speech without seeing Him, as what occurred with Mūsā, "or by the sending of a messenger," i.e., an angel such as Jibrīl ﷺ, "to reveal, with Allāh's permission, what Allāh wills, for He is Most High, Most Wise" (Qur'ān 42:51).

The above is different from the belief of the Muʿtazila, who negate the attribute of speech from Allāh and state that Allāh speaks using speech associated with someone else, and not through an attribute of His own. They say His speech is the letters and sounds that He creates in others like in the Preserved Tablet or in Jibrīl or a messenger (upon them be peace). This is also different from the opinion of the innovators among the Ḥanbalīs [excluding Imām Aḥmad and his companions] who say that His speech is composed of letters and sounds associated with His essence and hence eternal. Some have reached an extreme in their ignorance by saying, even the cover and paper [of copies of the Qur'ān] are eternal. [74]

The Use of the Word "Kun" for Creation

[Qārī] Qūnawī states in *Sharḥ al-ʿUmda,*[88] "As for the word *kun,* which is the imperative "be," the [majority of the] Ahl al-Sunna do not consider it necessary to bring things into being. Rather, they consider their existence dependent upon His *ījād* (originating) and *takwīn* (bringing into being), and that these are His eternal attributes. This is the opinion of Abū Manṣūr al-Māturīdī and of the majority of Qur'ānic exegetes. As for Imām Ashʿarī and those who follow him, they consider the existence of things to be dependent upon His attribute of eternal speech (*kalām nafsī*), the word *kun* being the indicator of that speech, as mentioned in the *Sharḥ al-Ta'wīlāt.*"[89] A third opinion on the matter is that of some Māturīdī scholars like Fakhr al-Islām al-Bazdawī in his *Uṣūl,* who said creation was from the word *kun* and from Allāh's attribute of *ījād,* and that it is invalid to deem *"kun"* a metaphorical expression for *takwīn.*

---

88 This is the commentary of Ḥāfiẓ al-Dīn ʿAbdullāh ibn Aḥmad al-Nasafī's (d. 710/1310) *ʿUmdat al-ʿAqā'id.* Nasafī compiled some of the most important rulings of Islamic theology in this short treatise, and then wrote a commentary on it which he called *Al-Iʿtimād.* Many others also wrote commentaries on this work, such as Jamāl al-Dīn Maḥmūd ibn Aḥmad al-Qūnawī (d. 770/1368) and Muḥammad ibn Yūsuf ibn Ilyās al-Rūmī al-Qūnawī (d. 788/1386). See *Kashf al-Ẓunūn* 2:1128.

89 This is ʿAlā' al-Dīn Muḥammad ibn Aḥmad ibn Abī Aḥmad, Abū Manṣūr al-Samarqandī's (d. 539/1144) commentary of Abū Manṣūr al-Māturīdī's *Ta'wīlāt,* frequently mistaken as being the work of Muḥammad ibn ʿAbd al-Ḥamīd ibn al-Ḥasan ibn Ḥamza al-Usmandī, ʿAlā' al-Dīn Abū Bakr al-Samarqandī (d. 552/1157).

Fakhr al-Islām says that it is in fact meant to indicate that the speech of Allāh itself is involved in the act of creation, but without the knowledge of exactly how this occurs. Sarakhsī[90] also takes this opinion.

However, it states in the *Tafsīr al-Taysīr*[91] under the verse "When He has decreed something, He says to it only, 'Be' and it is" (Qur'ān 3:47), "He Most High did not intend by this that He addresses it with the word *kun* and it come into being by it, because if we were to consider this a real address, it would either be to something nonexistent that comes into existence by it, or it is an address to the existent after it comes into existence. It cannot be the former since the nonexistent is not yet an entity, so how can it be addressed? It also cannot be the latter since it is already existent, so how does He order it to "Be" when it already is? Rather, it is merely to express that when He wills something to be, it is.

The scholars have understood the verse as showing how utterly simple it is for Him to do what He wills, to emphasize the speed and lack of effort required to put His will into action, and to exemplify His greatness and ability. It is in the same way that Allāh Most High resurrects those that are in their graves with His power, while the blowing of the Horn is simply an apparent cause of that occurrence, to express His might. There are many logical proofs that creation stems from *ījād*. However, after having said all this, the fact remains that Allāh Most High mentions the use of the word *kun* in the Qur'ān. It is, therefore, necessary to accept the verse and leave it as it is, without occupying oneself with seeking out its benefits, just as it is necessary to accept other ambiguous verses (*mutashābihāt*) in the Qur'ān without occupying oneself with seeking an interpretation. [72–73, 131]

hearing, Allāh Most High hears all sounds and words through His preeternal hearing, which is an eternal attribute of His. | seeing, for Allāh Most High sees all forms and colors with His preeternal sight, which is an eternal attribute of His.

---

90 Muḥammad ibn Aḥmad ibn Abī Sahl, Abū Bakr Shams al-A'imma al-Sarakhsī. He wrote commentaries on Muḥammad al-Shaybānī's *Al-Jāmiʿ al-Ṣaghīr* and *al-Kabīr* and *Al-Siyar al-Kabīr.* He also authored *Al-Mabsūṭ* and was known for his extensive memorization of various texts. He passed away around 482/1089, 490/1096, or 500/1106 (see *Tāj al-Tarājim* 18).

91 This most likely refers to the text written by ʿUmar ibn Muḥammad Najm al-Dīn al-Nasafī.

[Qārī] He uses no medium or sense by which to hear or see, nor can He ever be mistaken in what He hears and sees. His hearing and seeing are exact, absolute, definitive, and perfect. Neither attribute adds any new information to His already complete knowledge, in direct contrast to created beings who hear and see in order to add to their knowledge and understanding. [77]

and willing, for Allāh Most High has willed with His preeternal will that which is and that which is to be. Nothing in this world or the next, whether small or large, meager or great, good or bad, beneficial or detrimental, nor any success or ruin, or increase or decrease, occurs but through His will and desire. Whatever Allāh desires is, and what He does not is not. Allāh does all that He wills. There is no one to repulse His will and desire, nor one to defer His command. Among His essential attributes are oneness (*aḥadiyya*), sovereignty (*ṣamadiyya*), exaltedness (*ʿaẓama*), grandeur (*kibriyāʾ*), and others.

[Qārī] The will of Allāh over all things does not negate that the human too has a will, as Allāh says, "Do what you will, verily He sees (clearly) all that you do" (Qurʾān 41:40).[92] [78]

The Will and Desire of Allāh

[Qārī] The will (*irāda*) and desire (*mashīʾa*) of Allāh are both one and the same. If it is said that Allāh Most High demanded faith from the likes of Pharaoh and Abū Jahl by commanding it (*bi 'l-amr*), and yet they did not acquire faith, this seems in direct contradiction to what has been said regarding Allāh's will (*irāda*) and desire (*mashīʾa*) being the same. If they were both the same, then these people would have acquired faith, since desiring (*mashīʾa*) is bringing into being (*ījād*). The response to this is that the demands (*ṭalab*) from Allāh are of two types. One is the command (*amr*)—seeking the legally responsible one (*mukallaf*) to act but leaving him the choice—which does not necessitate [the thing's] existence since it relates to the discretion of the servant. The other type is that which has nothing to do with the choice of the servant, and is called desire (*mashīʾa*) or will (*irāda*) and comes into being immediately. If it

92 The will and desires of people, however, do not always come to be, whereas what Allāh wills always comes to be.

did not, then it would necessitate powerlessness on the part of Allāh, from which He is transcendent unlike created beings. [79]

[All action and occurrences are from the will of Allāh Most High. However, as for Allāh willing unbelief, disobedience, and evil, there are various opinions.] Some say that it should not be said in detail that whatever is ugly, evil, or sinful is from Allāh, but that one should say in general that He creates all that exists, just like we should not say in detail that He is the Creator of carrion and trash. Others say that one can mention such details, but in a way appropriate to Allāh Most High. It can be said that He wills unbelief for the unbeliever as an acquisition for him—an evil, foul, and prohibited one just as He wills belief for the believer as an acquisition for him—a good, wholesome, and commanded one. This is the preference of Imām Māturīdī and Ashʿarī.[93] [79–80]

According to the experts, there are two types of will (*irāda*) mentioned in the Qur'ān:

(1) the creative decreeing will (*irāda qadariyya kawniyya sharʿiyya*), which is the will that encompasses all created beings, as Allāh says, "Those whom Allāh (in His plan) wills to guide, He opens their breast to Islam; those whom He wills to leave astray, He makes their breast closed and constricted, as if they had to climb up to the sky" (Qur'ān 6:125),

(2) the legislative will (*irāda dīniyya amriyya sharʿiyya*). This is linked to His love and approval, as He says, "Allāh intends every facility for you; He does not want to put you to difficulties" (2:185). The commands (*amr*) of Allāh relate to this second category exclusively and not to the first. [80]

Other Essential Attributes

Imām Abū Ḥanīfa mentions here seven essential attributes. Others include oneness in essence (*aḥadiyya fī 'l-dhāt*), oneness in attributes (*aḥadiyya fī 'l-ṣifāt*), eternal independence from any possible being, greatness (*ʿaẓama*), exaltedness (*kibriyā'*). In explaining the difference between *ʿaẓama* (greatness) and *kibriyā'* (exaltedness), Imām Ghazālī says that one must believe in the difference between the two even though they may be subtle, since Allāh mentions each of them in a different context and has said [in a ḥadīth qudsī[94]],

---

93 In short, the evil is from the will and displeasure of Allāh, while the good is from the will, love and good pleasure of Allāh.

94 Ḥadīth Qudsī (Sacred Ḥadīth) is a sub-category of ḥadīth, which are sayings of the Prophet

"Greatness (*ʿaẓama*) is my upper garment and exaltedness (*kibriyāʾ*) is my lower garment (*Muslim*). [81]

A question may arise as a result of the above discussion: how is it that we can use terms such as preeternal (*qadīm*), present (*mawjūd*), and necessary (*wājib*) for Allāh when such words have not been related in the sacred texts (*Sharʿ*)? The answer is that this is approved through consensus (*ijmāʿ*),[95] which constitutes legal evidence.[96] [82]

And as for His active [attributes],

[Qārī] These are the attributes whose manifestation is dependent upon the existence of creation.[97] [82]

The Attribute Takwīn

[Qārī] As mentioned earlier, the Ashʿarī school holds that *takwīn* is originated, and thus not a preeternal attribute. They say that *takwīn* is nothing more than the attribute of power (*qudra*) in terms of its association (*taʿalluq*) with a particular effect. Hence, creating (*takhlīq*) is power in terms of its association with the "created being" (*makhlūq*), and similar is the case with sustaining (*tarzīq*). Therefore, all the active attributes are originated, since they are essentially the various associations (*taʿalluqāt*) of power (*qudra*), and associations are originated (*ḥādith*). The Muʿtazila hold that *takwīn* is an active attribute since the opposite—leaving in nonexistence—is also a possibility for Allāh,

---

Muḥammad ﷺ. They are considered revelation from Allāh transmitted by the Prophet ﷺ in his words. Sayyid Sharīf al-Jurjānī (d. 816/1413) offers the following definition in his lexicon *Al-Taʿrīfāt:* "A ḥadīth qudsī is, in its context, from Allāh Most High, and in its wording, from the Messenger of Allāh ﷺ. It is that which Allāh Most High has communicated to His Prophet through revelation or in a dream, and he ﷺ in turn, has transmitted it in his own words. The Qurʾān is superior to a ḥadīth qudsī because, aside from being revelation, it is the divine word."

95 *Ijmāʿ* literally means "resolve and agreement." Its technical meaning can be rendered as the following: "The agreement of the *mujtahids* on a matter of the *dīn* of the umma of Muḥammad ﷺ or a firm resolve by the *Ahl al-ḥall wa ʾl-ʿaqd* (lit. "the people who loose and bind) on an issue." The *ahl al-ḥall wa ʾl-ʿaqd* are defined more commonly as "respected representatives of the Muslim umma who act on its behalf in appointing and deposing a ruler or deciding another affair"). See *Taʿrīfāt al-Sayyid* 24–25.

96 Ibn Fūrak (d. 406/1015) has related a consensus in *Maqālāt al-Ashʿarī,* and Imām Ṭaḥāwī has used some of these terms in his work (*Al-Taʿlīq al-Muyassar* 82).

97 Thus, the difference between the active attributes and the essential attributes is that the essential attributes are always manifest, whereas the active attributes, though preeternally and forever present, remain hidden until there is creation.

and that it is created. The Māturīdīs hold that *takwīn* is an eternal attribute just as knowledge (*ʿilm*) is, even though many things knowable (*maʿlūmāt*) are created.

The confusion on the part of the Ashʿarīs and Muʿtazilīs regarding *takwīn* is that they say if it were eternal, it would have been associated eternally with "what is brought into being" (*mukawwan*) [i.e., the product of the *takwīn*] and thus the *mukawwan* would also necessarily have to be existent in eternity, because to say there is *takwīn* and no *mukawwan* is like saying there is "a beating" (*ḍarb*) but no one "beaten" (*maḍrūb*), which is impossible. Therefore, *takwīn* has to be originated.

The response to the Ashʿarīs and Muʿtazilīs is that if *takwīn* originated through another *takwīn*, then it is a *takwīn* in need of another *takwīn*, and this leads to infinite regress (*tasalsul*), which is unacceptable. If it stops at an "eternal" *takwīn*, then this is precisely what the Māturīdīs are saying. If it is taken as not originating from anyone's *takwīn* then it leads to denying the Maker (Allāh). In conclusion, the Māturīdīs say that *takwīn* is preeternal but it is associated with the *mukawwan* or created "effect," just as knowledge (*ʿilm*) is preeternal but some "things knowable" (*maʿlūmāt*) are created, along with the fact that *takwīn* existed preeternally not so that the universe could come into being in eternity, but so that it would come into being at its time. Hence, His *takwīn* is in eternal existence, and the existence of everything is associated to His eternal *takwīn*, as opposed to "a beating" (*ḍarb*) which is an accident (*ʿaraḍ*) and cannot be imagined to exist until the time of the existence of "the thing beaten" (*maḍrūb*). [83, 90]

they are creating, sustaining, bringing into being, originating, making, and others. For instance, giving life (*iḥyāʾ*), causing death (*imāta*), causing growth (*inbāt*), developing (*inmāʾ*), and shaping (*taṣwīr*). *Takhlīq* (creating), *inshāʾ* (bringing into being), and *ṣunʿ* (making) all bear the same meaning, that is, bringing into being something that was not existent, whether based on a previous model or not. *Ibdāʿ* (originating) means bringing into being something that was not existent and is not based on a previous model.[98] *Tarzīq*

98 In the published version and in *MS. 1062,* it is rendered affirmatively, that is, "is based on a previous model." However, the remaining manuscripts have it as "is not based on a previous model," which seems to be the more correct reading since Qārī (*Minaḥ al-Rawḍ al-Azhar* 85) has also defined it in this way.

(sustaining) is bringing into being the sustenance of something and enabling it to benefit therefrom.

[Qārī] All these attributes come under the collective attribute of *takwīn* but each deals with a specific aspect of it, such that if it were in relation to bringing to life, it would be called *iḥyā'*, if it were with respect to causing death, it would be called *imāta*, and so forth. Thus, the preeternal attributes according to the Māturīdīs are essentially eight. They are the attributes of life (*ḥayāt*), power (*qudra*), knowledge (*ʿilm*), speech (*kalām*), hearing (*samʿ*), sight (*baṣar*), will (*irāda*), and bringing into being (*takwīn*). All the active attributes are a subset of the eighth attribute, *takwīn*. [84]

Imām Abū Ḥanīfa sufficed by mentioning the above essential and active attributes and not others because these popular attributes are sufficient for believers to understand the existence of Allāh and His attributes. [86]

He was and is ever possessed of His names and attributes.[99] That is, Allāh Most

[99] The classification of the attributes of Allāh is quite simple according to the earlier works on *ʿaqīda* such as *Al-Fiqh al-Akbar, ʿAqīda Ṭaḥāwiyya, ʿAqā'id Nasafiyya,* Ūshī's *Bad' al-Amālī,* and even Ghazālī's *Kitāb Qawā'id al-ʿAqā'id,* which forms part of his *Iḥyā,* in that most of these works mention the attributes without any particular classification. However, many later works on *ʿaqīda,* especially the Ashʿarī commentaries on Laqānī's *Jawharat al-Tawḥīd* and Sanūsī's *Umm al-Barāhīn,* have a more detailed classification of the attributes along with details on their individual associations (*taʿalluqāt*). This is aside from the main difference of opinion between the Ashʿarīs and Māturīdīs on *takwīn* being an eternal attribute or just the associations (*taʿalluqāt*) of the attribute of power (*qudra*). These later commentaries classify the attributes into three primary categories: the personal attribute (*ṣifat nafsiyya,* or *thubūtiyya*), the negating or cancelling attributes (*ṣifāt salbiyya*), and the abstract or affirmative attributes (*ṣifāt maʿānī* or *wujūdiyya*). The personal attribute of Allāh is one: being (*wujūd*). There is disagreement over whether *wujūd* is one and the same as the *dhāt* (essence) or if it is an added description of the *dhāt.* Ashʿarī's opinion is that they are one and the same, while Rāzī and other scholars consider *wujūd* an added description of the *dhāt* (*Tuḥfat al-Murīd* 33). The negating attributes are five: beginninglessness (*qidam*), endlessness (*baqā'*), oneness (*waḥdāniyya*), self-subsistence (*qiyām bi 'l-nafs*), and absolute dissimilarity from created things (*mukhālafa li 'l-ḥawādith*). The affirmative attributes are seven: life (*ḥayāt*), knowledge (*ʿilm*), will (*irāda*), power (*qudra*), hearing (*samʿ*), sight (*baṣar*), and speech (*kalām*). Though completely different from the personal attributes mentioned above, the name *dhātiyya* (personal or essential) is also used sometimes to designate this category, as Abū Ḥanīfa does in *Al-Fiqh al-Akbar,* since they are inseparable from the essence of Allāh. Many also add a fourth category—the entitative attributes (*ṣifāt maʿnawiyya*)—to complete twenty attributes in all. There is some difference of opinion regarding this last category. Essentially, these are the attributes that require a *maʿnā,* or "entity." They are the active participle of the previous category and consist of the following: Allāh being the Ever-living (*ḥayy*), the All-knowing (*ʿālim*), the All-willing (*murīd*), the Almighty (*qādir*), the All-hearing (*samīʿ*), the All-seeing (*baṣīr*), and the Speaker (*mutakallim*). See *Tuḥfat al-murīd, Sharḥ al-Ṣāwī ʿala 'l-Jawhara,* and *Ḥāshiyat al-Bājūrī ʿalā Matn al-Sanūsiyya.*

High, with all His attributes and names, is preeternally beginningless and eternally limitless. No name or attribute originated later for Him, because if any attribute of Allāh Most High were to have originated anew for Him or to have ceased to exist [after being existent], He would have been incomplete before it originated or after it ceased to exist, which is inconceivable. Therefore, it is established that no attribute or name originated anew for Him, because whoever possesses knowledge in preeternity is the knower in preeternity [of everything that is to happen].

Use of Past Tense in the Qur'ān

[Qārī] Allāh is preeternal and everlasting and there is no past, present, and future with Allāh. From this, a question arises with respect to Allāh's use of the past tense in the Qur'ān when narrating events, such as "We *sent* Noah to his people" (71:1) and "He *said,* 'O my people'" (71:2). If the Qur'ān is the eternal speech of Allāh, then there should be no present, past, and future tense for Him, for it is considered falsehood to inform of happenings before they have occurred, and falsehood is inconceivable for Allāh. The answer is as follows: The eternal speech of Allāh does not use the same wording as the created speech we see in the Qur'ān. The Qur'ān is composed of special Arabic words and phrases of the highest eloquence that articulate the eternal speech of Allāh for us. The internal speech of Allāh (or the divine archetype) is preeternal and utilizes no words, sounds, syntax, or grammar as the language we use does. So in the revealed speech, events are characterized by tense based on the connection with the time in which they were revealed, whether before or after the time the Qur'ān was revealed. For instance, the speech of Allāh regarding the sending of Nūḥ عليه السلام is preeternally possessed by Allāh; however, before sending Nūḥ عليه السلام, the [created] words to articulate it would have been, "We *will* send," and after sending him they are, "We *sent.*" Hence, the change takes place in the words used to articulate the information and not in the informing itself that is possessed by Allāh. It is the same with the knowledge (*ʿilm*) that exists with Allāh of the event. The occurrence of the event does not change anything in the knowledge of Allāh; the only change is in the known event itself [that it has occurred, while it had previously not occurred]. [88]

He has forever been the All-knowing with His knowledge, and knowledge was an attribute in preeternity; the All-powerful with His power, and power was an attribute in preeternity; the Speaker with His speech, and speech was an attribute in preeternity; the Creator with His creating, and creating was an attribute in preeternity; and the Doer with his doing, and doing was an attribute in preeternity. The Great Imām's statement, "He has forever been the All-knowing . . ." is a rebuttal of the opinion of the Muʿtazila, who assert that the attributes of Allāh are His essence itself; that He is the All-knowing and Omnipotent in essence, and not through [the attributes of] knowledge and power. Adequate evidence for us is the statement of the Great Imām and that of all the imāms of guidance and religion among the Ahl al-Sunna wa 'l-Jamāʿa. We state as these imāms (may Allāh have mercy on them) do—that the attributes of Allāh are neither His essence itself, nor anything extraneous to His essence. And it is not necessary for us to investigate deeply into issues of this nature.

The Doer is Allāh Most High, while doing was an attribute in preeternity. That which is done [i.e., product of His doing] is created, while His doing is uncreated. This means whenever Allāh Most High does something, He does it through His doing,[100] which is His eternal attribute, not through a doing that has originated later. This is because the originated is the [tangible] impression (*athar*) of His doing, not the doing itself, as opposed to the thing done which is a locus (*maḥall*) for the impression of the doing to occur in—and that is created according to agreement [among the scholars] with no dissent.

His attributes in preeternity are neither originated nor created [by another]. Whoever says that they—His essential or active attributes—are created or originated, or wavers, that is, he neither maintains the existence of the attributes or their non-existence, because of obstinacy or ignorance, or is doubtful as to the existence of the attributes or their eternalness. Taken literally, *Shakk* (doubt) is an antonym of *yaqīn* (certainty), and *yaqīn* means awareness with the elimination of doubt. The Great Imām uses the words [he] is an unbeliever in Allāh Most High, because *īmān* means conviction (*taṣdīq*), which is defined as the submission of the heart and its acceptance of the existence of the Creator Most High, His Oneness, and all His attributes; this is because the attributes of Allāh Most High are from among the articles of true faith [belief in which is an obligation]. Therefore, whoever does not

100 This refers to the creative potential of Allāh or His capacity to do as He pleases, which is His eternal attribute.

believe in them is ignorant of Allāh Most High and His attributes and is an unbeliever in Him and His prophets.

[Qārī] If one has any doubt about any of the attributes of Allāh or His names, which are necessary to believe in "the way Allāh intends them to be," then one must actively seek to find out sufficient details to alleviate doubt and establish [faith] firmly in his heart. A person is responsible for knowing the essence of Allāh and all of His attributes; however, the attributes of which ignorance and doubt leads one to unbelief are the aforementioned well-known attributes of life (*ḥayāt*), power (*qudra*), knowledge (*ʿilm*), speech (*kalām*), hearing (*samʿ*), sight (*baṣar*), will (*irāda*), creation (*takhlīq*), and sustaining (*tarzīq*). [91]

THE QUR'ĀN: THE SPEECH OF ALLĀH MOST HIGH

وَالْقُرْآنُ كَلَامُ اللهِ تَعَالٰى فِي الْمَصَاحِفِ مَكْتُوْبٌ وَفِي الْقُلُوْبِ مَحْفُوْظٌ وَعَلَى الْأَلْسُنِ مَقْرُوْءٌ وَعَلَى النَّبِيِّ عَلَيْهِ الصَّلَاةُ وَالسَّلَامُ مُنَزَّلٌ. وَلَفْظُنَا بِالْقُرْآنِ مَخْلُوْقٌ وَكِتَابَتُنَا لَهُ مَخْلُوْقَةٌ وَقِرَاءَتُنَا لَهُ مَخْلُوْقَةٌ وَالْقُرْآنُ غَيْرُ مَخْلُوْقٍ. وَمَا ذَكَرَهُ اللهُ تَعَالٰى فِي الْقُرْآنِ حِكَايَةً عَنْ مُوْسٰى وَغَيْرِهِ مِنَ الْأَنْبِيَاءِ عَلَيْهِمُ السَّلَامُ، وَعَنْ فِرْعَوْنَ وَإِبْلِيْسَ، فَإِنَّ ذٰلِكَ كُلَّهُ كَلَامُ اللهِ تَعَالٰى إِخْبَارًا عَنْهُمْ. وَكَلَامُ اللهِ تَعَالٰى غَيْرُ مَخْلُوْقٍ، وَكَلَامُ مُوْسٰى وَغَيْرِهِ مِنَ الْمَخْلُوْقِيْنَ مَخْلُوْقٌ. وَالْقُرْآنُ كَلَامُ اللهِ تَعَالٰى فَهُوَ قَدِيْمٌ لَا كَلَامُهُمْ. وَسَمِعَ مُوْسٰى عَلَيْهِ السَّلَامُ كَلَامَ اللهِ تَعَالٰى كَمَا فِيْ قَوْلِهِ تَعَالٰى: ﴿وَكَلَّمَ اللهُ مُوْسٰى تَكْلِيْمًا﴾. وَقَدْ كَانَ اللهُ تَعَالٰى مُتَكَلِّمًا وَلَمْ يَكُنْ كَلَّمَ مُوْسٰى عَلَيْهِ السَّلَامُ، وَقَدْ كَانَ اللهُ تَعَالٰى خَالِقًا فِي الْأَزَلِ وَلَمْ يَخْلُقِ الْخَلْقَ، فَلَمَّا كَلَّمَ اللهُ مُوْسٰى كَلَّمَهُ بِكَلَامِهِ الَّذِيْ هُوَ لَهُ صِفَةٌ فِي الْأَزَلِ. وَصِفَاتُهُ كُلُّهَا بِخِلَافِ صِفَاتِ الْمَخْلُوْقِيْنَ: يَعْلَمُ لَا كَعِلْمِنَا، وَيَقْدِرُ لَا كَقُدْرَتِنَا، وَيَرٰى لَا كَرُؤْيَتِنَا، وَيَتَكَلَّمُ لَا كَكَلَامِنَا، وَيَسْمَعُ لَا كَسَمْعِنَا. وَنَحْنُ نَتَكَلَّمُ بِالْآلَاتِ وَالْحُرُوْفِ، وَاللهُ تَعَالٰى يَتَكَلَّمُ بِلَا آلَةٍ وَلَا حُرُوْفٍ، وَالْحُرُوْفُ مَخْلُوْقَةٌ، وَكَلَامُ اللهِ تَعَالٰى غَيْرُ مَخْلُوْقٍ.

The Qur'ān is the speech of Allāh Most High: written in texts, memorized by hearts, recited by tongues, and revealed upon the Prophet (upon him be blessings and peace). Our uttering of the Qur'ān is created, our writing of it is created, and our reciting it is created, but the Qur'ān is uncreated.

Whatever Allāh Most High has said in the Qur'ān in quoting Mūsā (Moses) and other prophets (upon them be peace), and Pharaoh and Iblīs (Satan), is all the speech of Allāh Most High informing [us] about them. The speech of Allāh Most High is uncreated, while the speech of Mūsā ﷺ and that of other created beings is created. The Qur'ān is the speech of Allāh Most High—therefore preeternally existent—unlike their speech.

Mūsā ﷺ heard the speech of Allāh Most High, as is [mentioned] in the words of Allāh: "And Allāh spoke directly unto Mūsā" [(Qur'ān 4:164)]. Allāh Most High was the Speaker when He had not yet spoken to Mūsā ﷺ. Allāh Most High was the Creator in preeternity when He had not yet created creation. So when Allāh spoke to Mūsā ﷺ, He spoke to him with His speech, which was His attribute in preeternity.

Every attribute of His is unlike the attributes of creation. He knows unlike the way we know. He is powerful unlike the way we are powerful. He sees unlike the way we see. He speaks unlike the way we speak. He hears unlike the way we hear. We speak [and communicate] by means of organs and letters, while Allāh Most High speaks without any organs or letters. Letters are created and the speech of Allāh Most High is uncreated.

❁

The Qur'ān is the speech of Allāh Most High/ The word "Qur'ān" is grammatically a verbal noun (*maṣdar*) meaning "gathering" and "joining," and also "reading." Hence, a Qur'ān is that which gathers the chapters together and joins them; that is why it is called the Qur'ān. In this case, the word holds the meaning of an active participle (*ism al-fāʿil*). One can also interpret it as "that which is read" (*al-maqrū'*), since it is read and recited. In this case, the verbal noun takes the meaning of the passive participle (*ism al-mafʿūl*). The "Qur'ān" here means the speech (*kalām*) of Allāh Most High, which is His attribute, not the Arabic composition (*naẓm*) [i.e. not the actual text or *muṣḥaf*]. It is also said [in a weaker opinion] that both the composition and meaning are intended by it. | written in texts, *maṣāḥif* (books) is the plural of *muṣḥaf*. That is, the speech of Allāh Most High, which is His attribute, is written in books with letters. | memorized by hearts through reflective (*mukhayyala*) words, recited by tongues through letters uttered and heard, and revealed upon the Prophet (upon him be blessings and peace) through the utterance of letters heard from an angel.

Our uttering of the Qur'ān is created, our writing of it is created, and our reciting it is created, because they are all part of our actions and our actions are all created through the creative act of Allāh but the Qur'ān, that is, the speech of Allāh, is uncreated. The letters, the paper, and the writing themselves are all created, because they are [the results of the] acts of people. [But] the speech of Allāh itself "is uncreated" because the writing, letters, words, and verses are necessary components of the Qur'ān [to service] the needs of people. The speech of Allāh Most High exists in His own essence (*qā'im bi dhātihī*), and its meaning is elucidated through the [use of such] tools. Therefore, whoever says that the speech of Allāh Most High is created is a disbeliever of Almighty Allāh. And whoever says that the Qur'ān is created and intends by it the uttered speech that exists in the essence of Allāh, as is the opinion of the Karrāmiyya, is an unbeliever; this is because he has negated an eternal attribute and rendered the Creator Most High a locus (*maḥall*) for originations (*ḥawādith*).[101] And it follows that a locus for originations is also originated (*ḥādith*). Moreover, whoever says that the Qur'ān is created and intends to negate by it the divine archetype is an unbeliever. But whoever says that the Qur'ān is created and intends by it uttered speech that does not exist in the essence of Allāh and also does not intend to negate by it the divine archetype, is not an unbeliever. However, this usage (*iṭlāq*) is flawed, because it suggests unbelief.

[Qārī] Our proof for the existence of the attribute of speech for Allāh is that it is established by consensus and uninterrupted transmission (*tawātur*) from the prophets (upon them be peace). This cannot mean anything other than that He possesses the attribute of speech, and since it is inconceivable that His speech be created, as created things do not subsist within His noble essence, it establishes an eternal-personal speech for Him. [95]

As for when there are two [or more] readings for one verse [according to the seven revealed readings of the Qur'ān],[102] if each reading has a meaning

---

101 Or finite occurrences.

102 The Messenger of Allāh ﷺ said, "This Qur'ān has been revealed [to be recited] in seven ways (*sab'at aḥruf*), so recite of them whichever is easier for you" (*Bukhārī*). There are several scholarly positions as to what is meant by the "seven ways." The stronger position seems to be that this refers to the seven types of variations found in the different readings of the Qur'ān, which essentially differ slightly in (1) some nouns (as in singular, plural, masculine, or feminine), (2) some verbs (for instance, in the tense, or the active or passive), (3) some vowelling, (4) addition or deletion of certain words, (5) placement of some words (before or after the other), (6) substitution of words (one word for another), and (7) the manner of reading and pronunciation (e.g., in elongation [*madd*], shortening [*qaṣr*], inclination [*imāla*], assimilation [*idghām*], etc.). For example, the name of the archangel Gabriel is pronounced differently in different recitations: Jibrīl and Jibra'īl. The word Qur'ān is pronounced without the glottal stop as "Qurān" in one recitation, and Prophet Ibrāhīm's ﷺ name is pronounced Ibrāhām in one recitation. It is important to mention that these variations in no way contribute to any form of confusion in the general meaning and message of

different than the other, then Allāh spoke both of them, and the two readings acquire the status of two separate verses. However, if the two readings retain a single meaning, then Allāh expressed one meaning, and allowed for the verse to be read in more than one way. [96]

Some scholars of theology (*kalām*) have used the word *qadīm* (preeternal) to describe Allāh, even though it is not related as one of His beautiful names. *Qadīm* is a relative term used to express that something comes before another thing. The related name al-Awwal (the First) is superior to *qadīm,* because it implies not only that He is before all else, but also that whatever comes after Him is in need of Him. Therefore, when the theologians use *qadīm* for Allāh, it is understood as embodying the meaning of al-Awwal, since whenever Allāh is described by an attribute, He is described by it in its fullest sense.

[Taken together,] the names al-Ḥayy (the Living) and al-Qayyūm (the Self-subsistent) have been considered the "great name" of Allāh (*ism Allāh al-aʿẓam*), which is supported by the fact that they are part of the Throne Verse (Āyat al-Kursī), which the Messenger ﷺ said was the greatest verse in the Qur'ān (*Bukhārī*). Also, these two names are the basis for all the other beautiful names of Allāh; His being "the Living" is necessary for any of the other names to exist. Moreover, being "Self-subsistent" includes within its definition the perfection of His power and authority and His not being in need of anyone. In effect, these two attributes permeate all the attributes of perfection to the utmost degree. [96–97]

Imām Abū Ḥanīfa says in *Al-Waṣiyya:*

> We declare that the Qur'ān is the uncreated speech of Allāh Most High, His inspiration and revelation. It is neither Him nor other than Him, but strictly speaking, it is His attribute, written in texts, read by tongues, and preserved in hearts, but not subsisting in them. The ink, the paper, and the writing are all created—for they are of the acts of servants—and the speech of Allāh is uncreated, and the writing, letters, words, and verses are indicators of the Qur'ān [i.e., of the divine archetype] because of the need of the servants for them, whereas the

---

the Qur'ān. These were the variations settled on by the Messenger of Allāh ﷺ in his final review of the Qur'ān with Jibrīl before he passed away. In the seven copies of the Qur'ān prepared by the third caliph, ʿUthmān ؓ, the script was written in a manner that allowed for all the seven variant readings to be read from it. The more widely used narrations today are those of Ḥafs from ʿĀṣim, Warsh from Nāfiʿ, Qālūn from Nāfiʿ and Dūrī from Abū ʿAmr. See Taqi Usmani, *ʿUlūm al-Qur'ān* 97–58; A. R. Doi, *The Sciences of the Qur'ān* 64.

> [internal] speech of Allāh Most High is associated with the essence of Allāh and its meaning is understood through these tools. Therefore, whoever said the speech of Allāh is created is an unbeliever in Allāh Most Great. Allāh Most High is the deity (*maʿbūd*) and has always been as He is, and His speech is recited, written, and preserved without it departing from Him.[103]

Whatever Allāh Most High has said in the Qur'ān in quoting Mūsā and other prophets (upon them be peace), and Pharaoh and Iblīs (Satan), is all the speech of Allāh Most High informing [us] about them. The speech of Allāh Most High is uncreated, while the speech of Mūsā عليه السلام and that of other created beings is created. The Qur'ān is the speech of Allāh Most High—therefore preeternally existent—unlike their speech. That is, whatever Allāh Most High has said in the Qur'ān in quoting Mūsā, ʿĪsā, and other prophets (upon them be peace), and Pharaoh and Iblīs (Satan), is all said with His preeternal speech, the words signifying which He inscribed on the Preserved Tablet prior to the creation of the heavens and earth, not with originated speech, nor with knowledge originated only after hearing it from them.

[In the Arabic text,] *Ikhbār* means to convey [something] in meaning, not in word, because the speech of Mūsā عليه السلام and other created beings is created, while the speech of Allāh Most High is uncreated. [This distinction] is reinforced by the notion that a set of three verses of the Qur'ān constitute the minimum for inimitability (*iʿjāz*), a rank not possible for a human being.[104] It is evident that whatever is quoted in the Qur'ān of [the speech of] created beings exceeds three verses, and so the [entire] Qur'ān constitutes the speech of Allāh Most High, not their [human] speech. Therefore, there is no difference between the stories mentioned in the Qur'ān, the "Throne Verse" (Āyat al-Kursī), and the "Chapter of Sincerity" (Sūrat al-Ikhlāṣ) in that they are the speech of Allāh Most High.

[Qārī] There is no difference between the verses and chapters of the Qur'ān

103 The truth of the matter is that when one refers to the speech of Allāh, one means by it both the internal speech (*kalām nafsī*), which is His eternal attribute, and the written and uttered Qur'ān that is present before us (*kalām lafẓī*), arranged into verses and chapters. Part of the proof for the sanctity even of this written word is the impermissibility of anyone in a state of impurity to touch it.

104 That is, a human being is not capable of composing three sentences that reach an inimitable degree.

that relate specific incidents or events of the past, and those that describe the attributes of Allāh, His actions, or His creation of the world; they are all His eternal speech. The internal speech (*kalām nafsī*) of Allāh, which is His eternal attribute, already contained all of these events and descriptions. They were merely articulated into the created form of letters, words, and sounds for us to understand at a time when their revelation was determined by Him.

The different languages into which the speech of Allāh is revealed, the Tawrāh (Torah) in Hebrew and the Qur'ān in Arabic, for example, are all still considered the speech of Allāh, as Allāh says, "Have you any hope that they will be true to you when a party of them used to listen to the *word* of Allāh" (Qur'ān 2:75) and then "If one among the polytheists asks you for asylum, grant it to him, so that he may hear the *word* of Allāh" (9:6). [These scriptures] came from Allāh and are the created articulation of the divine archetype [into the specific language for the people of the time]. [99–100]

Another proof for the eternal, uncreated nature of the speech of Allāh, is that the Prophet ﷺ is related to have said, "I seek refuge in the words of Allāh (*bi kalimāti 'Llāh*)" and the Prophet would not seek refuge in something created, just as he used to say, "I seek refuge in Your pleasure." [105]

About the Qur'ān, Imām Ṭaḥāwī and other pious predecessors (*salaf*) used to say, "From Him, it came without modality (*kayfiyya*) and to Him, it will return" as is indicated in the ḥadīths describing the removal of the Qur'ān from the hearts and texts prior to the Last Day. "To Him, it will return" means that He alone possesses the knowledge and understanding of the details of the description of His speech. [106–107]

Mūsā عليه السلام heard the speech of Allāh Most High, that is to say, Mūsā عليه السلام [directly] heard from Allāh Most High His preeternal speech, which exists in His entity, not through any medium [i.e., via an angel], as is mentioned in the words of Allāh: "And Allāh spoke directly unto Mūsā" [(4:164)]. Allāh Most High is capable of speaking to creation without [the use of] mediating tools from all directions (*jihāt*) or from a single direction, although human beings hear it through [the use of] mediating tools (e.g., utterances and sounds), as they need them to comprehend His preeternal speech. Allāh Most High is capable of it, for He has power over all things. It is said that when Allāh Most High spoke to Mūsā عليه السلام, he heard the speech from within a cloud that looked like a pillar, which other clouds had enveloped.

Allāh Most High was the Speaker when He had not yet spoken to Mūsā عليه السلام by saying to Mūsā عليه السلام in preeternity, without any sound or [without the utterance of a] letter, "O Mūsā! I am your Lord. So take off your shoes" [the complete verse being] "And when he reached it, he was called by name, 'O Mūsā! I am your Lord. So take off your shoes'" (Qur'ān 20:12). Allāh knew in preeternity that He would reveal the Qur'ān to Muḥammad ﷺ, inform him of the stories of the prophets and others, and give him some commands and prohibitions.

After the Great Imām expounded the attribute of speech—that it is not dependent on the existence of the addressed [e.g., Allāh's words to Mūsā عليه السلام existed in the limitless reaches of past eternity (*azal al-āzāl*), long before even the existence of Mūsā عليه السلام himself]—he intended to similarly expound all the attributes [of Allāh] and to repel the notion that this quality may be specific to the attribute of speech only. He states therefore, Allāh Most High was the Creator in preeternity when He had not yet created creation. He [the Imām] limits himself to the active attributes and does not expound any of the essential attributes, because the dependence of an active attribute on the existence of an association (*mutaʿallaq*) is more apparent than that of the essential attributes' [dependence on the existence of an association]. Thus, the position of the essential attributes is understood *a fortiori*. He also selected "creating" from among the active attributes, because it is common and present in all the other attributes. Then, after eliminating cause for doubt, he returns to continue explaining the subject of his discussion, saying, So when Allāh spoke to Mūsā عليه السلام, He spoke to him with His speech, which was His attribute in preeternity. This is because Allāh's speech is preeternal and everlasting; it does not change or alter.

Because the attributes of Allāh Most High are unlike the attributes of creation, just as His essence is unlike the essence of creation, the Great Imām says, Every attribute of His, whether essential or active, is unlike the attributes of creation. This is because He knows unlike the way we know since our knowledge is originated and prone to illusion (*wahm*), while His knowledge is preeternal, and beyond being necessary (*ḍarūrī*), acquired (*kasbī*), conceived (*taṣawwurī*), or asserted (*taṣdīqī*).

He is powerful unlike the way we are powerful. The power of Allāh Most High is preeternal and effective in creating, and our power is originated and ineffective. We are only able to do some things with tools, means, and assistants.

Allāh Most High, with His preeternal power, is able to do all things without the help of tools or the assistance of anybody.

He sees unlike the way we see. We see shapes and colors with the help of senses, and [our seeing is] subject to particular conditions [e.g., having our eyes open, sufficient brightness, etc.]. He sees shapes and colors through His seeing that is His preeternal attribute, without any organs and without being subject to any conditions, such as time, place, direction, or being face to face.

He speaks unlike the way we speak. We speak with [the help of communicative] tools, which are subject to particular conditions. He speaks without any organs and without being subjected to any conditions.

He hears unlike the way we hear. We hear through [our use of auditory] tools, which are subject to particular conditions. He hears all sounds and words with His preeternal hearing, without any aids like earlobes or earcanals, and without being subject to any conditions, such as time, place, direction, nearness, or farness.

We speak [and communicate] by means of organs and letters, while Allāh Most High speaks without any organs or letters. Letters are created because whatever is formed from the created is also created, and the speech of Allāh Most High is uncreated. His speech is preeternal and existent in His entity, and it does not become detached or separated [from Him] when being relayed to the hearts and ears [of created beings].

[Qārī] Allāh hears sounds and single and compound words with His attribute of hearing (*samᶜ*) and sees forms, colors, and various shapes with His attribute of sight (*baṣar*), all without aids or assistance from anyone. His listening to and seeing them is preeternal in its essence, even though what is seen and heard is originated [and their prior occurrence or existence is not a pre-requisite for His hearing or seeing them]. The contingent object occurring later does not negate the prior occurrence of the eternal association [i.e., His attributes]. Do you not observe that a person when dreaming sometimes sees colors and shapes and hears noises, despite their nonexistence in the real world? Later, in a wakeful state, that person may see and hear those same things in exactly the same way they had appeared in his dream. How is it then, that one has doubts about or is surprised by the fact that Allāh, the Sovereign Most High, who possesses all the attributes of completeness and excellence, can see things and hear things before their actual occurrence? After all, it is He who shows the sleeping person shapes and colors in his sleep and allows him to hear sounds in [his dream] before their actual occurrence. [108]

The greatest blessing for the people of Paradise in the Hereafter will be the Beatific Vision and hearing His speech. Denying this fact is denying the ultimate pleasure in Paradise without which Paradise would not be enjoyable to its inhabitants. Similarly, the greatest punishment for the unbelievers will be His not speaking to them and the erecting of a firm veil between them and Him as mentioned in the Qur'ān: "Allāh will not speak to them on the Day of Resurrection" (2:174), i.e., with the speech of honor, and "Nay! most surely they shall on that day be barred from their Lord" (83:15). [112]

ALLĀH IS UNLIKE ANYTHING, AND HIS HAND, COUNTENANCE, AND SELF

وَهُوَ شَيْءٌ لَا كَالْأَشْيَاءِ. وَمَعْنَى الشَّيْءِ الثَّابِتُ بِلَا جِسْمٍ وَلَا جَوْهَرٍ وَلَا عَرَضٍ، وَلَا حَدَّ لَهُ، وَلَا ضِدَّ لَهُ، وَلَا نِدَّ لَهُ، وَلَا مِثْلَ لَهُ. وَلَهُ يَدٌ وَوَجْهٌ وَنَفْسٌ كَمَا ذَكَرَهُ اللهُ تَعَالَى فِي الْقُرْآنِ، فَمَا ذَكَرَهُ اللهُ تَعَالَى فِي الْقُرْآنِ مِنْ ذِكْرِ الْوَجْهِ وَالْيَدِ وَالنَّفْسِ فَهُوَ لَهُ صِفَاتٌ بِلَا كَيْفٍ. وَلَا يُقَالُ إِنَّ يَدَهُ قُدْرَتُهُ أَوْ نِعْمَتُهُ، لِأَنَّ فِيْهِ إِبْطَالَ الصِّفَةِ، وَهُوَ قَوْلُ أَهْلِ الْقَدَرِ وَالْإِعْتِزَالِ، وَلٰكِنْ يَدُهُ صِفَتُهُ بِلَا كَيْفٍ، وَغَضَبُهُ وَرِضَاهُ صِفَتَانِ مِنْ صِفَاتِ اللهِ تَعَالَى بِلَا كَيْفٍ.

Allāh is an entity (*shay'*) unlike any other entity. The meaning of [Allāh being a] *shay'* [unlike any other] is that He is without body, substance, or accident. He has no definition, no opposite, no equal, and no peer. He possesses a hand, a countenance, and a self, as He has mentioned in the Qur'ān.

What Allāh Most High has mentioned in the Qur'ān—His countenance, hand, and self—they are His attributes without description. It should not be stated that His hand is His power or blessing, because saying that would be invalidating the attribute, which is the view of the Qadariyya and the Muʿtazila. His hand is His attribute without description, and His anger and pleasure are from among His attributes without description.

❁

Allāh is an entity (*shay'*) as He says, "Say (O Muḥammad): 'What *entity* is greatest in testimony?' Say, 'Allāh'" (Qur'ān 6:19), [for He is] unlike any other entity as Allāh Most High says, "Nothing is as His likeness" (42:11). The meaning of [Allāh being a] *shay'* [unlike any other] is that He is/ Most editions have it as *ithbāt* "to establish" or "to affirm," i.e., "The meaning of [Allāh being a] *shay'* [unlike any other] is to affirm His existence . . . ." | without body/[105] This is an explanation of the author's statement "unlike any other entity," because every body (*jism*) is divisible (*munqasim*), every divisible thing is complex (*murakkab*), every complex thing is originated (*muḥdath*), and every originated thing requires an originator (*muḥdith*). Therefore, every possible (*mumkin*)[106] body is in need of the necessarily existent (*wājib al-wujūd*) [which is Allāh]. | substance because a substance is a locus (*maḥall*) for accidents (*aʿrāḍ*) and originations (*ḥawādith*), and Allāh Most High is transcendent of that. | or accident because an accident (*ʿaraḍ*) is not self-subsisting, but depends on a locus (*maḥall*) in which to subsist, and is therefore possibly existent [in nature] (*mumkin*).

[Qārī] We are unable to comprehend Allāh Most High. Whatever occurs to one's mind, Allāh is other than that, for Allāh says, "But they shall not encompass Him with their knowledge" (Qur'ān 20:110). For one to ascertain one's inability to completely comprehend is, in fact, to comprehend, as the Messenger of Allāh ﷺ said, "I cannot enumerate enough praise for You, You are as You have praised Yourself" (*Muslim*). [117]

The word *shay'* (entity), a verbal noun, can express two meanings: one, as a passive participle, as in "And Allāh has power over all entities (*ashyā',* sing. *shay'*)" (Qur'ān 2:274), and second, as an active participle, as in, "Say, 'What entity (*shay'*) is most weighty in evidence?' Say, 'Allāh is witness between me and you'" (6:19). It is in the second meaning that the word *shay'* can be used for Allāh Most High. In fact, Allāh being the Necessary Existence

---

105 Abu 'l-Faḍl al-Tamīmī said that Aḥmad ibn Ḥanbal condemned those who said that Allāh is a "body" (*jism*), since names are derived from the Sharīʿa and lexicography. Lexicographers have coined the term *jism* (body) to indicate things that have length, width, depth, and a compound nature. Therefore, this term cannot be applied to Allāh, since if He were a body, He would be spatial (*mutaḥayyiz*), which would also entail Him being compound (*tarkīb*) and originated (*ḥudūth*). It is then surprising that Ibn Taymiya said, "It is also known that the Book, Sunna, and consensus did not state that all bodies (*ajsām*) are created and that Allāh is not a body (*jism*); neither did any imām from among the imāms of the Muslims say this. Hence, my not saying this [i.e., that Allāh is *not* a body] is not a dissent from the natural way (*fiṭra*) or the Sharīʿa." Contrast this statement to his shaykh Imām Aḥmad's remarks; the difference is quite startling (*Al-Taʿlīq al-Muyassar* 118–119).

106 *Mumkin* (*or Mumkin al-wujūd*). Contingent being or possible being. This refers to one whose existence is contingent. It can be or not be, and its existence is through the existence of that which necessarily exists through itself, namely the Necessary Being. All creation beside Allāh is *mumkin*. This is similar to *ḥādith* or being contingent. See also note 58.

(*wājib*) makes Him most deserving of the term *shay'* (entity), since He is the only necessary entity in existence, and all others are merely possible entities (*mumkin al-wujūd*) [—their existence and non-existence being equal in this context]. [118]

Fakhr al-Dīn al-Rāzī (may Allāh be pleased with him) once made a beautiful statement, "The anthropomorphist (*mujassim*) is the one who never worshipped Allāh because he worships the forms he imagines, and Allāh Most High is free from that." [119]

He has no definition/ *ḥadd* means to define a quiddity (*māhiya*) by mentioning its parts (*ajzā'*), whereas the Necessarily Existent (*wājib al-wujūd*) [Allāh] is single without parts. Therefore, it is not possible for Him to have a definition (*ḥadd*). Sometimes *ḥadd* also means "end" or "boundary," but there is no end or boundary to Allāh Most High. | no opposite, no equal, and no peer, that is, He has no partner in species (*nawᶜ*), because there is no species for Him, just as there is no genus (*jins*) for Him. Having a peer (*mithl*) means to be a co-member in species.

He possesses a hand, a countenance, and a self, as He has mentioned in the Qur'ān where He says, "The hand of Allāh is above their hands" (48:10), "Yet still abides the countenance of your Lord" (55:27); and, quoting ᶜĪsā عليه السلام, He says, "You know what is within my self, and I know not what is within Your self" (5:116).

What Allāh Most High has mentioned in the Qur'ān—His countenance, hand, and self—they are His attributes without description. This means that their reality is known but their description is unknown to us. The known reality is not eliminated despite the ambiguity and incomprehensibility of the description. It is related of Aḥmad ibn Ḥanbal (may Allāh have mercy on him) that the modality (*kayfiyya*) is unknown and inquiry into it is an innovation.[107]

It should not be stated that His hand is His power or blessing, because saying that would be invalidating the attribute, which is established in the Qur'ānic verse. | which is the view of the Qadariyya and the Muᶜtazila. This is a specific [term] following a general [term], because the Qadariyya (Ahl al-

107 Although this reflects the view held by all the scholars of the Ahl al-Sunna wa 'l-Jamāᶜa, this statement is more popularly ascribed to Imām Mālik.

Qadar) are the Muʿtazila, as well as the Imāmiyya among the Shīʿa (or Shi'ites). Hence, all Muʿtazila are Qadariyya, but all Qadariyya are not Muʿtazila. The Messenger of Allāh ﷺ said, "In every umma, there are Magians (Majūs),[108] and the Magians of this umma are those who say there is no predestination (*qadar*). If someone dies from among them, do not attend his funeral, and if someone falls ill from among them, do not visit him. They are the faction of the Antichrist (Dajjāl), and it is upon Allāh to place them [in the ranks] with the Antichrist" (*Abū Dāwūd,* "al-Sunna," 4027). The Messenger of Allāh ﷺ has spoken the truth. He ﷺ also said, "Belief in destiny removes grief and worry."[109] Again, the beloved of Allāh has spoken the truth.

His hand is His attribute without description just as is His countenance and self (*nafs*). Imām Fakhr al-Islam ʿAlī al-Bazdawī says in his *Uṣūl al-Fiqh,* "Likewise, the establishment of the hand and countenance is known to us in their reality but ambiguous in their description. Moreover, it is not permissible to invalidate their reality on the inability to comprehend their description. The Muʿtazila deviated in this regard, because they rejected the reality of certain things based on their ignorance of the descriptions." | and His anger and pleasure are from among His attributes without description, that is, without any explanation of their description. Their description is unknown, because His anger and pleasure are dissimilar to our anger and pleasure. Anger in us is the boiling of the blood in the heart, and pleasure in us is becoming equipped with free will until it reaches manifestation, which include psychological states, such as happiness, joy, love, and amazement. All are subject to a disposition that entails being a complex being, which is contrary to [the nature of one endowed with] necessary existence (*wujūb al-dhāt*).

[Qārī] Abū Ḥanīfa says in his book *Al-Waṣiyya,* "We agree that Allāh is established (*istawā*) on the Throne without His needing it or resting (*istiqrār*) on it, and He is the Guardian of the Throne and all besides the Throne. If He were in need, He would not have been able to bring into existence the universe or administrate over its affairs, just as created beings cannot. If He was in need

108 The Majūs are the Magians. They are the Thanawiyya or dualists who believed the universe originated from two sources, light and darkness, both mutually exclusive of the other; they also believed that good came from the light and from the darkness came evil. They are also referred to as the Zoroastrians and Mazdians.

109 *Kanz al-ʿUmmāl* 481; from Ḥākim's *Tārīkh* and Shihāb al-Quḍāʿī's *Musnad* on the authority of Abū Hurayra ﷺ.

of sitting or settling [on it], then before the creation of the Throne, where was He Most High? In effect, He is transcendent of all this." [126]

When asked about the establishment (*istiwā'*) on the Throne, Imām Mālik responded by saying, "The establishment is known, the 'how' (*kayf*) is unknown;[110] asking about it is an innovation, and belief in it is obligatory." This is the way of the pious predecessors (*salaf*) and it is the safest path, and Allāh knows best. The interpretations (*ta'wīl*)[111] of some of the successors

---

110 This is also transmitted as "the 'how' is not comprehensible" (*ghayr maʿqūl*) in more authentic chains of narration. See the introduction to Ibn Jamāʿa's *Īḍāḥ al-Dalīl fī Qaṭʿ Shubah al-Taʿṭīl* (*Al-Taʿlīq al-Muyassar* 127). Ibn ʿAbd al-Barr relates that Ayyūb ibn Ṣalāḥ al-Makhzūmī reported, "We were by Mālik when an Iraqi came and said, 'O Abū ʿAbdillāh, "Allāh became established on His Throne," how did He become established?' Mālik replied, 'You have asked about what is not unknown [i.e., the establishment], and you have spoken about what is incomprehensible [i.e., the modality]'" (*Al-Tamhīd* 7:151–152). (Saʿīd Fawda, *Al-Farq al-ʿAẓīm Bayna al-Tajsīm wa 'l-Tanzīh* 22)

111 *Ta'wīl* means to "interpret, make sense of, assign a meaning to, give an interpretation or explanation to" as in interpreting the saying "The king defeated the enemy" as the defeat occurring at the hands of the king's army. *Tafwīḍ* (relegation) [lit. "to refer to another for decision or judgment"] means to leave any statement revealed about Allāh Most High as it was revealed, without elucidating or interpreting it, and consigning its intended explanation to Allāh. For instance, Allāh says, "(Allāh) Most Gracious is firmly established (*istawā*) on the Throne" (20:5). Hence, this information is mentioned in the Qur'ān, but the "how" of it is not known, and asking about it is an innovation, as Imām Mālik (may Allāh have mercy on him) said.

In detail, it can be said that the word *ʿarsh*, "throne," is used and the "elevated seat that is encircled by angels" is intended; this is the apparent understanding in the Sharīʿa. The word can also be used to mean "dominion" (*mulk*), as the poet said, "When the thrones (*ʿurūsh*) of the sons of Marwān were diminished," meaning their power and dominion diminished. The word *istawā'* can be used to mean "resting" or "becoming settled" (*istiqrār*) as in the words of Allāh Most High: "The Ark rested on Mount Judi" (11:44). It is also used to mean "to straighten" or "stand up" as opposed to "become crooked" as in the words of Allāh Most High: "Then it [the plant] stands on its own stem" (48:29). It is also used to mean "completeness" as Allāh Most High says, "When he reached full age and was firmly established" (28:14), that is, he had achieved his full body strength. It is also used to mean physical elevation or highness above something, but this meaning is inconceivable for Allāh Most High, along with the fact that physical elevation does not necessarily imply exaltedness, since it is possible that a leader be physically situated below his guard despite being superior. Rather, what is meant by *istiwā'* [with respect to Allāh] is elevation in status and rank.

Interpretation of the Physical Attributes of Allāh. As for those who say that "Hand" in the verse "the Hand of Allāh is over their hands" (48:10) means an actual physical limb, but the "how" of it is unknown, this is not the opinion of the predecessors (*salaf*) because the literal meaning of "hand" is the limb, and it is impossible to attribute a limb to Allāh. This is corporealism (*tashbīh*) and anthropomorphism (*tajsīm*). Thus, the difference of opinion regarding *ta'wīl* (interpretation) lies in the understanding of the Companions and those after them of the verse: "And no one knows its [the ambiguous verses'] meaning except Allāh" (3:7). Hence, whoever consigns the matter to Allāh affirms that one must pause at this point in the verse necessarily, [leaving interpretation of the ambiguous verses completely to Allāh], and begin again at "And those who are firmly grounded in knowledge say, 'We believe in it, the whole of it is from our Lord,' and none will grasp the Mes-

(*khalaf*) has already been mentioned, and it has been said, that their way is more judicious (*aḥkam*) [according to the exigencies of their times].[112] However, it has been related from some Shāfiʿīs that Imām al-Ḥaramayn al-Juwaynī initially engaged in *ta'wīl* but left doing so at the end of his life and rendered it unlawful. He related the consensus of the predecessors on its prohibition as he has explained in his *Risāla Niẓāmiyya,* and this is in accordance with the position of our Māturīdī scholars.[113]

Ibn Daqīq al-ʿĪd[114] has followed a middle path in which he says that the *ta'wīl* of these attributes is acceptable if the meaning is close to the popular usage (*takhāṭub*) of the Arabs; it is unacceptable if it is distant. Ibn al-Humām says it depends on the situation, and *ta'wīl* is called for if there is a problem in the understanding of the people, otherwise it is to be left alone. [126–127]

---

sage except men of understanding." But some hold that the "and" in this verse is conjunctive (*ʿaṭf*) with the previous phrase ending with "except Allāh," such that it reads: "And no one knows its interpretation except Allāh and those who are firmly grounded in knowledge." By this reading, they propose that the knowledgeable ones also know its interpretation. Regardless of this difference, they were all in agreement regarding the transcendence (*tanzīh*) of Allāh and His dissimilarity from any of His creation [confirming the absurdity of attributing a limb to him], and they were in agreement regarding establishing those attributes of Allāh that are established in the Qur'ān and the rigorously authenticated narrations (*Al-Taʿlīq al-Muyassar* 301–302).

112 The opinion of the *khalaf* was more judicious and wiser in light of the resistance they met with from the Muʿtazila and more specifically the anthropomorphists, who tried to influence the masses to turn toward their heretical ideas. The practice of the *salaf* of maintaining silence regarding such texts was no longer viewed as an adequate approach to overcome such heresy, and thus, some of the *khalaf* attempted to make *ta'wīl* but at the same time, they maintained the opinion that the way of the *salaf* was safer.

113 Imām al-Ḥaramayn, mentions what can be taken as a general principle for approaching the subject of the attributes of Allāh: "Any attribute in created beings whose affirmation indicates [the need of] an allocator, who assigns the attribute and confers upon it [movement, limitations, etc.], without whose affirmation the attribute cannot be otherwise imagined, then such an attribute is impossible to apply to Allāh; if it were established for Allāh, it would indicate His need for an allocator too, just as it does in the originated created being" (*Al-ʿAqīda al-Niẓāmiyya fi 'l-Arkān al-Islāmiyya* 21). The Imām also said, "Whoever sets out to seek its [i.e., the universe's] administrator and settles on something existent that his thinking concluded for him, then he is one who equates others with Allāh (*mushabbih*), and if he settles on complete repudiation then he is one who negates Allāh's attributes (*muʿaṭṭil*). If he achieves conviction regarding something existent but confesses his inability of comprehending its reality, then he is a monotheist (*muwaḥḥid*) (*Al-ʿAqīda al-Niẓāmiyya* 23). See Saʿīd Fawda, *Al-Farq al-ʿAẓīm Bayn al-Tanzīh wa 'l-Tajsīm* 19.

114 The ḥadīth scholar and jurist Muḥammad ibn ʿAlī ibn Wahb ibn Muṭīʿ, Abu 'l-Fatḥ al-Qushayrī al-Qūṣī al-Ḥāfiẓ al-Miṣrī al-Mālikī al-Shāfiʿī (at the time of his passing, he adhered to the Shāfiʿī school of law) more well known as Ibn Daqīq al-ʿĪd. A great scholar, he died in Cairo in 702/1302.

THE ATTRIBUTES OF CREATING, KNOWLEDGE, PREDESTINATION, AND HIS WRITING IN THE PRESERVED TABLET

خَلَقَ اللهُ تَعَالَىٰ الْأَشْيَاءَ لَا مِنْ شَيْءٍ. وَكَانَ اللهُ تَعَالَىٰ عَالِمًا فِي الْأَزَلِ بِالْأَشْيَاءِ قَبْلَ كَوْنِهَا، وَهُوَ الَّذِيْ قَدَّرَ الْأَشْيَاءَ وَقَضَاهَا، وَلَا يَكُوْنُ فِي الدُّنْيَا وَلَا فِي الْآخِرَةِ شَيْءٌ إِلَّا بِمَشِيْئَتِهِ وَعِلْمِهِ وَقَضَائِهِ وَقَدَرِهِ وَكَتْبِهِ فِي اللَّوْحِ الْمَحْفُوْظِ، وَلٰكِنْ كَتْبُهُ بِالْوَصْفِ لَا بِالْحُكْمِ. وَالْقَضَاءُ وَالْقَدَرُ وَالْمَشِيْئَةُ صِفَاتُهُ فِي الْأَزَلِ بِلَا كَيْفٍ، يَعْلَمُ اللهُ تَعَالَىٰ الْمَعْدُوْمَ فِي حَالِ عَدَمِهِ مَعْدُوْمًا وَيَعْلَمُ أَنَّهُ كَيْفَ يَكُوْنُ إِذَا أَوْجَدَهُ، وَيَعْلَمُ اللهُ الْمَوْجُوْدَ فِي حَالِ وُجُوْدِهِ مَوْجُوْدًا وَيَعْلَمُ أَنَّهُ كَيْفَ يَكُوْنُ فَنَاؤُهُ، وَيَعْلَمُ اللهُ الْقَائِمَ فِي حَالِ قِيَامِهِ قَائِمًا وَإِذَا قَعَدَ فَقَدْ عَلِمَهُ قَاعِدًا فِيْ حَالِ قُعُوْدِهِ مِنْ غَيْرِ أَنْ يَتَغَيَّرَ عِلْمُهُ أَوْ يَحْدُثَ لَهُ عِلْمٌ، وَلٰكِنَّ التَّغَيُّرَ وَالْإِخْتِلَافَ يَحْدُثُ عِنْدَ الْمَخْلُوْقِيْنَ.

Allāh Most High created all things from no thing. Allāh Most High knew in preeternity all things prior to their being. It was He who apportioned all things and ordained them. There is in this world nothing, nor in the next, except through His will, knowledge, ordination, decree, and in accordance with His writing it in the Preserved Tablet. Yet His writing entails descriptions, not commands.

Ordaining, decreeing, and willing are His attributes in preeternity without description. Allāh knows that the nonexistent is nonexistent in the state of its nonexistence, and He knows how it will be when He brings it into existence. And Allāh knows that the existent is existent while it is in a state of existence, and He knows how it will perish. Allāh knows that somebody standing is standing while he is standing; then when he sits, He knows that he is sitting while he is sitting, without there being any alteration or origination in His knowledge. Alterations and differences only occur in the knowledge of created beings.

❁

Allāh Most High created all things from no thing, that is, Allāh Most High created all things existent from no substance. Allāh Most High knew in preeternity all things prior to their being, that is, before their origination. It was He who apportioned all things and ordained them. This sentence is a justification for the previous statement. It is as though the author is saying, "How can it not be that He knew in preeternity all things prior to their origination, when it is He who apportions all things and ordains them?" The apportioning and ordaining of things do not occur but before their origination, and they do not occur but with [His] knowledge. It is also stated that *qaddarnā* ("we apportioned") means *katabnā* ("we wrote"). Zajjāj[115] states that *qaddarnā* means *dabbarnā* ("we devised"), and the root meaning of *qaḍā'* (ordaining or decreeing) is to either conclude and complete (*itmām*) something by word, as when Allāh Most High says, "Your Lord has *decreed* that you worship none but Him" (Qur'ān 17:23) or by action, as Allāh Most High says, "Then He *ordained* them [to be] seven heavens" (41:12). This is stated in the *Tafsīr* of Qāḍī [Bayḍāwī].

The Essence of Things is Real

[Qārī] The essence of things is indeed real, as indicated by the creation of the Pen first and Allāh ordering it to write all that will come to exist until the Day of Judgment (*Abū Dāwūd, Tirmidhī*). This is a direct rebuttal to the Sophists (*sūfisṭā'iyya*) and others who deny the real essences of things (*ḥaqā'iq al-ashyā'*) and believe that the world is all imaginary and fantasy like dreams. Close to this opinion is that of the heretic pantheists (*wujūdiyya ilḥādiyya*), the incarnationists (*ḥulūliyya*),[116] and those like them from among the ignorant *ṣūfis.*[117] [130–131]

---

115 Ibrāhīm ibn Muḥammad ibn al-Sarī ibn Sahl, Abū Isḥāq al-Zajjāj al-Baghdādī, the grammarian of his era and famous lexicographer (d. 311/923).

116 The incarnationists (*ḥulūliyya*) are of two types. Those who say that Allāh indwells in physical forms, and those who say that when a servant endeavors to fulfill his obligations, does his best to put the laws into action, abstains from the unlawful, and is abundant in performing supererogatory acts, Allāh inhabits him. Allāh is transcendent of what [such] polytheists claim (*Kashshāf Iṣṭilāḥāt al-Funūn*). (*Al-Taʿlīq al-Muyassar* 132)

117 Shaykh Ghāwjī writes, "The ignorant *ṣūfis* are among those who hold the opinion of

Imām Abū Ḥanīfa says in *Al-Waṣiyya:* "The ordainment of all good and evil is from Allāh Most High. If one declared that it was from other than Allāh, he would become an unbeliever in Allāh Most High, and his declaration of divine oneness (*tawḥīd*) would be invalidated."

There is in this world nothing, whether substance (concrete) or accident (abstract), nor in the next, except through His will, knowledge, ordination, decree, and in accordance with His writing it in the Preserved Tablet. The Messenger of Allāh ﷺ said, "The first thing Allāh created was the Pen, after which He commanded it to write. The Pen asked its Lord what it should write. Allāh said, "Write all that is to occur until the Day of Resurrection" (*Tirmidhī*,

---

pantheism (*waḥdat al-wujūd*), and this is blasphemy and falsehood, because how can the created become the Creator and the Creator the created; may Allāh protect us from such [thoughts]. Whenever a true *ṣūfī* rises to a high station and reaches self-annihilation, he recognizes that he is created and that the Creator is Allāh, a being other than him. The ignorant *ṣūfīs*, just like every other deviant group, will bear their burden, and true *ṣūfism* is far removed from this group" (*Al-Taʿlīq al-Muyassar* 132).

Basically there is a difference between "pantheism" and "oneness or unity of existence." Though very different ideas, both terms are sometimes used to explain the concept of *waḥdat al-wujūd*. *Waḥdat al-wujūd* "the unity or oneness of being" in the true sense is a *ṣūfī* philosophy which means "there is no true existence except that of the Ultimate Truth (Allāh)." The reason for this is that all created beings are possibly existent and only gain their existence through Allāh, the Necessarily Existent. Since the existence of Allāh is the only true existence, as it is essential and by merit of itself, and that of His creation relatively speaking is not a true existence, as it is not essential, or necessary, the *ṣūfīs* consider there to be no other existence except Allāh; this is their definition of *waḥdat al-wujūd*. Another definition of this provided by Imām Ghazālī in his *Iljām al-ʿAwāmm* and other books is that since creation is no more than [created by] the actions of Allāh, the only thing that exists is Allāh and His actions. Hence, nothing exists except for Him (see *Iljām al-ʿAwāmm ʿan ʿIlm al-Kalām* 76). As such, this concept cannot be denied, since it makes it clear that Allāh is Allāh and created beings are created beings. However, when exaggerated, it can become pantheism, which emphasizes that everything is Allāh, and there is no reality at all for anything else.

Bājūrī says, "This is what is called *waḥdat al-wujūd* according to them, and those who have immersed themselves in it have immersed themselves in it, so much so that what has been reported of some of the *awliyā'* gives a notion of indwelling (*ittiḥād*) and incarnation (*ḥulūl*), like Ḥallāj saying, 'I am Allāh,' and another's saying, 'There is none in this dress other than Allāh.' Such statements are not legally permitted because of the impression they give; however, the *ṣūfīs* (*qawm*) sometimes are overcome by their [spiritual] states, and thus such statements should be interpreted appropriately. Among those who gave a decree to kill Ḥallāj when he made the statement he made was Junayd [al-Baghdādī], as has been mentioned in *Sharḥ al-Kubrā*. Another misleading statement that has become common on the tongue of the laity is '[Allāh] is existent in every existence' (*mawjūd fī kulli 'l-wujūd*). Although in this statement, there is an indication of *waḥdat al-wujūd* [in the accepted sense, that is, 'He is never absent from any being, but is always aware of them' (see *Ṣāwī ʿala 'l-Jawhara* 146)], such a pronouncement is prohibited because it gives the impression of indwelling (*ḥulūl*)" (*Tuḥfat al-Murīd* 33). And Allāh knows best.

"al-Qadar," 2081). Yet His writing entails descriptions, not commands, that is, everything is written in the Preserved Tablet in complete detail as regards its attributes, such as beauty, ugliness, width, breadth, smallness, largeness, paucity, abundance, lightness, heaviness, hotness, coldness, wetness, dryness, obedience, disobedience, will, power, acquisition, and other descriptions, conditions, and characteristics. Nothing is written in it as merely a command to occur without description or cause. For example, "Let Zayd be a believer and ʿAmr an unbeliever" is not written in the Tablet as such. Had it been written that way, Zayd would have been involuntarily compelled to believe and ʿAmr to disbelieve, because whatever Allāh Most High commands necessarily transpires. Allāh Most High commands, and there is none to rescind (*muʿaqqib*) His command. Rather, it is written in the Tablet that Zayd will be a believer through his own choice and power, and he will desire true faith (*īmān*) and not unbelief; and ʿAmr will be an unbeliever through his own choice and power, and he will desire unbelief and not true faith. Therefore, the purpose of the Great Imām's statement "His writing entails descriptions, not commands" is to deny compulsion in the actions of servants and to refute the belief of the Jabriyya.[118]

Ordaining, decreeing, and willing are His attributes in preeternity without description, that is, without any explanation of their description. This means that while the reality of the attributes is established through the Qur'ān, Sunna, and consensus of the umma, they are from the ambiguities (*mutashābihāt*); in short, their interpretation is not known but by Allāh. Their descriptions are unknown, and no amount of effort can lead the intellect to comprehend them. The same holds for all the attributes of Allāh Most High, because His

118 An example by which the issues of predestination and compulsion may become more understandable is that of a teacher who works with a group of students for a number of years. Before administering a set of exams, he speculates on the grades his students will receive, writes them down on a piece of paper, and then leaves for vacation. When he comes back, he receives their actual scores and finds that most of his estimates are accurate or extremely close to the actual scores. It is quite clear that he was able to achieve such close approximations because of having worked with these students long enough to determine their capabilities and potential. As Allāh is the Creator of all and is endowed with eternal knowledge of both the whole and particular of things, His knowledge of all His creation is also on a very highly detailed and definitive level. In fact, He has knowledge of all things before they even occur. A ḥadīth states that He had the Pen write all that was to happen until the Day of Judgment. Then as each person comes into this world and does what they want to do with their free will, their acts are in accordance with what is written by the Pen on the Preserved Tablet, because Allāh had this information from before, and not because they are being forced to do what is written.

attributes are unlike the attributes of creation just as His essence is unlike the essence of creation.

[Qārī] Though *qaḍā'* (ordaining) and *qadar* (decreeing) have similar meanings, there is a difference between the two terms. The first term means a non-detailed general command and the other a more defined and detailed command.[119] Under the topic of ordaining and decreeing emerges the critical issue of the existence of unbelief. The Muʿtazila claim that if unbelief was from the decree of Allāh, it would be necessary for one to be satisfied with it, since satisfaction with the decree of Allāh (*riḍā' bi 'l-qaḍā'*) is necessary. They say this is problematic since satisfaction with unbelief is unbelief too, and thus unbelief cannot be from the decree of Allāh. In effect, all the actions of servants are not from the decree of Allāh as the Ahl al-Sunna wa 'l-Jamāʿa maintain [but some of their actions—the evil ones—are from themselves].

The rejoinder to this is that the claim of the Muʿtazila is fundamentally flawed since unbelief is not the decree (*qaḍā'*) of Allāh but is the decreed (*maqḍī*); moreover, it is necessary to have satisfaction with the decree of Allāh and not necessarily with the decreed. To elaborate, unbelief can be attributed to Allāh in that He created it according to His wisdom. There is no questioning Him on His desire (*mashī'a*), since He is the Sovereign Most High and is free to act toward His creation as He wills. However, unbelief also has another consideration, which applies to the responsible human being (*mukallaf*). It [unbelief] becomes the trait of such a person by his own acquisition (*kasb*) and choice. Accordingly, he is questioned for his actions, since he has angered his Lord by his acquisition and become worthy of uninterrupted punishment. Whoever is pleased with his own unbelief, by agreement [of the scholars], is guilty of unbelief.

Following this, scholars have differed regarding one who is pleased with the unbelief of another. The stronger opinion is that one is not guilty of unbelief in this situation as long as he dislikes unbelief itself. This is because his being pleased may well be because he wishes that Allāh take away true faith from that person so he may be given retribution for his harms and wrongdoings. This

119 This seems to be a unique definition of *qaḍā'* and *qadar*. A more well-known definition is that *qaḍā'* is His foreknowledge of events prior to their occurrence, while *qadar* is His bringing into existence those events in accordance with how He knows them to be. Some reverse the two definitions.

[opinion] is mentioned in the *Tatārkhāniya*[120] and supported by what Allāh relates about Mūsā 🕮 in the Qur'ān where he said, "Our Lord! Destroy the power of their [Pharaoh and his cohorts] wealth and send hardness to their hearts, so much so that they will not believe until they have seen the great punishment" (10:88). [133–134]

Imām Abū Ḥanīfa says in *Al-Waṣiyya:* "We declare that Allāh Most High ordered the Pen to write. The Pen asked, 'What should I write, O Lord,' so Allāh Most High said, 'Write what is to occur until the Day of Judgment,' as He Most High says, 'And everything they did is in the scriptures, and every small and great deed is recorded'" (54:52–53).

Whatever the mind tries to entertain by way of the description of these three attributes (*qaḍāʾ, qadar,* and *mashīʾa*) is false, since it is impossible to truly understand their reality; this is true for all the attributes of Allāh. Hence, it is necessary for one to believe in them and hold that anything that the intellect may conclude about them be invalid. Shams al-Aʾimma [al-Sarakhsī] (may Allāh have mercy on him) says, "There are two types of believers in this regard. The first are those who, due to their ignorance of these attributes, are tested in their endeavor to seek out their meanings. The second group consists of those who, due to being honored with some type of [inspired] knowledge about them, are tested with abstinence from seeking their meanings. The second type of believer is sometimes in far greater trial than the first, since after possessing some knowledge, he has to refrain from seeking the intellectual satisfaction of deeper understanding and realize that such is impossible."

The position of the second group is also the stronger position, since it encompasses belief in an unseen reality, in which there is neither a role for the intellect nor satisfaction for the human nature [in attaining complete knowledge of these attributes]. Rather, it is merely [forcing the self] to follow the truth that has been transmitted in the sacred sources. This is in contrast to the first position, in which one is relying completely on one's intellect and reason. This affirms that complete resignation and submission in acts of ritual worship (*ʿibādāt taʿabbudiyya*)[121] is superior and more complete than it is in

---

120 This is the famous compendium of formal legal opinions (*fatāwā*) of ʿĀlim ibn ʿAlāʾ al-Dīn, Farīd al-Dīn al-Andarpatī (al-Dihlawī) al-Hindī al-Ḥanafī (d. after 777/1375), in which he compiled rulings from *Al-Muḥīṭ al-Burhānī, Al-Dhakhīra, Al-Ẓahīriyya, Al-Khāniya,* and others. This compendium is also known as *Zād al-Musāfir fī 'l-Furūʿ* and was compiled in the 8th/14th century.

121 These are laws that are strictly and precisely determined by Allāh through the Qurʾān and Sunna of His Messenger 🕮, as opposed to non-ritual (*ʿādī*) acts.

other forms of worship because there is no gain in it for the lower self (*nafs*); in order to achieve this submission, complete following of Allāh's command is essential.[122]

Allāh says, "And of knowledge you have been given but little" (Qur'ān 17:85). About this, it has been related that "I don't know" (*lā adrī*) is half of knowledge and that "to realize one's inability to comprehend is, in fact, to comprehend." The caliph ʿAlī ibn Abī Ṭālib ﷺ was asked about a matter while he was standing on the pulpit, to which he responded, "I don't know." It was said to him, "How can you ascend this pulpit and say you do not know?" His reply was, "I ascended it according to my knowledge of things, had I ascended it according to my level of ignorance, I would have reached the heavens." It was similarly asked of Abū Yūsuf, "You take such and such from the treasury and yet you are unable to solve this matter?" He said, "Yes, I take from the treasury according to my knowledge. If I were to take according to my ignorance, I would take it all."[123]

Imām Abū Ḥanīfa mentions the will (*irāda*) of Allāh again to emphasize its status as a preeternal attribute of Allāh that designates a created being to be a certain way at a certain time; it is also a rejoinder to the Karrāmiyya and some Muʿtazila, who claim that the will of Allāh is created (*makhlūq*). As for the majority of the Muʿtazila, they deny that Allāh Most High wills evil and abominable things, such that they say Allāh Most High wills for the unbeliever and the sinner belief and obedience, not unbelief and disobedience; their assumption is that willing the abominable is also abominable as is the creation and origination [of evil equally abominable]. This position is negated and rejected by the fact that the abomination is what the person has acquired and become characterized by [and not Allāh creating or willing the

---

122 The human free will is limited, and its boundaries can be understood from the following. A person has the free will and ability to lift one foot off the ground and stand on just the other foot. However, lifting both feet off the ground at the same time is not within the free will granted to the human being. Therefore, the human has the ability to perform a number of things through his will but does not have control over many other things such as the span of his life, the timing of his death, the venue of his death, the number of children he has, the identity of his parents, the extent of his wealth, etc. Allāh says in the Qur'ān, "It is He who knows what is in the wombs. Nor does any one know what it is that he will earn tomorrow. Nor does any one know in what land he is to die. Verily with Allāh is full knowledge and He is well acquainted (with all things)" (31:34).

123 This statement emphasizes that mankind can only reach a certain level of understanding, even at the most advanced level, and that true knowledge is to recognize the limit of one's knowledge, intellect, and understanding.

act]. Consequently, according to them, most of what occurs of the actions of creation would be against the will of Allāh in this world—an extremely reprehensible consequence, which not even the head of a small village would tolerate! [134–136]

Discussing Destiny

[Qārī] Wahb ibn Munabbih[124] said, "I looked into the matter of destiny (*qadar*), and I was bewildered. I looked into it again, and I was still bewildered. I then concluded that the most knowledgeable of people regarding destiny are those who keep the farthest away from it, and the most ignorant of people regarding destiny are those who talk most about it." This is supported by what the Messenger of Allāh ﷺ said, "When destiny is discussed, restrain yourself from it" (*Ṭabarānī*). [140]

Regarding Attributing Good and Evil to Allāh

[Qārī] Good is attributed to Allāh, as He is responsible in every sense for its favorable bestowal. As for [what seems to be] "evil," He created it for some wise purpose, and based on that wise purpose, it is counted from among His favors; Allāh Most High does not do evil. Everything He does is good and for the best, as the Messenger ﷺ said, addressing Allāh, "The good is all in Your hands and the evil cannot be imputed to You (*Muslim*), which means, "You do not create anything purely and wholly evil, because everything You create consists of some wisdom by which it is considered good, even though it is sometimes considered evil for some people; this makes it a partial and relative evil. As far as it being pure or completely evil, Allāh is transcendent of that. This is why evil cannot be solely attributed to Allāh; instead, it can be counted as being from among the generality of His creation, as in, "Allāh is the creator of all things" (Qur'ān 13:16) and "Say, 'All things are from Allāh'" (4:78). Alternatively, it can be attributed to its cause, as in "From the evil of what He has created" (113:2), or it can be mentioned in the passive as in "And

124 The imām and erudite scholar Wahb ibn Munabbih ibn Kāmil ibn Sayaj ibn Dhī Kibār al-Yamānī al-Ṣaghānī, the brother of Hammām ibn Munabbih. He was born during the caliphate of ʿUthmān ؓ in 34/654. He traveled and studied under many Companions and Followers and was known for his extensive knowledge of the Israelite traditions. He passed away in 110 or 113 AH. See *Siyar Aʿlām al-Nubalāʾ* 4:544–557.

we understand not whether ill is *intended* to those on earth, or whether their Lord (really) intends to guide them to right conduct" (72:10). [141–142]

Regarding the Ability to Do the Impossible

[Qārī] As a final note [regarding the power (*qudra*) of Allāh], it has been said that every general term (*ʿāmm*) [in texts] is specified (*yukhaṣṣu*) as is reflected in the verse: "For Allāh has power over *all* things" (2:284). The general term here ["all" (*mā*)] has been qualified as being "everything He desires (*shāʾa*)." This excludes His essence and attributes, the things He does not desire from among His creation, and the things whose occurrence is an impossibility in His creation. In conclusion, the power of Allāh (*qudra*) is associated with everything with which His desire (*mashīʾa*) is associated. Otherwise, it is not to be said that He has power over the impossible, since it is nonexistent and will necessitate the falsehood [of the supposition]. Having said this, it should not be said that He does not have the power over it out of utmost respect and shyness toward one's Lord. [143]

Allāh knows that the nonexistent is nonexistent in the state of its nonexistence, and He knows how it will be when He brings it into existence. And Allāh knows that the existent is existent while it is in a state of existence, and He knows how it will perish. Allāh knows that somebody standing is standing while he is standing; then when he sits, He knows that he is sitting while he is sitting, without there being any alteration or origination in His knowledge. Alterations and differences only occur in the knowledge of created beings. Allāh Most High is aware of all things through His eternal knowledge, which has no beginning, not through any new knowledge. And He has possessed it since the limitless reaches of past eternity (*azal al-āzāl*), because His knowledge does not change due to change, alteration, and origination in things. The knowledge of Allāh is one (*wāḥid*), while the things known (*maʿlūmāt*) are numerous.

ALLĀH CREATED PEOPLE PURE AND THE COVENANT OF THE BEGINNING

خَلَقَ اللهُ تَعَالٰى الْخَلْقَ سَلِيْمًا مِنَ الْكُفْرِ وَالْإِيْمَانِ ثُمَّ خَاطَبَهُمْ وَأَمَرَهُمْ وَنَهَاهُمْ، فَكَفَرَ مَنْ كَفَرَ بِفِعْلِهِ وَإِنْكَارِهِ وَجُحُوْدِهِ الْحَقَّ بِخِذْلَانِ اللهِ تَعَالٰى إِيَّاهُ، وَآمَنَ مَنْ آمَنَ بِفِعْلِهِ وَإِقْرَارِهِ وَتَصْدِيْقِهِ بِتَوْفِيْقِ اللهِ تَعَالٰى إِيَّاهُ وَنُصْرَتِهِ لَهُ. أَخْرَجَ ذُرِّيَّةَ آدَمَ مِنْ صُلْبِهِ فَجَعَلَهُمْ عُقَلَاءَ فَخَاطَبَهُمْ وَأَمَرَهُمْ بِالْإِيْمَانِ وَنَهَاهُمْ عَنِ الْكُفْرِ، فَأَقَرُّوْا لَهُ بِالرُّبُوْبِيَّةِ، فَكَانَ ذٰلِكَ مِنْهُمْ إِيْمَانًا فَهُمْ يُوْلَدُوْنَ عَلٰى تِلْكَ الْفِطْرَةِ. وَمَنْ كَفَرَ بَعْدَ ذٰلِكَ فَقَدْ بَدَّلَ وَغَيَّرَ وَمَنْ آمَنَ وَصَدَّقَ فَقَدْ ثَبَتَ عَلَيْهِ وَدَاوَمَ. وَلَمْ يُجْبِرْ أَحَدًا مِنْ خَلْقِهِ عَلَى الْكُفْرِ وَلَا عَلَى الْإِيْمَانِ وَلَا خَلَقَهُمْ مُؤْمِنًا وَلَا كَافِرًا، وَلٰكِنْ خَلَقَهُمْ أَشْخَاصًا وَالْإِيْمَانُ وَالْكُفْرُ فِعْلُ الْعِبَادِ. وَيَعْلَمُ اللهُ تَعَالٰى مَنْ يَكْفُرُ فِي حَالِ كُفْرِهِ كَافِرًا فَإِذَا آمَنَ بَعْدَ ذٰلِكَ عَلِمَهُ مُؤْمِنًا فِي حَالِ إِيْمَانِهِ وَأَحَبَّهُ مِنْ غَيْرِ أَنْ يَتَغَيَّرَ عِلْمُهُ وَصِفَتُهُ.

Allāh Most High created all created beings free from unbelief and true faith. He then addressed them, commanded them, and prohibited them [from certain acts]. Thereafter, whoever disbelieved did so through his own doing by rejecting and repudiating the truth, Allāh having forsaken him; and whoever believed did so through his own choosing by affirming [the truth] and being convinced [of it], Allāh having granted him divine guidance and assistance.

Allāh extracted the progeny of Ādam ﷺ from his loins and endowed them with intelligence. He then addressed them, commanding them to believe and prohibiting them from unbelief. They affirmed His lordship, and that was faith on their part. Thus, they are born on this natural faith. Thereafter, whoever disbelieves has indeed replaced and altered [his natural faith], and whoever believes and affirms has indeed remained steadfast on it and persevered.

Allāh does not compel anyone to unbelief or true faith. He does not create people believers or unbelievers, but creates them as [pure] individuals; to believe or disbelieve is the action of the servants.

Allāh Most High knows one who disbelieves as an unbeliever while in the state of unbelief. Thereafter, if the person believes, Allāh knows him as a believer, while in the state of belief and loves him, without His knowledge or attribute [of love] undergoing any change.

❁

Allāh Most High created all created beings free from unbelief and true faith, which they acquire after coming into this world. He then addressed them at maturity when they possessed intellect and commanded them to have true faith and obedience and prohibited them from unbelief and disobedience. Thereafter, whoever disbelieved did so through his own doing by rejecting and repudiating the truth—*juḥūd* (repudiating) means to reject something while knowing it to be true—Allāh having forsaken him, that is, the rejection and repudiation is a result of Allāh Most High forsaking the person who disbelieves. | and whoever believed did so through his own choosing by affirming with his tongue [the truth] and being convinced [of it] from the depth of his inner heart (*janān*), Allāh having granted him divine guidance and assistance. *Tawfiq* (divine guidance and assistance) means to bind and harmonize the will of the servant with the ordainment and decree of Allāh Most High. This includes [matters of both] good and evil, and those involving both the bliss (*saʿāda*) and misery (*shaqāwa*) [of people]. But common usage has come to assign the noun specifically to what is in harmony with bliss (*saʿāda*) from among the ordainments and decrees of Allāh Most High. This is similar to the word *ilḥād* (deviation), which literally means "to incline toward," but became assigned specifically to one who inclines toward wrong. This is stated in *Iḥyā ʿUlūm al-Dīn*.

Allāh extracted the progeny of Ādam عليه السلام from his loins and endowed them with intelligence. He then addressed them, commanding them to believe and prohibiting them from unbelief. They affirmed His lordship, and that was faith on their part. Thus, they are born on this natural faith, that is, on true faith. It is called *fiṭra* because mankind has been created upon it, and *fiṭra* means natural disposition (*khilqa*). Most commentators of the Qur'ān and all the Companions (*ṣaḥāba*) and Followers (*tābiʿīn*) are in agreement regarding the extraction of the progeny of Ādam from his loins and the taking of the covenant (*mīthāq*) from them in his lifetime. Some are of the opinion that it occurred with the souls [of the progeny] and not the bodies.

[One could bring up the following objection: how can the words of Allāh Most High "Am I not your Lord? They say, 'Yes, we testify'—lest You should say on the Day of Resurrection, 'We were unaware of this'" (Qur'ān 7:172) be binding evidence against us when we are unable to remember the covenant, even if we try our best to remember? Our answer is that Allāh has caused us to forget it in order to test us, because this world is a testing ground, and we are obligated to believe in the unseen from the onset [of the age of discernment]. If we remembered the covenant, there would no longer be a test and we would not be in need of the reminder of messengers (upon them be peace). Moreover, an evidence (*ḥujja*) does not become invalid, nor an excuse valid on the basis of something forgotten. Allāh Most High says regarding our actions, "Allāh has kept account of it, yet they forgot it" (58:6).][125] Allāh renews the covenant and reminds us of it by sending messengers and revealing scriptures. Therefore, there is no valid excuse. This is stated in *Tafsīr al-Taysīr*.[126]

Regarding the Extraction of the Progeny of Ādam

[Qārī] Allāh extracted all of the progeny of Ādam in the similitude of tiny ants, some of which were white and some of which were black, and they spread out to the right and left of Ādam. Allāh endowed them with intelligence before making them bear witness that He is their Lord. [146]

Qūnawī states, "There are two opinions regarding the interpretation of the verse [on the extraction of Ādam's progeny]. The opinion of the commentators (*mufassirīn*), which is also the opinion of many other great scholars and the majority of the Ahl al-Sunna wa 'l-Jamāʿa, is what is related from ʿUmar ﷺ. He said, "I heard the Messenger of Allāh ﷺ say, 'Allāh Most High created Ādam, then rubbed his back with His right hand, whereupon He extracted from him some of his progeny, and said, "I have created these for Paradise, and they will perform the actions of the people of Paradise." Then He rubbed

125 This bracketed portion does not exist in any of the manuscripts of Maghnīsāwī's commentary I consulted. It seems to have been added in the published edition from Qārī's commentary and with some inaccuracies. I have translated the correct version here from Qārī's commentary.

126 Although the published edition had *Al-Tafsīr al-Shahīr* (the well-known *tafsīr*) here, nearly all the manuscripts have it as *Tafsīr al-Taysīr*, which seems more correct. See also note 91.

the back of Ādam with His left hand, and extracted from him others of his progeny and said, "I have created these for the Fire, and they will perform the actions of the people of the Fire."' Upon this, a man asked, 'O Messenger of Allāh, what is then the purpose of action?' He ﷺ replied, 'When Allāh Most High creates a servant for Paradise, He employs him in the work of the people of Paradise until he dies upon the deeds of the people of Paradise, and He therefore enters him into Paradise. Likewise, when Allāh creates a servant for the Fire, He employs him in the work of the people of the Fire until he dies doing the deeds of the people of the Fire, and He therefore enters him into the Fire'" (*Muwaṭṭā, Abū Dāwūd, Tirmidhī*).

The Jabriyya took the literal interpretation of this ḥadīth, saying that Allāh created the believers as believers and the unbelievers as unbelievers. They say, Iblīs was always an unbeliever [even when he was worshipping Allāh before his rejection], Abū Bakr and ʿUmar were believers before [embracing] Islām, and the prophets were prophets before [receiving] revelation.[127]

The Ahl al-Sunna wa 'l-Jamāʿa say that the prophets became prophets after receiving revelation, and Iblīs became an unbeliever afterwards; however, this does not negate the fact that it was preeternally known by Allāh that he would become an unbeliever. If there were compulsion, then Iblīs would never have performed an obedient act [which he did before becoming the rejected one]. Similarly, Abū Bakr and ʿUmar would never have committed disobedience. Therefore, their saying that unbelievers are forced into unbelief and disobedience and believers are forced into belief and obedience is baseless, and we say that a servant has the ability to believe or not believe and earns his belief or disbelief. He is not forced into one or the other [by Allāh]. If believers were created believers then He would not have commanded them to believe, nor would He have taken from them the covenant. Success and guidance (*tawfīq*), however, is ultimately from Allāh.

The second opinion regarding the verse is that of the people of speculation (*arbāb al-naẓar*) who maintain that Allāh extracted the progeny from the loins of their fathers. This extraction entails that they were first drops [of semen], then they were in the wombs of their mothers and became clots [of blood], then clumps of flesh until He finally made them into full and complete human

127 Thus, the servant in general has no choice in any matter since everyone according to them is designated one way or the other from the beginning.

being. He made them bear witness upon themselves by what He instilled in them of proofs of His Oneness. By their witnessing these proofs, it is as if they have replied in the affirmative to the covenant. This opinion does not negate the opinion of the majority mentioned above, because the two opinions are easily reconcilable; therefore, ponder it.

As for the Muʿtazilīs, they denied that the verse can be interpreted in the first manner [as found in the ḥadīth of ʿUmar] and have taken the verse to be metaphorical. This is completely in line with their overriding philosophy of giving preference to the intellect over the transmitted by saying whatever cannot be comprehended by the intellect is not permissible to adopt as an opinion.

In conclusion, it is out of the grace of Allāh that He made belief beloved to us and beautified it in our hearts and made unbelief and disobedience reprehensible to our hearts. Praise be to Allāh, who has guided us to this, for we would not have been guided if Allāh had not guided us. It is from His justice that He did not guide the unbelievers, and He made beloved to them disobedience, and made belief reprehensible to them. Thus, glory be to Allāh! "Thus does Allāh leave astray whom He pleases" (Qur'ān 74:31), "And those whom Allāh leaves astray, no one can guide" (13:33), and "And he whom Allāh guides, for him there can be none to lead astray" (39:37). This is all of the secrets of destiny (*qadar*) according to the preeternal judgment, and "He will not be questioned as to what He does, but they will be questioned" (21:23). [148–152]

Thereafter, whoever disbelieves has indeed replaced and altered [his natural faith] with unbelief that he acquired through his own choice after reaching maturity. Similarly, whoever believes and affirms after entering into the abode of legal responsibility (*dār al-taklīf*) and reaching the age of discretion has indeed remained steadfast on it, that is, on the natural true faith he inherited on the day of the covenant (*mīthāq*) and persevered in true faith. If it is claimed that this explanation contradicts the author's previous statement that Allāh created the creation free from unbelief and true faith, then our answer would be that it means Allāh created the creation free from "acquired" faith (*īmān kasbī*), but characterized by "natural" faith (*īmān fiṭrī*). The Messenger of Allāh ﷺ said, "Every newborn is born upon the natural faith (*fiṭra*). Thereafter, his parents either turn him to Judaism, Christianity, or Magianism" (*Bukhārī,* "al-Janā'iz," 1296; *Muslim,* "al-Qadar," 4803). This is proof that the children of believers and unbelievers possess natural faith [not acquired faith].

Allāh does not compel anyone to unbelief or true faith. Allāh Most High does not create unbelief or faith in a person's heart by compulsion or force, but creates it through the servant's [own] choice, satisfaction, and love [for it]. Do you not see that true faith is beloved to a believer, that unbelief is detestable, loathsome, and repulsive, and to the unbeliever, [unbelief] is beloved? He does not create people believers, that is, Allāh Most High does not create people on acquired faith (*īmān kasbī*) | or unbelievers with acquired unbelief (*kufr kasbī*) but creates them as [pure] individuals; to believe or disbelieve is the action of the servants, that is, unbelief, true faith, obedience, and disobedience are acts of the servants.

Allāh Most High knows one who disbelieves as an unbeliever while in the state of unbelief. Thereafter, if the person believes, Allāh knows him as a believer, while in the state of belief, and loves him, without His knowledge or attribute [of love] undergoing any change, because everything changeable is originated, and everything originated requires a knowledgeable, powerful, living, and independent (*mukhtār*) originator. If the knowledge of Allāh were changeable, it would be originated, and that would require that Allāh be a locus (*maḥall*) for originations (*ḥawādith*), whereas Allāh Most High is exalted above that.

[Qārī] Despite the fact that Allāh with His eternal knowledge knows before the existence of creation who will become a believer and who will become an unbeliever, He, out of His grace and generosity, does not act based on this knowledge [and thus force people into belief or unbelief]. He allows servants to make their own choices and perform their actions, until the time of judgment comes when they are judged; there, they receive punishment or reward based upon those choices and actions. And Allāh knows best. [152]

THE CREATOR AND THE ACTIONS OF HIS CREATION

وَجَمِيْعُ أَفْعَالِ الْعِبَادِ مِنَ الْحَرَكَةِ وَالسُّكُوْنِ كَسْبُهُمْ عَلَى الْحَقِيْقَةِ وَاللهُ تَعَالَى خَالِقُهَا. وَهِيَ كُلُّهَا بِمَشِيْئَتِهِ وَعِلْمِهِ وَقَضَائِهِ وَقَدَرِهِ. وَالطَّاعَاتُ كُلُّهَا كَانَتْ وَاجِبَةً بِأَمْرِ اللهِ تَعَالَى وَبِمَحَبَّتِهِ وَبِرِضَائِهِ وَعِلْمِهِ وَمَشِيْئَتِهِ وَقَضَائِهِ وَتَقْدِيْرِهِ، وَالْمَعَاصِيْ كُلُّهَا بِعِلْمِهِ وَقَضَائِهِ وَتَقْدِيْرِهِ وَمَشِيْئَتِهِ لَا بِمَحَبَّتِهِ وَلَا بِرِضَائِهِ وَلَا بِأَمْرِهِ.

All actions of servants pertaining to their motion and stillness are in reality their acquisition, while Allāh Most High is their Creator. They are all through His will, knowledge, ordainment, and decree. All acts of obedience are obligatory through the command of Allāh, His love, approval, knowledge, will, ordainment, and decree; and all acts of disobedience are through His knowledge, ordainment, decree, and will, but not through His love, approval, or command.

❁

All actions of servants pertaining to their motion and stillness are in reality their acquisition, while Allāh Most High is their Creator. *Kasb* (acquisition) literally means to seek sustenance, and its root meaning is "to gather." Technically, it constitutes the connection of the servant's will and power to his action. Thus, his motion, with respect to its relation to his own power and will, will be called *maksūb* (acquired), and with respect to its relation to the power and will of Allāh Most High, will be called *makhlūq* (created). Likewise is his stillness. Therefore, his motion and stillness are creations of the Lord and attributes and acquisitions of the servant. The power and will of the servant are the creation of the Lord and attributes of the servant, not his acquisitions. This explanation is indicated in *Sharḥ al-Maqāṣid*. They, that is, the actions of the servants—unbelief, true faith, obedience, and disobedience—are all through His will, knowledge, ordainment, and decree. The Messenger of Allāh ﷺ said, "Everything is subject to decree, even incapability and intelligence" (*Muslim,* "al-Qadar," 4799). Know that the doctrine of the Muʿtazila is that if Allāh Most High wishes true faith and obedience for a servant and the servant wishes unbelief and disobedience for himself, the wish of the servant is fulfilled and the wish of Allāh Most High is not fulfilled; therefore, the wish of the servant prevails and the wish of Allāh Most High is disregarded. Our belief, however, is that whatever Allāh Most High wills occurs. It is Allāh Most High who wills unbelief for the unbeliever and true faith for the believer. Therefore, Allāh's will prevails and the will of the servant is disregarded.

Acquisition (Kasb) and Creation (Khalq)

[Qārī] The difference between acquisition (*kasb*) and creation (*khalq*) is that in acquisition, the acquirer (*kāsib*) is not completely independent, while in creation (*khalq*), the creator is completely independent. It is also said that whatever occurs through the use of an implement or aid is considered acquisition, and whatever occurs without them is considered creation. Therefore, what Allāh brings into existence without His power (*qudra*) associating with the power or will (*irāda*) of the servant is considered an attribute of the servant but not his action [rather the act is ascribed to Allāh], like the involuntary trembling of someone [due to Parkinson's disease or some other cause]. On the other hand, that which Allāh brings into existence in association with the servant's ability and choice is described as the attribute (*ṣifa*), action (*fiʿl*), and acquisition (*kasb*) of the servant, like his purposeful movements. Similarly, effects such as pain from striking, or the breaking of glass are the creation of Allāh Most High, whereas according to the Muʿtazila, they are from the creation of the person. [154]

One of the great Imāms of the Ahl al-Sunna, ʿAllāma Bāqillānī,[128] said that the power (*qudra*) of Allāh is associated with the source (*aṣl*) of the action. The ability of the servant is associated with the action's identification with obedience or disobedience. Hence, the associations of the effect of the two abilities [of Allāh and His servant] upon the action are different.[129] [160]

---

128 The great Ashʿarī theologian Muḥammad ibn al-Ṭayyib ibn Muḥammad ibn Jaʿfar ibn al-Qāsim, Abū Bakr al-Baṣrī al-Qāḍī al-Bāqillānī. He resided in Baghdad and died there in 403/1013.

129 Take for example the case of punishing someone for the sake of disciplining them or for injuring them. The act of the punishment occurs through the power of Allāh and His effecting

ʿAlī ﷺ said, "I recognized Allāh by the annulment of determinations." Despite what one may plan or resolve to do, Allāh is ultimately the one who decides what will come to pass.

Abū Ḥanīfa says in *Al-Waṣiyya,* "We declare that the servant with all his actions, confessions, and knowledge (*maʿrifa*) is created, and thus, when the actor is created, it is all the more proof that his actions are also created." [155]

Ability and Action

[Qārī] The will of the servant as well as his power are both created at the moment of the action, neither before nor after. Abū Ḥanīfa explains this in *Al-Waṣiyya:*

> Ability (*istiṭāʿa*) coincides with the action, not before it or after it. If the ability were given before the action, the servant would not be in need of Allāh at the moment of the action, and this contradicts what is mentioned in the Qur'ān: "Allāh is free of all wants, and it is you who are needy" (47:38). And if the ability were to be after the action, then the performance of the action would have been impossible without it. Allāh created all created beings without power, and they are weak and feeble. Allāh Most High is their Creator and Sustainer as He Most High says, "Allāh is He who created you and then sustained you, then causes you to die, then gives life to you again" (30:40).
>
> To earn is lawful, and so accumulating wealth from the lawful is lawful, and accumulating wealth from the unlawful is unlawful. People are of three types: the believer who is sincere in his faith, the denying unbeliever in his unbelief, and the deceitful hypocrite in his hypocrisy. Allāh Most High has obligated deeds on the believer, belief on the unbeliever, and sincerity on the hypocrite, as He Most High says, "O mankind! Attend to your duty to your Lord" (4:1), which means, "O believers, be obedient; O unbelievers, be believers; and O hypocrites, be faithful." [156–157]

All acts of obedience are obligatory through the command of Allāh, that is, devotional worship that is obligatory on the servant is from the command of Allāh Most High and out of His love, approval, knowledge, will, ordainment,

---

it, but it constitutes an act of obedience on the part of the person performing it when it is for discipline, and an act of disobedience when intended solely to injure. This is because it is being done through the person's power and ability as a result of his firm resolve.

and decree; and all acts of disobedience are through His knowledge, ordainment, decree, and will, but not through His love, approval, or command. Allāh Most High says, "And Allāh loves not mischief" (2:205), and "And He approves not ingratitude in His servants" (39:7), and "Say: 'Allāh does not command indecency'" (7:28), that is, the evils of unbelief and disobedience.

The Author [Abū Ḥanīfa] states in *Kitāb al-Waṣiyya,*

> We state that actions are of three types: an obligation (*farīḍa*), a virtue (*faḍīla*), and a sin (*maʿṣiya*). Obligations are by the order, will, love, approval, ordainment, decree, creation, command, knowledge, and divine guidance of Allāh, and through His writing it in the Preserved Tablet. Virtues are not by the order of Allāh, (otherwise they would be obligatory); instead, they are through His will, love, approval, ordainment, decree, command, knowledge, creation, and divine guidance (by His conferring the soundness of means and associated ability [upon His servant]), and His writing it in the Preserved Tablet. Sins are not [committed] on the order of Allāh. Rather, they occur through His will, not through His love; through His ordainment, not through His approval; through His decree and creation, not through His divine guidance; through His forsaking the sinner and with His knowledge of it, and through His writing it in the Preserved Tablet.

Know that sins are of two kinds: enormities and minor sins. As for the enormities, there are nine. Ṣafwān Ibn ʿAssāl relates, "A Jew told his friend, 'Take us to this prophet.' His friend told him, 'Don't say prophet. If he heard you he would grow four eyes.' They came to the Messenger of Allāh ﷺ and asked him regarding the nine clear signs (*āyāt bayyināt*). The Messenger of Allāh ﷺ replied, "Do not partner anything with Allāh, squander wealth, perform unlawful intercourse, take any life that Allāh has sanctified except with due right, report an innocent person to someone in authority to have him killed, practice sorcery, consume interest, slander a chaste woman, or flee on the day of battle, and, specifically for you, O Jews! Do not transgress on [your Sabbath] of Saturday." Ṣafwān states that they both kissed the Messenger's hands and feet and said, "We testify that you are a prophet." The Messenger of Allāh ﷺ asked, "Then what prevents you from following me?" They replied, "Dāwūd ﷺ prayed to his Lord that prophets should remain in his descendants, and therefore, we are afraid that if we were to follow you, the Jews would kill us" (*Tirmidhī,* "al-Isti'dhān wa 'l-ādāb," 2657; *Nasāʾī,* "Taḥrīm al-dam," 4010).

Allāh's Pleasure with Regard to Good and Evil Actions

[Qārī] The good actions of the servants are those that are associated with praise in this world and reward in the Hereafter, in accordance with the good pleasure of Allāh Most High, His will, and His ordination. Evil actions, on the other hand, are those that are associated with blame in this world and punishment in the Hereafter. They are not in accordance with the good pleasure of Allāh, but in accordance with His will and ordination. Allāh says, "He is not pleased with ingratitude from His bondsmen" (Qur'ān 39:7). Therefore, His desire (*mashī'a*), will (*irāda*), and decree (*taqdīr*) are associated with all actions, whereas His good pleasure (*riḍā'*), love (*maḥabba*), and command (*amr*) are only associated with the good actions, and not evil ones. This is because He ordered His servants to believe, with His full knowledge from preeternity that some of them would die on unbelief. [165–166]

Regarding Ability and Accountability

[Qārī] Obedience is according to ability, as Allāh says, "On no soul does Allāh place a burden greater than it can bear" (Qur'ān 2:286). The ability (*istiṭāʿa*) by which a person is accountable for obedience is the soundness of the means by which one may fulfill what is required with regards to knowing Allāh and worshiping Him. It is for this reason that the child and the mentally incompetent are not held accountable for belief, and that a mute person is not required to articulate his belief with his tongue, and that the bedridden is not required to stand while praying. [166]

Conclusion Regarding Ability

[Qārī] In conclusion, ability (*istiṭāʿa*) is an attribute that Allāh creates upon the acquisition of an action, after the soundness of the means and causes are in place. If the servant intends to do a good deed, Allāh creates in him the ability to do that good deed. If the servant intends to do a bad deed, Allāh creates in him the ability to do that bad deed. It is the servant, then, who squanders his [God-given] ability to do good actions, and thus becomes blameworthy and deserving of punishment.

The word *istiṭāʿa* also applies to the soundness of the causes, means, and limbs [mentioned earlier] as Allāh says [describing the one who ought to perform the greater pilgrimage], "Who is able to undertake (*istaṭāʿa*) the journey to it" (Qur'ān 3:97). It is this type of ability that must be ascertained for accountability to be determined in the first place, not the ability mentioned above [which is the power or energy Allāh creates at the actual time of the action that enables a person to carry out the act]. Imām Abū Ḥanīfa holds that it is the same ability (*qudra*) that may be employed for performing the good or the evil deed—the servant links to it one or the other depending on his intention. Thus, the unbeliever is intrinsically capable of belief, for which he is also accountable, except that he squanders his ability on unbelief, diverting it away by his own choice from belief. It is this that makes him deserving of reproach and punishment.[130] [167–168]

Accountability for What One Lacks Ability

[Qārī] As far as what is inconceivable for other reasons, such as Allāh preeternally knowing or willing the contrary, namely the belief of an unbeliever and the obedience of a sinner, there is no difference of opinion regarding whether the person is accountable, since [believing and doing good deeds] are intrinsically within one's ability. Hence, Allāh holding one responsible is not considered making one responsible for what one has no power over. [Especially when one] considers a person's intrinsic ability. The one who thinks this is holding one responsible for what one has no power over has considered the occurrence of the association in preeternity of the knowledge of Allāh and His will to its contrary, but not the intrinsic ability of the person himself.

Otherwise, if one were not responsible for faith and obedience, the one who leaves it would not be considered disobedient. Hence, the belief of an unbeliever and the obedience of a sinner could only be considered inconceivable based upon the association of this to Allāh's preeternal knowledge and will.[131] [168]

---

130 An example may elucidate this point. When a driver gets behind the wheel of a car, turns on the ignition, and engages the gears, the engine is ready to respond to the pressure the driver applies to the foot pedal. The driver can use the power and energy created in the vehicle for good and virtuous acts such as going to the masjid for prayer or running an errand for someone, or to commit an evil act such as going to the bar, running someone over, or even driving oneself over a cliff. It is his free will to do with the vehicle as he likes, and it is the same energy from the vehicle that will be employed. Ultimately, though, he is also held responsible for what is done with the car, not the vehicle itself or its manufacturer. This is similar to the physical and mental ability Allāh creates in the human being, allowing him to dispose of it as he wishes, albeit with limitations.

131 This ultimately means that the difference between saying that Allāh holds a servant responsible for what he is unable to do, or that He does not, is only semantic; ultimately the acquisition of good and bad deeds relate back to the servant's intentions and his action regardless of Allāh's preeternal knowledge of what he was going to do.

THE PROPHETS (UPON THEM BE PEACE), MUḤAMMAD ﷺ, AND THE COMPANIONS ﷺ

وَالْأَنْبِيَاءُ عَلَيْهِمُ الصَّلَاةُ وَالسَّلَامُ كُلُّهُمْ مُنَزَّهُوْنَ مِنَ الصَّغَائِرِ وَالْكَبَائِرِ وَالْكُفْرِ وَالْقَبَائِحِ، وَقَدْ كَانَتْ مِنْهُمْ زَلَّاتٌ وَخَطَايَا. وَمُحَمَّدٌ عَلَيْهِ الصَّلَاةُ وَالسَّلَامُ حَبِيْبُهُ وَعَبْدُهُ وَرَسُوْلُهُ وَنَبِيُّهُ وَصَفِيُّهُ وَنَقِيُّهُ. وَلَمْ يَعْبُدِ الصَّنَمَ وَلَمْ يُشْرِكْ بِاللهِ تَعَالٰى طَرْفَةَ عَيْنٍ قَطُّ وَلَمْ يَرْتَكِبْ صَغِيْرَةً وَلَا كَبِيْرَةً قَطُّ. وَأَفْضَلُ النَّاسِ بَعْدَ النَّبِيِّيْنَ عَلَيْهِمُ الصَّلَاةُ وَالسَّلَامُ أَبُوْ بَكْرٍ الصِّدِّيْقُ ثُمَّ عُمَرُ بْنُ الْخَطَّابِ الْفَارُوْقُ ثُمَّ عُثْمَانُ بْنُ عَفَّانٍ ذُو النُّوْرَيْنِ ثُمَّ عَلِيُّ بْنُ أَبِيْ طَالِبٍ الْمُرْتَضٰى، رِضْوَانُ اللهِ تَعَالٰى عَلَيْهِمْ أَجْمَعِيْنَ، عَابِدِيْنَ ثَابِتِيْنَ عَلَى الْحَقِّ وَمَعَ الْحَقِّ، نَتَوَلَّاهُمْ جَمِيْعًا، وَلَا نَذْكُرُ أَحَدًا مِنْ أَصْحَابِ رَسُوْلِ اللهِ إِلَّا بِخَيْرٍ.

The prophets (upon them be blessings and peace) are all free from minor sins, enormities, unbelief, and wicked acts. However, some slips and mistakes have escaped them.

Muḥammad ﷺ is Allāh's beloved, His servant, His Messenger, His Prophet, His chosen one, and His purified one. Never did he worship idols or partner anything with Allāh even for a blink of an eye, nor did he ever commit a minor sin or enormity.

The most noble person after the prophets (upon them be blessings and peace) is Abū Bakr, the Most Truthful, then ʿUmar ibn al-Khaṭṭāb, the Differentiator, then ʿUthmān ibn ʿAffān, Possessor of Two Lights, and then ʿAlī ibn Abī Ṭālib, the Chosen One (may the pleasure of Allāh be with them all). They were [devout] worshippers and steadfast on the truth and with the Truth. We love them all and do not mention any Companion of the Messenger of Allāh ﷺ except only by way of praise.

The prophets (upon them be blessings and peace) are all free from minor sins, enormities, unbelief, and wicked acts before and after receiving prophethood (*nubuwwa*).

The Major and Minor Sins

[Qārī] It must be known that leaving obligatory (*farḍ*) or necessary (*wājib*) acts even once without excuse is considered an enormity (*kabīra*). Likewise, committing the unlawful (*ḥarām*) is also considered an enormity. Leaving the *sunna*[132] act once without excuse due to laziness or taking the matter lightly is considered a minor sin (*ṣaghīra*), as is committing a disliked action (*makrūh*). However, habitually leaving the *sunna* or committing disliked actions also becomes an enormity, though they are considered enormities beneath other [established] enormities. This is because major and minor are relative terms, and thus it is said, "The good deeds of the pious are the sins of the intimate (*muqarrabīn*)." [170]

However, some slips and mistakes have escaped them. An example of a slip (*zalla*) is when Ādam عليه السلام ate from the tree, and an example of a mistake (*khaṭa'*) is when Mūsā عليه السلام killed a member of Pharaoh's people. He did not intend to kill him, but only to strike him with his hand in order to push him away from the Israelite. Thus, the strike was intentional, but the killing a mistake. The killing was also a slip, because every mistake is a slip, but not every slip is a mistake. Therefore, between the two is the universal-particular relationship. A slip sometimes occurs by mistake, sometimes out of forgetfulness, sometimes out of inattentiveness, and sometimes out of leaving the more worthy or preferred action. Imām ʿUmar al-Nasafī states in his *Tafsīr*, "The Imāms of Samarqand do not use the word *zalla* for acts committed by the prophets (upon them be blessings and peace) because a *zalla* [according to them] is a type of sin. Instead, they say, "They [the prophets] performed the good act (*fāḍil*) and left the preferred one (*afḍal*), and they were lightly

132 *Sunna* here is taken in the juridical sense where it refers to an action regularly performed by the Messenger of Allāh ﷺ and left at times in order for it not be taken as an obligation. This is then subcategorized into the emphasized *sunnas* and the non-emphasized *sunnas,* the latter being more like the *mustaḥabb* (preferred) acts, i.e., those performed by the Messenger ﷺ sometimes or encouraged in general.

reproved for it, because for prophets to leave the more preferred act is equivalent to others leaving an obligation (*wājib*)."

Another view is that the slip of a Prophet or a Friend of Allāh Most High is a means of closeness to Him. Abū Sulaymān al-Dārānī (may Allāh have mercy on him) states, "'Dāwūd ﷺ did not perform an act more beneficial for him than a misdeed. He continued to flee from it toward his Lord until he reached Him. Hence, the misdeed was the cause of his fleeing toward Allāh, away from himself and the world."

[Qārī] As for Ādam ﷺ, there are a number of explanations for why he ate from the forbidden tree. One is that he ate from it out of forgetfulness. Another is that he did not eat from the specific tree that Allāh forbade, but from another tree of the same type, assuming that the prohibition of Allāh was only regarding the specific tree, as Allāh said, "but approach not *this* tree."[133] He thus chose the less superior or suboptimal (*rukhṣa*) path, in accord with the wisdom of Allāh in order [that He] illustrate the weakness of the human ability and condition and to express the strength of divine forgiveness. This is why a ḥadīth states, "If you did not sin, Allāh would bring forth a people who would sin and [then] seek forgiveness and Allāh would forgive them" (*Muslim, Tirmidhī*). This is the opinion of the majority of scholars. [172]

"Verily a Cloudiness Comes Over My Heart"

[Qārī] As for the ḥadīth of the Messenger of Allāh ﷺ that states, "Verily a cloudiness comes over my heart (*la yughānu ʿalā qalbī*), and verily I seek forgiveness from Allāh one hundred times daily" (*Muslim, Abū Dāwūd*), Rāzī explains in *Al-Tafsīr al-Kabīr* that this cloudiness is like the light mist in the air that does not block the sun's light but does prevent its complete light from penetrating it. Scholars have interpreted this statement in many ways. First, that Allāh would inform His Messenger ﷺ of the disputations and problems that were to occur among his followers in the future, and whenever he would think about these events, a cloudiness would come over his heart, and he would seek forgiveness from Allāh for his umma. However,

133 Also Ādam's ﷺ offense was in Paradise, which was not considered an abode of accountability (*dār al-taklīf*), in spite of the fact that Allāh forbade him from eating from the tree. In other words, he had no knowledge of the consequences for disobedience. Thus his disobedience was not open defiance as in the case of Satan.

saying that he would be constantly occupied by such a thought seems clearly far-fetched, since he occupied too high a station for it [to overcome him in such a manner]. Second, it is interpreted to mean that the Messenger ﷺ would constantly ascend from one state to the next, each successive state being loftier than the previous state. He would thus seek forgiveness for thinking that he had reached the highest state. This is the more appropriate opinion due to its coherence with the verse "And the latter is better for you than the former" (Qur'ān 93:4). The third interpretation is that of the People of Reality (*arbāb al-ḥaqīqa*), namely that the cloudiness was the state of ecstasy that would overcome him due to his absorption in the divine love from which he would reach the state of self-annihilation. When returning to normal consciousness, he would seek forgiveness from Allāh for this return. Some have said that he meant he was seeking forgiveness for the cloudiness that would come about after returning from that state, as he ﷺ himself says, "Verily a cloudiness comes over my heart so much so that it prevents me from witnessing my Lord" (*Muslim, Abū Dāwūd*). The fourth explanation is that this cloudiness came over him whenever anything other than Allāh passed through his mind and heart, moving him out of the state of complete absorption in Allāh, and so, he would seek forgiveness for these moments. This conforms with the famous statement: "The good deeds of the pious are the sins of the intimate." Fifth, the literalists interpreted it as referring to the [worldly] desires that would enter his heart, from which he would seek recourse to his Lord. Sixth, that it was as a result of his viewing his acts of worship as falling short of what was due of him or his inability to show gratefulness in certain circumstances. It is for these reasons that he used to seek forgiveness immediately after the prayer and also after relieving himself. [172–175]

The Purposeful Actions of Allāh's Messenger ﷺ

[Qārī] According to Qāḍī Abū Zayd[134] in *Uṣūl al-Fiqh,* the purposeful actions of the Messenger of Allāh ﷺ [and other prophets] fall into four categories: the necessary (*wājib*), the preferred (*mustaḥabb*), the permissible (*mubāḥ*), and the

134 Qāḍī ʿAbdullāh ibn ʿUmar ibn ʿĪsā, Abū Zayd al-Dabūsī al-Bukhārī. He was known for his depth of inference in legal issues and the science of differences. He wrote *Kitāb al-Asrār, Al-Amad al-Aqṣā, Ta'sīs al-Naẓar,* and his most famous work *Taqwīm al-Adilla* better known as *Uṣūl al-Dabūsī.* He passed away at the age of 63 in Bukhārā in 430/1038 (*Al-Wāfī bi 'l-Wafayāt* 5:445, *Al-Aʿlām* 4:109).

slip (*zalla*). As for what happened unintentionally, such as that which occurred during sleep or by mistake, this deserves no attention, since these acts are not subject to [Allāh's] address. As for the slip, it would not go unnoticed, either by a proclamation made by the prophet himself, such as when Mūsā ﷺ after killing the Egyptian (*qibṭ*) with his blow declared, "This is of Satan's doing" (Qurʾān 28:18),[135] or by Allāh declaring it as such, as in the case of Ādam ﷺ when Allāh said, "Thus did Ādam disobey his Lord, and allow himself to be seduced" (20:121). This was before his prophethood, as Allāh then says, "Then his Lord chose him, and turned to him, and guided him" (20:122). Since the slips are [always] made obvious via revelation, it is evident to all that they are not practices to be emulated [by the followers of the prophets]; this is a main concern with regards to the actions of the prophets, for they are exemplars of upright action. Thus, it is the other three types that remain of importance [in terms of emulation]. [175–176]

Regarding Minor Sins and Enormities and Prophethood

[Qārī] All that is soundly transmitted about the prophets which may indicate falsehood or disobedience should be distanced from its apparent meaning if possible. If this is not possible, the occurrence has to be considered as their leaving the more preferred position, or as having occurred before prophethood.

Ibn al-Humām says that the preferred opinion with regards to the actions of the prophets is that they are protected from committing both major and minor sins, with the exception of those minor sins committed out of forgetfulness or mistake and which are not considered repulsive. Thus, the conclusion is that none of the Ahl al-Sunna wa 'l-Jamāʿa hold that it is possible for a prophet to intentionally perform a forbidden act [because of their infallibility], though this is possible inadvertently or out of forgetfulness, and this is what is termed a slip.

According to Abū Manṣūr al-Māturīdī, the infallibility (*ʿiṣma*) is a favor and boon bestowed on the prophets from Allāh that does not eliminate the trials or tribulations [they experience in this world]. It does not "force" the prophets to be obedient, nor does it render them incapable of committing disobedience. Rather, it is a mercy from Allāh Most High in that it encour-

---

135 Mūsā ﷺ did not intend to kill the man. His intention was only to defend the Israelite; repelling the offense of the Egyptian required some physical force, which resulted in the man's death.

ages them to do good, prevents them from committing evil, all the while preserving their ability to choose and not removing their state of trial and tribulation. [176–177]

Muḥammad ﷺ is Allāh's beloved/ The Messenger of Allāh ﷺ said, "We are the last ones [to come into the world], but we will be the first [to enter Paradise] on the Day of Resurrection. I am going to say something without pride: Ibrāhīm is the friend of Allāh, Mūsā is the interlocutor of Allāh, Ādam is the chosen one of Allāh, and I am the beloved of Allāh. In my possession will be the flag of praise on the Day of Resurrection."[136] Thereafter, the Great Imām indicates toward two useful benefits from his statement, His servant, that is, the conferring of honor on Muḥammad ﷺ and the protection of the Muslim umma from [adopting] the belief of the Christians [that their prophet was the son of God].

Abu 'l-Qāsim Sulaymān al-Anṣārī relates that when Muḥammad ﷺ reached the lofty stages and high ranks during the Ascension (*miʿrāj*), Allāh spoke to him and asked him, "Through what shall I honor you?" He replied, "O Allāh, by associating me to You in servitude (*ʿubūdiyya*)." Upon this, the words of Allāh Most Purified, Most High were revealed: "Glorified is He who carried His servant by night" (Qur'ān 17:1). The Messenger of Allāh ﷺ cautioned, "Do not praise me the way ʿĪsā ﷺ was praised, but say [I am] Allāh's servant and Messenger" (*Bukhārī,* "al-Ḥudūd," 6328). This is transmitted in *Mashāriq* [*al-Anwār*].[137] This statement means, "Do not transgress the limits in praising me as the Christians exaggerated in praising ʿĪsā ﷺ, until they committed unbelief, saying, 'He is the son of Allāh.' Say regarding me that I am the servant and Messenger of Allāh, lest you become like them."

His Messenger, His Prophet because of the words of Allāh: "Muḥammad is the Messenger of Allāh" (Qur'ān 48:29) and His words, "O Prophet, fear Allāh, and obey not the unbelievers" (33:1). *Nabī* (prophet) is more general than *rasūl* (messenger). What demonstrates this point is that the Messenger of Allāh ﷺ was asked regarding the [number of] prophets. He said, "One hundred and twenty-four thousand." He was then asked how many of them

---

136 Recorded in *Dāramī,* "al-Muqaddima," 54 with some variation; Mūsā ﷺ is mentioned as the chosen one, and there is no mention of Ādam ﷺ.

137 *Mashāriq al-Anwār al-Nabawiyya ʿalā Ṣiḥāḥ al-Akhbār al-Muṣṭafawiyya* by Raḍī al-Dīn Abu 'l-Faḍā'il Ḥasan ibn Muḥammad ibn al-Ḥasan al-ʿAdawī al-Ṣaghānī al-Ḥanafī (d. 650/1252).

were messengers, and he said, "A large group of three hundred and thirteen."[138] His chosen one, that is, His selected and preferred one. The Messenger of Allāh ﷺ said, "Allāh chose [the tribe of] Kināna from the descendants of Ismāʿīl (Ishmael) ﷺ, and chose Quraysh from Kināna, and chose the tribe of Hāshim from Quraysh. He then chose me from the tribe of Hāshim." This is transmitted in *Al-Maṣābīḥ*.[139] | and His purified one because Allāh cleansed and purified his heart in childhood from all the substances that would hinder his advancement. Anas ﷺ reports that Jibrīl came to the Messenger of Allāh ﷺ while he was playing with some boys. He took hold of him and laid him down. He split open his chest and took out a portion of clotted blood and said, "This is the portion of Satan in you." After washing it in a gold vessel with the water of Zamzam, he mended it, and returned it to its place. The other children ran to his mother (i.e., his wet-nurse), and cried that Muḥammad had been killed. When they reached him, they found that he had changed color. Anas ﷺ says, "I used to observe the mark left by the stitches on his chest" (*Muslim*, "al-Īmān," 236).

Never did he worship idols or partner anything with Allāh even for a blink of an eye before or after receiving prophethood, because prophets are protected from ignorance of Allāh. ʿAlī ﷺ reports that the Messenger of Allāh ﷺ was asked whether he had ever worshipped idols. He said no. They asked whether he had ever consumed alcohol. He said no, and then said, "I knew all along that the path they were on was of unbelief, at a time when I knew not the Qur'ān nor true faith."[140] | nor did he ever commit a minor sin or enormity before or after receiving prophethood.

[Qārī] The full lineage of the Messenger of Allāh ﷺ is Muḥammad son of ʿAbdullāh, son of ʿAbd al-Muṭṭalib, son of Hāshim, son of ʿAbd Manāf, son of Quṣayy, son of Kilāb, son of Murra, son of Kaʿb, son of Lu'ay, son of Ghālib, son of Fihr, son of Mālik, son of Naḍr, son of Kināna, son of Khuzayma, son of Mudrika, son of Ilyās, son of Mudar, son of Nizār, son of Maʿad, son of

138 *Aḥmad*, "Bāqī Musnad al-Anṣār," 21207; though this narration mentions three hundred and fifteen instead of three hundred and thirteen.

139 This is *Maṣābīḥ al-Sunna*, a ḥadīth collection by the Shāfiʿī scholar Abū Muḥammad Ḥusayn ibn Masʿūd ibn Muḥammad al-Farrā' al-Baghawī (d. 516/1122). It was on this text that Walī al-Dīn Muḥammad al-Khaṭīb al-Tabrīzī (d. 740/1340 or 748/1347) based his work *Mishkāt al-Maṣābīḥ*.

140 Recorded in *Kanz al-ʿUmmāl* 35439 from Abū Nuʿaym's *Dalā'il al-Nubuwwa*.

ʿAdnān (*Bukhārī*). There is no difference of opinion regarding this lineage up to ʿAdnān, as the Messenger ﷺ himself confirmed. [178]

After completing his explanation of the prophets (upon them be peace), the Great Imām begins his explanation of the caliphs. He states, The most noble person after the prophets (upon them be blessings and peace) is Abū Bakr, the Most Truthful. The Messenger of Allāh ﷺ said, "The sun has neither risen nor set on anyone after the prophets and messengers superior to Abū Bakr."[141] It is narrated that when the Messenger of Allāh ﷺ related the incident of the Ascension (*miʿrāj*) [to the people of Makka], they rejected him and went to Abū Bakr saying, "Your friend is saying such and such." Abū Bakr replied that if the Messenger of Allāh ﷺ had said it, he was telling the truth. He then went to the Messenger of Allāh ﷺ, who related the details of the incident to him. Every time the Messenger of Allāh ﷺ made a statement, Abū Bakr ؓ would say, "You have spoken the truth." When he had finished informing him, Abū Bakr ؓ said, "I testify that you are the true Messenger of Allāh," upon which the Messenger of Allāh ﷺ said, "And I testify that you are indeed most truthful (*ṣiddīq*)." This is stated in *Al-Tafsīr al-Kabīr.*

[Qārī] Abū Bakr's name before Islam was ʿAbd al-Kaʿba; the Messenger ﷺ changed his name to ʿAbdullāh after Islam. His full lineage is: Abū Bakr son of Abū Quḥāfa ʿUthmān, son of ʿĀmir, son of Kaʿb, son of Saʿd, son of Taym, son of Murra, son of Kaʿb, son of Lu'ay, son of Ghālib, son of Fihr al-Qurashī al-Taymī. He was called the Most Truthful One (al-Ṣiddīq) due to his profound honesty, his devotion to the truth, the strength of his belief, and his being divinely guided (*tawfīq*). He is the best of all of the friends (*awliyā'*) of Allāh from among the earlier ones and the later ones. [182]

then ʿUmar ibn al-Khaṭṭāb, the Differentiator/ The Messenger of Allāh ﷺ said, "Every prophet has two ministers (*wazīrān*) from the inhabitants of the heavens and two ministers from those of the earth. As for my two ministers of the heavens, they are Jibrīl and Mīkā'īl, and my two ministers of the earth are Abū Bakr and ʿUmar" (*Tirmidhī*, "al-Manāqib," 3613). This is from *Al-Maṣābīḥ*. It is

141 Recorded in *Kanz al-ʿUmmāl* 36112 from the accounts of Ibn ʿAsākir with a slight variation. Also recorded in *Al-Musnad al-Jāmiʿ* 11069 from the *Musnad* of ʿAbd ibn Ḥumayd on the authority of Abu 'l-Dardā' ؓ.

related from Ibn ʿAbbās ﷺ that a hypocrite had a dispute with a Jew. The Jew summoned him to the Messenger of Allāh ﷺ, and the hypocrite summoned him to Kaʿb ibn al-Ashraf. They [finally] took the case to the Messenger of Allāh ﷺ, who passed a ruling in favor of the Jew. The hypocrite was not pleased and insisted that they go to ʿUmar for a ruling. The Jew told ʿUmar that the Messenger of Allāh ﷺ had already ruled in his favor and the hypocrite had not been pleased. He had insisted that they come to ʿUmar. ʿUmar asked the hypocrite whether that was true, and he replied that it was. ʿUmar instructed them to remain where they were until he returned. He went inside, picked up his sword, and came out and beheaded the hypocrite. He then said, "This is my ruling for the person who is not satisfied with the ruling of Allāh and His Messenger." Jibrīl ﷺ states, "ʿUmar differentiated between the truth and untruth, so he was named the Differentiator (al-Fārūq)." This is as stated in the *Tafsīr* of Qāḍī [Bayḍāwī].

[Qārī] His lineage is: ʿUmar son of Khaṭṭāb, son of Nufayl, son of ʿAbd al-ʿUzzā, son of Riyāḥ, son of ʿAbdullāh, son of Qurṭ, son of Zarāḥ, son of ʿAdī, son of Kaʿb al-Qurashī al-ʿAdawī. He was called the Differentiator (al-Fārūq) because of his tremendous ability to differentiate between the truth and falsehood, as also mentioned by the Messenger of Allāh ﷺ: "Verily the truth flows from the tongue of ʿUmar" (*Abū Dāwūd*). [185]

then ʿUthmān ibn ʿAffān, Possessor of Two Lights/ [The title was given to him] because the Messenger of Allāh ﷺ gave him his daughter Ruqayya in marriage. When she passed away, the Messenger of Allāh ﷺ gave him [his other daughter] Umm Kulthūm, and when she passed away, the Messenger of Allāh ﷺ remarked, "If I possessed a third daughter, I would marry her to you, too." This is why he was given the title "Possessor of Two Lights" (Dhu 'l-Nūrayn). It is related by Anas ﷺ that when the Messenger of Allāh ﷺ ordered the Pledge of Riḍwān (*Bayʿat al-Riḍwān*), ʿUthmān was the envoy of the Messenger of Allāh ﷺ to Makka [and thus not present]. The Messenger of Allāh ﷺ took the pledge from everybody and remarked, "ʿUthmān is occupied in the work of Allāh and His Messenger," and thereafter struck his one hand over the other. This way, the two hands of the Messenger of Allāh ﷺ for ʿUthmān were superior to everybody else's hands for themselves (*Tirmidhī,* "al-Manāqib," 3635). This is from *Al-Maṣābīḥ*.

[Qārī] His lineage is: ʿUthmān son of ʿAffān, son of ʿĀṣ, son of Umayya, son of ʿAbd Shams, son of ʿAbd Manāf, son of Quṣayy al-Qurashī al-Umawī. [185]

and then ʿAlī ibn Abī Ṭālib, the Chosen One/ The Messenger of Allāh ﷺ remarked to ʿAlī, "'You are to me like Hārūn عليه السلام was to Mūsā عليه السلام, except that there is to be no prophet after me" (*Muslim*, "Faḍāʾil al-Ṣaḥāba," 4418).

[Qārī] His lineage is: ʿAlī son of Abū Ṭālib, son of ʿAbd al-Muṭṭalib, son of Hāshim, son of ʿAbd Manāf, son of Quṣayy al-Qurashī. [186]

(May the pleasure of Allāh be with them all). They were [devout] worshippers of Allāh Most High and steadfast on the truth and with the Truth. That they were with the True One Most High [Allāh] in their worship, meaning that they worshipped Him with truthfulness, sincerity, fearfulness, and humility.

We love them all—all four caliphs. We do not differentiate between them by expressing love for some and hatred for the others. The Rawāfiḍ[142] detested

---

142 Rawāfiḍ or Rāfiḍa: Rejectionists. They were a group of Shīʿa who pledged their allegiance to Zayd ibn ʿAlī ibn al-Ḥusayn ؓ, and then demanded from him to dissociate himself from Abū Bakr and ʿUmar ؓ. He refused, saying that they were the ministers of the Messenger of Allāh ﷺ, so they abandoned him and dissented from him. This was at the time Zayd had embarked to fight Hishām ibn ʿAbd al-Malik (*Al-Bidāya wa ʾl-Nihāya* 9:231). It has also been said that they were called Rāfiḍa, because they rejected (*rafaḍū*) the majority of Companions and the leadership of Abū Bakr and ʿUmar ؓ (Ashʿarī, *Maqālāt al-Islāmiyyīn* 1:87). (*Al-Taʿlīq al-Muyassar* 65)

The eponymous founder of the Sabaʾiyya sect, an extreme sect of the Rawāfiḍ, is ʿAbdullāh ibn Sabaʾ. He was originally a Yemeni Jew who expressed his belief in Islam; he was also called Ibn al-Sawdāʾ because of his mother being black. Ibn Sabaʾ traveled throughout the Muslim lands, turning people away from obedience to their Muslim leaders and spreading mischief in their midst. He began in Ḥijāz (a region in the northwest of present-day Saudi Arabia where Makka and Madīna are located), then went to Baṣra, Kūfa, and finally Damascus during the days of ʿUthmān ibn ʿAffān ؓ. He was not able to realize his goals in the Levant (Shām) and they expelled him, so he set out for Egypt. He made some claims there, and said, "It is surprising that one can believe in the impending return of ʿĪsā, but outright deny the return of Muḥammad, despite the fact that Allāh Most High has said, 'Verily He who ordained the Qurʾān for you, will bring you back to the place of return' (Qurʾān 28:85). Muḥammad has more right to return than ʿĪsā." They accepted this belief from Ibn Sabaʾ. He then said, "There were a thousand prophets and every prophet had an assistant who afterward succeeded him." He then claimed that Muḥammad was the Seal of Prophets and ʿAlī was the Seal of the Successors (ʿAbd al-Qādir Badrān, *Tahdhīb Tārīkh Ibn ʿAsākir* 7:431). Dhahabī said in his *Mīzān*, "'Abdullāh ibn Sabaʾ was from the extreme heretics, misguided and a misguider. I reckon that ʿAlī had him burnt" (3:426). He influenced some of the Muslims just as Paul influenced the followers of ʿĪsā عليه السلام and turned them away from monotheism. ʿAbdullāh ibn Sabaʾ called for the divinity of ʿAlī, and ʿAlī had him burnt along with some of his followers. However, those who managed to escape said, "This makes it even more clear that

the three caliphs [Abū Bakr, ʿUmar, and ʿUthmān], and have therefore rejected (*rafaḍū*) and left the true belief. The Khawārij have hatred for ʿAlī, and so have left the Straight Path.

Regarding the Superiority of Abū Bakr ﵁

[Qārī] The foremost proof of the superiority of Abū Bakr ﵁ over all of the Companions is the Messenger's ﷺ assignment of him to lead the prayers during his illness. It is for this reason that the great Companions all said, "He ﷺ was satisfied with him for our religion, are we not satisfied with him for our worldly affairs?" Thus, the agreement of the majority of the Companions was to appoint him caliph, and the remaining ones also ultimately agreed. [186]

My belief is that the superiority of Abū Bakr ﵁ is definitive (*qaṭʿī*) by virtue of the Messenger ﷺ appointing him as his representative to lead prayers (*imāma*), as it is established in the religion that the one most worthy of leading the prayer is the most superior. Other great Companions were available for the Messenger ﷺ to appoint, among them ʿAlī ﵁, but he ﷺ insisted upon Abū Bakr ﵁. One time, Abū Bakr ﵁ was late coming to the prayer and ʿUmar ﵁ stepped forward to lead it. The Messenger ﷺ said, "Allāh and the believers refuse other than Abū Bakr." Even ʿĀ'isha's opinion regarding her father is well known [in that she thought he was too soft-hearted for the post of leading the prayers (*imāma*), but the Messenger ﷺ strongly insisted on it (*Bukhārī*, "al-Adhān," 684)]. After much discussion and consultation in the shelter of the Sāʿida tribe (*saqīfa Banī Sāʿida*), both the Emigrants (*muhājirīn*) and Helpers (*anṣār*) unanimously agreed on Abū Bakr ﵁ becoming caliph. The consensus (*ijmāʿ*) of the scholars is definitive proof since the Messenger of Allāh ﷺ said, "My umma will not gather together on deviance" (*Abū Dāwūd, Ibn Māja*). [189]

ʿAlī's ﵁ *Pledge of Allegiance to Abū Bakr*

[Qārī] ʿAlī ﵁ pledged his allegiance to Abū Bakr in front of many people after having held back for a period. He had not had time to contemplate the matter because of the grief and sadness from the Messenger's ﷺ death, and his

---

ʿAlī is God, for the Messenger of Allāh ﷺ said, "Only the Lord of the Fire punishes with the fire" (*Al-Taʿlīq al-Muyassar* 38–39).

preoccupation with the burial rites and inheritance issues. The Shīʿa consider his action to be based on dissimulation (*taqiyya*) even though it is impossible to know this, because only the person performing the dissimulation would be aware of that. Furthermore, a single person's disagreement would not in any case affect the consensus of a large group, even if it had been an openly-expressed difference. The most it could have been is that he declared himself equal or superior to Abū Bakr ♦, but without any proof. [189–190]

The Superiority of Abū Bakr and ʿUmar over the Companions and ʿUthmān's Superiority over ʿAlī

[Qārī] The superiority of Abū Bakr and ʿUmar over all the Companions ♦ according to the Ahl al-Sunna wa 'l-Jamāʿa is agreed upon. The superiority of ʿUthmān over ʿAlī ♦ is also the opinion of the majority of the Ahl al-Sunna wa 'l-Jamāʿa, as the opposite has been related from some Kūfans and Baṣrans, but the correct judgment is that of the majority. [187]

Imām Abū Ḥanīfa says in *Al-Waṣiyya:*

> We declare that the most noble person after our Prophet Muḥammad ♦ is Abū Bakr the Most Truthful, then ʿUmar, then ʿUthmān, then ʿAlī (may Allāh be pleased with them all), because Allāh said, "And those foremost (in faith) will be foremost (in the Hereafter). These will be those nearest to Allāh in gardens of bliss" (56:10–12). And all those who were earlier [in embracing the faith] are superior, and every believer loves them, and every wretched hypocrite hates them.

Succession after Abū Bakr ♦

[Qārī] ʿUmar's succession to Abū Bakr ♦ is based directly upon his appointment in writing. Abū Bakr's ♦ letter, as recorded in *Sharḥ al-Mawāqif,*[143] is as follows:

> In the name of Allāh, Most Gracious, Most Merciful. This is what Abū Bakr son of Abū Quḥāfa commissions during his final moments in this world and the beginning moments of the next, a state in which [even] the transgressor becomes righteous and the unbeliever becomes a believer. I designate ʿUmar, son of Khaṭṭāb, my successor over you. If he performs well, then that is my opinion about him, and it is

---

143 Sayyid al-Sharīf ʿAlī ibn Muḥammad al-Jurjānī's (d. 816/1413) commentary on *Al-Mawāqif fī ʿIlm al-Kalām* of ʿAḍud al-Dīn ʿAbd al-Raḥmān ibn Aḥmad al-Ījī (d. 756/1355).

only the good that I have intended, and if it is other than that, then "soon will the unjust know what vicissitudes their affairs will take" (Qurʾān 26:227). [190]

Then when ʿUmar was struck and was on his deathbed, he called for a council to be formed consisting of six of the remaining seven members of the ten Companions to whom Allāh's Messenger ﷺ had given glad tidings of Paradise [Saʿīd ibn Zayd ❀ was not included].[144] The council consisted of ʿUthmān, ʿAlī, ʿAbd al-Raḥmān ibn ʿAwf, Ṭalḥa, Al-Zubayr, and Saʿd ibn Abī Waqqās ❀. The purpose was for them to discuss the matter and choose one from among themselves to be the next leader. He did this, because he felt they were superior to all other Muslims at the time and the most worthy of leadership; he also chose to leave it to their opinion rather than exercise his judgment alone. His instructions were, "If they split into a group of four and two, then be in the one among whom is ʿAbd al-Raḥmān ibn ʿAwf, and thus five of them delegated the decision to ʿAbd al-Raḥmān ibn ʿAwf. He settled on ʿUthmān ❀ and they all pledged their allegiance to him. ʿUthmān took up the responsibilities of the position and began to lead the Muslims in their Friday and ʿĪd prayers [without any opposition] and thus a consensus was formed [on his successorship]. [191]

Thereafter, ʿUthmān ❀ was martyred and the succession was left open and unassigned. The great Companions from among the Emigrants and Helpers agreed on ʿAlī ❀ as the successor. He was no doubt the most superior among the people of his time. As for those Companions who did not side with ʿAlī and did not aid him in fighting [against the enemies], and those who took up arms against him in the battles of the Camel and Ṣiffīn, none of this proves that his succession was incorrect. Their disagreement and fighting was not due to a refusal or doubt in his position as caliph, but rather a mistake in their inference (*ijtihād*) on the issue at hand, in that they rejected his decision to postpone capturing and punishing the murderers of ʿUthmān ❀ until he took control of the prevailing situation. [According to what the Messenger of Allāh ﷺ has said], those who reach an incorrect conclusion while endeavoring to extract the correct ruling (*ijtihād*) are not considered transgressors or deviant

---

144 As related by Ibn Kathīr, ʿUmar ibn al-Khaṭṭāb ❀ excluded Saʿīd ibn Zayd from the selection committee for choosing the caliph only because he was a relative of his and ʿUmar did not want him to be considered by the others for the position because of this relationship (*Al-Bidāya wa 'l-Nihāya* 7:155).

[as long as they are qualified to undertake such an exercise; this was certainly true for Companions like Muʿāwiya and ʿĀʾisha ☙].

Further proof of the correctness of ʿAlī's succession to ʿUthmān over anybody else is the ḥadīth in which the Messenger ﷺ said, "The caliphate after me is thirty years, after which it will become an unjust (ʿaḍūḍ) kingdom" (Abū Dāwūd, Tirmidhī). ʿAlī ☙ was martyred just before the end of the thirty years from the Messenger's ﷺ death. [192–193]

The breakdown of the thirty years is: Abū Bakr ☙ ruled for two years and three months, ʿUmar ☙ for ten years and six months, ʿUthmān ☙ for twelve years, ʿAlī ☙ for four years and nine months, and Ḥasan ibn ʿAlī ☙ for six months to complete the thirty years, and Allāh knows best. [202]

Details of ʿAlī's Caliphate

[Qārī] After the grave martyrdom of ʿUthmān ☙, there was an urgent desire among the Companions to bring back calmness and security. They presented the caliphate to ʿAlī ☙ but he refused. He was severely affected by the death of ʿUthmān ☙ and confined himself to his home. They then offered it to Ṭalḥa ☙, but he also refused and expressed his loathing for the position. They offered it to Al-Zubayr ☙ who also refused due to the seriousness of the martyrdom. It was three days after the martyrdom of ʿUthmān ☙ that the Emigrants and Helpers gathered and asked ʿAlī ☙ once more to take it up imploring him by Allāh to protect Islam and the City of Migration (Madīna) for the sake of Allāh's Messenger ﷺ. After much difficulty, he finally accepted seeing that it was for the best. They knew as he knew that he was the most knowledgeable, superior, and preferred of the remaining Companions, so they pledged allegiance to him. It is important to note here that it is not the vote of the majority that counts as far as who is elected to leadership, but rather, when some of the righteous from the Islamic community confer their allegiance to one who is worthy of the position, it becomes established, and it is not permissible for others then to conflict with it. There cannot be any reason to stipulate the need for consensus when there is such an urgent need. [197–198]

[After becoming caliph], ʿAlī ☙ did not immediately seek out and execute the murderers of ʿUthmān ☙ because they had the status of rebels (bughāt), the rebel being one with military strength and [technically speaking] one who justifies his actions through a [corrupt] interpretation of the issues. These rebels considered what they had done to be lawful because of some things they disliked about the Caliph [ʿUthmān ؓ]. The law regarding the rebel is that if he submits to the Imām of the just ones, he is no longer liable for the destruction he has perpetrated against the property of the just ones, for spilling their blood, or for afflicting wounds to their bodies. Therefore, it was not legally obligatory upon ʿAlī ؓ to execute these people or hand them over to the one making demands for them. And according to those who consider the rebel liable for his crimes, it would be obligatory on the Imām to exact retribution from him only after his strength and support has been broken, and his ability to create more civil strife and dissension has been destroyed. None of these factors had been achieved at the time, in fact the power and strength of the rebels remained strong and so too their military might. Therefore, [according to both opinions], it was not legally obligatory upon ʿAlī ؓ to immediately round them up and execute them [nor was it practically feasible. Thus ʿAlī ؓ chose the correct course of action for that moment].

Consequently, two of the prominent Companions, Al-Zubayr and Ṭalḥa, who after initially having gone out against ʿAlī ؓ based on their incorrect judgment on the matter, later regretted opposing him, as did ʿĀ'isha ؓ. In fact, ʿĀ'isha ؓ used to cry profusely over what she had done, so much so that her scarf would become wet.[145] [198–200] Muʿāwiya ؓ was also incorrect in his judgment [demanding that ʿUthmān's murderers be caught and dealt with immediately and then marching out against ʿAlī ؓ]. Because it was through [genuine] scholarly endeavor [and not out of a personal vendetta], he too does not become classified as unrighteous (*fāsiq*).

ʿAlī ؓ was correct in his arbitration, but the Khawārij thought he was

---

145 ʿĀ'isha had gone out against ʿAlī ؓ with the intention of reforming the situation and protecting the lives of many of the great Companions. She had with her many of her relatives and kinsfolk among whom were ʿAbdullāh ibn al-Zubayr, Umm Kulthūm, wife of Ṭalḥa, and Asmā', wife of Al-Zubayr. In fact, every male who was with her was like her son in terms of unmarriageability (*maḥramiyya*), and she herself was carried in a metal litter. It is related that the Messenger of Allāh ﷺ said to ʿAlī ؓ, "A dispute (*amr*) will soon arise between you and ʿĀ'isha." . . . ʿAlī ؓ said, "Yes, and I will be in the wrong, Messenger of Allāh?" He ﷺ said, "No, but when it does arise, take her back to her place of safety" (*Musnad Aḥmad*). Qays relates that one night [during the expedition] when ʿĀ'isha ؓ reached the waters of the ʿĀmir tribe, dogs began to bark. She asked which waters these were and they told her that they were the waters of Ḥaw'ab. She remarked, "It seems to me that I am heading back." Someone who was with her said, "You are going forward so that the Muslims may see you, and Allāh Most High will bring reconciliation between them through it." However, she replied that once the Messenger of Allāh ﷺ had said to us [i.e., his wives], "How it will be when the dogs of Ḥaw'ab will bark at one of you" (*Aḥmad, Abū Yaʿlā, Bazzār*). (*Al-Taʿlīq al-Muyassar* 199–200)

wrong and claimed that he had committed unbelief by not pursuing the war. According to them, it was obligatory to do so, because of [their interpretation of the verse in the Qur'ān]: "If one of them transgresses beyond bounds against the other, then fight against the one that transgresses until it complies with the command of Allāh" (49:9). We say that the purpose of this verse is to order the repelling of evil and uniting the hearts of the believers, and this is exactly what ʿAlī ﷺ was trying to achieve [by not fighting the rebels at that moment]. [200]

After the Five Caliphs

[Qārī] The first ruler to follow the five caliphs was Muʿāwiya ﷺ, and he was the most superior of them. He became the legitimate ruler when Ḥasan ibn ʿAlī ﷺ transferred the caliphate to him. The people of Iraq had pledged their allegiance to Ḥasan ﷺ after his father's death, and after six months, he delegated it to Muʿāwiya ﷺ [who managed to reinstate calmness and order in the Muslim lands]. [202]

Speaking Ill of the Companions

[Qārī] One should guard one's tongue from speaking anything but good about the Companions of Allāh's Messenger ﷺ, and particularly from cursing them. The Messenger of Allāh ﷺ said, "Do not curse any one of my Companions, for if any of you were to give gold to the amount of Mount Uhud in charity, it would not reach even a *mudd*[146] of one of them, or even half of it" (*Muslim, Abū Dāwūd*). [201]

ʿĀ'isha ﷺ was once told, "Some people are criticizing the Companions of the Messenger ﷺ, even Abū Bakr and ʿUmar." She responded, "Do not be surprised by this! Their ability to work good deeds has been cut off [by their death], so Allāh has preferred that their reward not be cut off" (*Muslim*). Ibn Baṭṭa has related with an authenticated chain from Ibn ʿAbbās ﷺ that he said, "Do not curse the Companions of Muḥammad ﷺ for their one moment spent with the Prophet ﷺ is superior to your performing forty years of deeds. [202] Ibn ʿAbbās ﷺ also said, "Do not curse the Companions of Muḥammad ﷺ, because verily Allāh ordered that one seek forgiveness for them, for He knew that they would soon be driven to conflict" (*Aḥmad*). [214]

146 Approximately 0.51 liters or 792.068 milligrams.

The Companionship of Abū Bakr ❦

[Qārī] There is agreement among the scholars that denying the Companionship of Abū Bakr ❦ is considered unbelief since it is established by Qur'ānic text: "If you help him not (it is no matter), for Allāh did indeed help him, when the unbelievers drove him out, the second of two; they were in the cave, and he said to his Companion, 'Have no fear, for Allāh is with us'" (9:40). The commentators are unanimous that "Companion" here refers to Abū Bakr ❦. [208]

A Special Distinguishing Attribute of Abū Bakr and ʿUmar

[Qārī] The commentator of ʿAqīda Ṭaḥāwiyya [Ibn Abi 'l-ʿIzz][147] says that the order of superiority for the rightly-guided caliphs is the same as their order in succession. However, Abū Bakr and ʿUmar have another distinguishing attribute. The Prophet ﷺ ordered us to follow the general way (Sunna) of the rightly-guided caliphs, but did not order us to emulate (iqtidāʾ) each and every action (afʿāl) legislated by any except Abū Bakr and ʿUmar ❦. He said, "Follow the two after me: Abū Bakr and ʿUmar" (Tirmidhī), and there is a difference between ittibāʿ (following their way in general) and iqtidāʾ (taking them as complete exemplars).[148] [203]

---

147 Despite Ibn Abi 'l-ʿIzz being a Ḥanafī in fiqh and having the most well-known commentary on Ṭaḥāwī's ʿAqīda, he is not considered the most authoritative person in matters of creed. As a matter of fact, his beliefs were highly influenced by the creed and writings of Ibn Taymiya (may Allāh have mercy on him), after which Ibn Abi 'l-ʿIzz adopted his aberrant positions regarding Islamic creed in his commentary. This was done covertly since the name of Ibn Taymiya was not associated with much good in Islamic doctrine during the time of Ibn Abi 'l-ʿIzz. Therefore, he stealthily injected his readers with these teachings to avoid criticism. This is also acknowledged by Zuhayr Shāwīsh in his introductory note on this commentary (5). Qārī quotes him when his opinion is correct and he provides a unique insight into the matter under discussion. Otherwise, Qārī quotes an aberrant opinion of his and then refutes it. It is unfortunate that this commentary has been published by some Ḥanafī publishers and become widespread among many Ḥanafīs under the false assumption of it being a reliable Ḥanafī Māturīdī commentary of Ṭaḥāwī's ʿAqīda.

148 This does not give them any superiority over the Messenger of Allāh ﷺ, but just means that we follow their guidance [regarding aspects of the dīn], since the fundamentals of the dīn are the same, and there is no difference of opinion regarding them (Majmaʿ Biḥār al-Anwār 4:234). This is not an oft-mentioned point, but it seems that the difference the commentator is attempting to make here between the two statements of the Messenger ﷺ is that it is necessary to take everything that Abū Bakr or ʿUmar ❦ command, infer, or legislate, as opposed to what ʿUthmān and ʿAlī ❦ infer. It is not necessary to take everything from them, though following their general way is required, and taking their opinions would be superior to taking from other Companions due to their being from among the rightly-guided caliphs. And Allāh knows best.

The Ten Companions Promised Paradise

[Qārī] Saʿīd ibn Zayd said, "Verily, the participation of one of the ten Companions with the Prophet ﷺ and getting their face dusty [in battle] is better than the works of any of you, even if you were to be given the life of Nūḥ ﷿" (*Abū Dāwūd, Tirmidhī, Ibn Māja*). So how ignorant can the one be who dislikes using the term "ten" or doing an action in "tens" because of his hatred for the privileged of the Companions who were promised Paradise (they exempt ʿAlī ؓ from this hatred).[149] Except for a group of ten or so, they have hatred for all the Companions among the Emigrants and Helpers regarding whom Allāh said, "Well-pleased is Allāh with them, as are they with Him" (Qurʾān 9:100). The absurdity of this is further emphasized by the fact that there are many other praiseworthy associations with the number ten, such as the holiness of the last ten days of Ramaḍān, the virtuous first ten days of Dhu 'l-Ḥijja, etc. [204]

The Twelve Imāms

[Qārī] The Rawāfiḍ have chosen instead of the ten Companions twelve Imāms. The textual evidence suggests no support for this, but actually refutes it. This is from what has been transmitted in both *Ṣaḥīḥs* on the authority of Jābir ibn Samura, who said, "I visited the Prophet ﷺ with my father, and I heard him say, 'The religion (*amr*) of the people will continue [strongly] until twelve men have led them, all of whom will be from the Quraysh'" (*Bukhārī, Muslim*). In another version, it states, "The state [of Islam] will be mighty and powerful until twelve caliphs." What occurred was exactly as the Messenger ﷺ prophesied. The twelve after him were the four rightly-guided caliphs, Muʿāwiya and his son Yazīd, ʿAbd al-Malik ibn Marwān and his four sons, and in between them ʿUmar ibn ʿAbd al-ʿAzīz. Thereafter, things unraveled. According to the Rāfiḍīs, however, the state of the umma during the above times was corrupt and disturbed, [their affairs] being managed by unjust oppressors, hypocrites and unbelievers. The people of truth were more humiliated than the Jews. This is clearly a false and untenable allegation, and recourse is only to Allāh. [206]

---

149 The ten Companions promised Paradise (*al-ʿashara al-mubashshara bi 'l-janna*) by the Messenger of Allāh ﷺ in a sitting are the following: Abū Bakr al-Ṣiddīq, ʿUmar ibn al-Khaṭṭāb, ʿUthmān ibn ʿAffān, ʿAlī ibn Abī Ṭālib, Ṭalḥa ibn ʿUbaydillāh, Al-Zubayr ibn al-ʿAwwām, ʿAbd al-Raḥmān ibn ʿAwf, Saʿd ibn Abī Waqqāṣ, Saʿīd ibn Zayd, and Abū ʿUbayda ʿĀmir ibn ʿAbdillāh ibn al-Jarrāḥ (may Allāh be pleased with them all).

and [we] do not mention any Companion of the Messenger of Allāh ﷺ except only by way of praise. This means that the view of the Ahl al-Sunna wa 'l-Jamāʿa is to attest to the honor and integrity of all the Companions and to praise them just as Allāh Most High and His Messenger ﷺ have praised them. Whatever occurred between ʿAlī and Muʿāwiya proceeded from personal inference (*ijtihād*). This is stated in *Iḥyā' ʿUlūm al-Dīn.* It is related by ʿUmar ؓ that the Messenger of Allāh ﷺ said, "Honor my Companions, for they are the best among you, followed by those after them, followed by those after them, after which untruth will appear" (*Tirmidhī,* "al-Fitan," 2091). This is from *Al-Maṣābīḥ.*

[Qārī] Ibn Daqīq al-ʿĪd states in *Al-ʿAqīda,*

> That which has been related regarding the conflicts between them [i.e., the Companions] and their disagreements: some of it is falsehood and lies and should not be given any attention. Whatever is true, we should interpret it with the best possible interpretation because the praise of Allāh for them has already transpired [and has been definitively established in the Qur'ān], and what has been transmitted to us thereafter is open to interpretation. The doubtful or imagined cannot invalidate the firmly established and well-known.

Regarding delving into such matters, Imām Shāfiʿī said, "Those were bloody [times] from which Allāh has kept our hands purified, so why defile our tongues with it?"[150] Imām Aḥmad was asked regarding the conflict between ʿAlī and ʿĀ'isha ؓ, and he replied, "Those are a people who have passed away. Theirs is what they earned, and yours is what you earn. And you will not be asked regarding what they did" (Qur'ān 2:134). Imām Abū Ḥanīfa once said, "If it had not been for ʿAlī, we would not have known the proper way to deal (*sīra*) with the Khawārij" (*Manāqib al-Muwaffaq al-Makkī*). [209–210]

150 The same is also related by ʿUmar ibn ʿAbd al-ʿAzīz (may Allāh be pleased with him). (*Al-Taʿlīq al-Muyassar* 210)

THE EFFECTS OF SIN ON A PERSON, WIPING LEATHER SOCKS, *TARĀWĪḤ*, AND OTHER MATTERS

وَلَا نُكَفِّرُ مُسْلِمًا بِذَنْبٍ مِنَ الذُّنُوْبِ وَإِنْ كَانَتْ كَبِيْرَةً إِذَا لَمْ يَسْتَحِلَّهَا، وَلَا نُزِيْلُ عَنْهُ اسْمَ الْإِيْمَانِ وَنُسَمِّيْهِ مُؤْمِنًا حَقِيْقَةً، وَيَجُوْزُ أَنْ يَكُوْنَ مُؤْمِنًا فَاسِقًا غَيْرُ كَافِرٍ. وَالْمَسْحُ عَلَى الْخُفَّيْنِ سُنَّةٌ، وَالتَّرَاوِيْحُ فِي لَيَالِيْ شَهْرِ رَمَضَانَ سُنَّةٌ، وَالصَّلَاةُ خَلْفَ كُلِّ بَرٍّ وَفَاجِرٍ مِنَ الْمُؤْمِنِيْنَ جَائِزَةٌ. وَلَا نَقُوْلُ إِنَّ الْمُؤْمِنَ لَا تَضُرُّهُ الذُّنُوْبُ، وَلَا نَقُوْلُ إِنَّهُ لَا يَدْخُلُ النَّارَ، وَلَا نَقُوْلُ إِنَّهُ يُخَلَّدُ فِيهَا وَإِنْ كَانَ فَاسِقًا بَعْدَ أَنْ يَخْرُجَ مِنَ الدُّنْيَا مُؤْمِنًا. وَلَا نَقُوْلُ إِنَّ حَسَنَاتِنَا مَقْبُوْلَةٌ وَسَيِّئَاتِنَا مَغْفُوْرَةٌ كَقَوْلِ الْمُرْجِئَةِ، وَلٰكِنْ نَقُوْلُ مَنْ عَمِلَ حَسَنَةً بِجَمِيْعِ شَرَائِطِهَا خَالِيَةً عَنِ الْعُيُوْبِ الْمُفْسِدَةِ وَلَمْ يُبْطِلْهَا بِالْكُفْرِ وَالرِّدَّةِ وَالْأَخْلَاقِ السَّيِّئَةِ حَتّٰى خَرَجَ مِنَ الدُّنْيَا مُؤْمِنًا، فَإِنَّ اللهَ تَعَالٰى لَا يُضِيْعُهَا بَلْ يَقْبَلُهَا مِنْهُ وَيُثِيْبُهُ عَلَيْهَا. وَمَا كَانَ مِنَ السَّيِّئَاتِ دُوْنَ الشِّرْكِ وَالْكُفْرِ وَلَمْ يَتُبْ عَنْهَا صَاحِبُهَا حَتّٰى مَاتَ مُؤْمِنًا، فَإِنَّهُ فِيْ مَشِيْئَةِ اللهِ تَعَالٰى: إِنْ شَاءَ عَذَّبَهُ بِالنَّارِ وَإِنْ شَاءَ عَفَا عَنْهُ، وَلَمْ يُعَذِّبْهُ بِالنَّارِ أَصْلًا. وَالرِّيَاءُ إِذَا وَقَعَ فِيْ عَمَلٍ مِنَ الْأَعْمَالِ فَإِنَّهُ يُبْطِلُ أَجْرَهُ. وَكَذٰلِكَ الْعُجْبُ.

We do not charge any believer with unbelief for any sin he commits, even if it is an enormity, as long as he does not regard it as lawful. We do not remove the title of true faith from him, and we call him a real believer. It is possible that the person be an unrighteous believer, without being an unbeliever.

Wiping over leather socks is a *sunna. Tarāwīḥ* prayer during the nights of the month of Ramaḍān is a *sunna.* Prayer is permissible behind any righteous or unrighteous believer.

We do not claim that a believer is unharmed by sin or that he will not enter Hellfire. Nor do we claim that he will remain in the fire of Hell forever, even if he is unrighteous, after leaving the world a believer. We do not claim that our good deeds are [surely] accepted and bad deeds [surely] forgiven, as the Murji'a do. But we state that whoever performs a good deed in conformity with all its conditions and free from corruptive defects, and does not invalidate it by unbelief, apostasy, or bad character until he leaves the world a believer, then Allāh Most High will not disregard the deed, but will accept it from him and reward him for it.

For any sin lesser than partnering others with Allāh or unbelief altogether, in which the perpetrator did not repent, but died a believer, he will be within the will of Allāh Most High—If Allāh wills, He will punish him with the Fire, and if He wills, He will forgive him and not punish him with the Fire at all.

If ostentation becomes part of any action, it eliminates its reward; similar is vanity.

❁

We do not charge any believer with unbelief for any sin he commits, even if it is an enormity, as long as he does not regard it as lawful. We do not charge any believer with unbelief because of a sin, as the Khawārij do by charging the perpetrator of an enormity with unbelief. However, a person who regards a sin that has been established through definitive proof lawful is an unbeliever in Allāh Most High, because to regard it as lawful is tantamount to rejecting Allāh and His Messenger. We do not remove the title of true faith from him, that is, from a believer who perpetrates an enormity without regarding it lawful, and we call him a real believer. The Imām [author] indicates here that a *muslim* can be called a *mu'min* (believer) in the true sense [of the word]. This indicates the oneness of *īmān* (true faith) and *islām* (submission), [much like the oneness] of the back and stomach. It is possible that the person be an unrighteous believer, without being an unbeliever. *Fisq* (unrighteousness) means to depart from the obedience of Allāh Most High by committing an enormity. Ṣadr al-Sharīʿa[151] states, "An enormity is everything that is classified as immoral, such as sodomy, marrying the wife of one's own father, or anything that has a punishment (*ʿuqūba*) associated with it in this world or

151 ʿUbaydullāh ibn Masʿūd ibn ʿUbaydillāh ibn Maḥmūd, Ṣadr al-Sharīʿa al-Bukhārī al-Maḥbūbī. A great scholar of the Ḥanafī school, he wrote *Al-Tanqīḥ* on the fundamentals of jurisprudence, its commentary *Al-Tawḍīḥ*, and *Sharḥ al-Wiqāya*. He died in 747/1346 (*Tāj al-Tarājim* 13, *Al-Aʿlām* 4:198).

the Hereafter and is established by a definitive sacred text (*naṣṣ qaṭʿī*)." The Muʿtazila believe that the perpetrator of an enormity is unrighteous (*fāsiq*) and can neither be a believer nor an unbeliever. By this, they have created a condition between the two conditions (*al-manzila bayn al-manzilatayn*), i.e., between unbelief and true faith.

[Qārī] Abū Ḥanīfa rejects calling sinners from the people of the *qibla* unbelievers, even if they are people of innovation. This indicates that cursing Abū Bakr or ʿUmar is not unbelief, as has been confirmed by Abu 'l-Shakūr al-Sālimī in his *Tamhīd*.[152] Cursing a believer is a sin (*fisq*) as is mentioned in a well authenticated ḥadīth: "Cursing a believer is a sin and fighting him is unbelief" (*Bukhārī, Muslim*). Hence, Abū Bakr, ʿUmar, and others would be equal in this regard, and if it were hypothesized that someone killed them and ʿUthmān and ʿAlī, it would still not take the murderer outside the folds of Islam according to the Ahl al-Sunna wa 'l-Jamāʿa, and cursing is certainly lesser than killing. Yes, if one were to hold it lawful to curse or kill [them or any] believer, that would indeed be unbelief. [211]

In conclusion, sinning and disobedience do not eliminate true faith from a believer. Similarly, innovation (*bidʿa*) does not eliminate true faith from a person; for instance, the Muʿtazilīs deny the attributes (*ṣifāt*) of Allāh, that Allāh is the Creator of all the actions of His servants, and the possibility of the Beatific Vision in the Hereafter; since these [innovations] are all based on an interpretation, albeit a corrupt one, with the exceptions of anthropomorphism (*tajsīm*)[153] and denying that the knowledge of Allāh encompasses the particulars of things (*juzʾiyyāt*), for these two beliefs will unquestionably render one an unbeliever according to all. [212]

---

152 This is *Al-Tamhīd fī Bayān al-Tawḥīd* of Muḥammad ibn ʿAbd al-Sayyid ibn Shuʿayb, Abu 'l-Shakūr (and Abū Jaʿfar) al-Muhtadī al-Kishshī (or al-Kashshī) al-Sālimī al-Ḥanafī. He died after 463/1070.

153 As for anthropomorphism (*tajsīm*), if it is believed that Allāh is a physical body (*jism*), this is unbelief. If it is stated that Allāh has a body (*jism*) unlike any other body, this is misguided innovation and not unbelief according to the majority. As for the anthropomorphists (*mujassima*) of Khurāsān among the Karrāmiyya, identifying them as unbelievers is necessary because they affirm that Allāh has a physical limit and boundary from underneath, from whence He is in contact with His Throne. An innovation (*bidʿa*) does not lead one to unbelief unless it is an extreme one that takes one out of faith, such as claiming that ritual prayer (*ṣalāt*) can be fulfilled by mere supplication (*duʿāʾ*), claiming that Jibrīl mistakenly went to the Prophet ﷺ with the revelation instead of ʿAlī ؓ, the true recipient, or denying the exoneration of ʿĀʾisha ؓ from immorality in the Qurʾān; such ideas certainly constitute unbelief (*Al-Taʿlīq al-Muyassar* 212).

Reconciling the Conflicting Opinions Regarding the Takfīr of the People of the Qibla

[Qārī] It is difficult, as the commentator of *Al-ʿAqā'id* [Taftāzānī] has stated, to reconcile the various statements [of scholars] regarding *takfīr* (considering one an unbeliever) of the people of the *qibla.* For instance, one statement says, "No one from the people of *qibla* should be rendered unbelievers,"[154] and another says "One who says the Qur'ān is created, the beatific vision is impossible, or curses the *Shaykhayn* [Abū Bakr and ʿUmar] is an unbeliever." Similarly, the commentator of *Al-Mawāqif* states, "The majority of the theologians and jurists hold that *takfīr* should not be made of anyone of the people of the *qibla,* although it is also mentioned in the books of *fatāwā* that cursing the *Shaykhayn* is unbelief, as is denying their leadership (*imāma*). There is no doubt that rulings like this are accepted by the majority of Muslims, and therefore, reconciling between the two [types of] statements is difficult."[155]

---

154 Dhahabī relates in his *Siyar Aʿlām al-Nubalā'* that Zāhir al-Sarakhsī said: "When Abu 'l-Ḥasan al-Ashʿarī drew close to death in my house in Baghdad he called me and I went to him. He said, 'Be witness that I do not make *takfīr* of anyone from the people of the *qibla,* because they all make reference to the same deity, just their verbiage is different.'" Dhahabī then says, "I also take the same as my belief. Similarly, during the end of his life, our shaykh Ibn Taymiya used to say, 'I do not make *takfīr* of anyone from this umma.' He would say that the Messenger of Allāh ﷺ said, 'Only the believer is regular in performing *wuḍū'* (ritual ablution),' so whoever is regular on their *ṣalāt* with *wuḍū'* is a believer" (10:16). (*Al-Taʿlīq al-Muyassar* 427)

155 Many exhortations have been reported from the scholars regarding *takfīr* of Muslims. The Syrian Ḥanafī jurist Ḥaskafī says, "Know that a formal legal opinion (*fatwā*) will not be issued regarding a Muslim whose statements can be interpreted in a positive way, or when there is a difference of opinion regarding the unbelief of a person [who makes such a statement], even if that [difference] is based on a weak narration" (*Al-Durr al-Mukhtār* 3:287). Ibn Nujaym states, "I have made it binding on myself not to issue a formal legal verdict of unbelief regarding any matter in which the scholars have differed" (*Al-Baḥr al-Rā'iq* 5:210). The Shāfiʿī scholar Ibn Ḥajar al-Haytamī says, "What our scholars have clearly said is that no judgment should be made against a person who has uttered something that could constitute unbelief until he is questioned, that is, he is asked of his intention. If he says, 'I intended such and such' and such a thing can be clearly taken as unbelief, then a judgment of *takfīr* will be made. If he has intended a meaning that is not of unbelief, then *takfīr* will not be made (*Al-Fatāwā al-Kubrā* 4:239). Qārī has quoted that Ibn Ḥajar [al-ʿAsqalānī] said, "The correct opinion according to the majority of the *salaf* and *khalaf* is that we do not make *takfīr* of the innovators and sectarians unless they declare open unbelief and not just words whose implications may be construed as unbelief (*kufr istilzāmī*). This is because the soundest opinion is that the necessary implications of a position cannot be taken as the position itself (*lāzim madhhabin laysa bi madhhabin*). Based on this, the Muslims have been dealing with such people as believers in terms of intermarriage, praying on their deceased, and burying them in their cemeteries, because even though such people are considered to be in error, unexcusable, and correctly labeled unrighteous and deviant, their intention by what they have uttered is not to adopt unbelief (*Mirqāt al-Mafātīḥ* quoted by Mubārakpūrī in his *Tuḥfat al-Aḥwadhī* 2:362).

The difficulty essentially lies in the disparity between the legal rulings (*masāʾil farʿiyya*) and the theological proofs (*dalāʾil uṣūliyya*) among which is the agreement of the theologians that *takfīr* should not be made of the people of the *Muḥammadī qibla.* This difficulty can be removed by the fact that the reports contained in the books of *fatāwā* cannot be used as a proof from their transmitters due to the names of the reporters being unknown and their evidences not presented. Typically, the basis for belief in religious rulings is on definitive proofs. Moreover, there are many manifest and hidden harms that result from doing *takfīr* of the Muslim. Thus, the explanation by some that the authors of such books included the reports for the sake of creating a deterrence and exhorting people is not convincing.

Ibn al-Humām, in his commentary on [Marghīnānī's] *Al-Hidāya* attempts to provide a solution to this problem. He says, "Know that the basis for the judgment of *takfīr* of the sectarians we mentioned earlier, despite the ruling related from Abū Ḥanīfa and Shāfiʿī (may Allāh have mercy on them) of not making *takfīr* of all the innovators from among the people of the *qibla,* is that such a belief is an unbelief in and of itself. Although the proponent of such a belief disseminates an unbelief, he should not be considered an unbeliever. This is because his belief is the result of his utmost endeavor to ascertain the truth. However, the conviction of [the jurists] that the *ṣalāt* (ritual prayer) behind such a person is invalid does not support this explanation, unless we take 'invalid' to mean 'not permissible,' that is, 'impermissible to do but not invalidating the *ṣalāt* if performed.' Without this explanation, reconciling [the two statements] is difficult."

To resolve this conflict, it could be argued that their judgment of *ṣalāt* being invalid behind such people is a precautionary measure that does not necessitate that they be judged unbelievers. Do you not see that the jurists have ruled on the invalidity of *ṣalāt* facing in the direction of the *ḥijr*[156] [only] as a precautionary measure while not judging that the *ḥijr* be excluded from the House [of Allāh]? Rather they judge it to be from the House based on their

---

Shaykh Ghāwjī after compiling the above statements concludes by saying, "We should constantly keep in mind the words of Allāh: "The Believers are but a single brotherhood. So make peace and reconciliation between your two (contending) brothers; and fear Allāh, that you may receive mercy" (Qur'ān 49:10). (*Al-Taʿlīq al-Muyassar* 534)

156 The semicircular walled area adjoining the Kaʿba, also know as the Ḥaṭīm.

best opinion regarding it. Thus, they obligate that the *ṭawāf* (circumambulation) be around it [and not between it and the House].

Know that the people of the *qibla* are those who agree on all the necessary beliefs of the religion, such as the createdness of this world, resurrection of bodies, Allāh knowing the whole and the particular of all things, and other issues. Therefore, whoever is regular in his worship and obedient his entire life but believes in the world being preeternal, denies resurrection, or the knowledge of Allāh of the particulars, he is not from among the people of the *qibla*. Furthermore, according to the Ahl al-Sunna, the meaning of not doing *takfīr* of anyone from among the people of the *qibla* is that they not be considered unbelievers unless some [clear] unbelief or a sign of it is found in them, or if something necessitating unbelief issues from them.

Once you have understood the above, then know that the people of *qibla* who agree upon the fundamentals of beliefs we mentioned earlier do differ in regard to other fundamentals, such as the divine attributes, the creation of [all] actions [by Allāh], [His] encompassing will, the eternality of [His] speech, the permissibility of the beatific vision, and [all] such things for which there is no difference of opinion [among the Ahl al-Sunna] that the reality and truth in them is only one. They also differ as to whether or not *takfīr* can be made of one who opposes the truth in such matters and holds conflicting beliefs.

Imām Ashʿarī and the majority of his followers hold that such a person is not an unbeliever, and this is also indicated by what Imām Shāfiʿī (may Allāh have mercy on him) said: "I do not reject the testimony of the sectarians except the Khaṭṭābiyya,[157] because they consider lying to be lawful. Similarly, in *Al-Muntaqā*, it is related from Abū Ḥanīfa: "We do not do *takfīr* of anyone from among the people of the *qibla*." And this is the opinion of the majority of jurists. Nonetheless, some scholars have made *takfīr* of those who differ [in the fundamental beliefs mentioned above], and the earlier Muʿtazila have said that *takfīr* will be made of those who claim the eternality of the attributes or that [Allāh] creates the [evil] actions [of the servants]. Ustādh Abū Isḥāq [al-Isfirāyīnī] (d. 418/1027) said, "We do *takfīr* of those who make *takfīr* of us, and those who do not, we do not [made *takfīr* of them]. On the other hand,

157 The Khaṭṭābiyya are attributed to Abu 'l-Khaṭṭāb Muḥammad ibn Abī Zaynab al-Asadī. He persisted on his deviance and falsehood until the ʿAbbāsid governor of Kūfa ʿĪsā ibn Mūsā killed him in 143/760 (see *Al-Milal wa 'l-Niḥal* 1:179–180 and *Al-Farq Bayn al-Firaq* 188).

Rāzī's preference is that *takfīr* should not be made of anyone from among the people of the *qibla.*

Another way to resolve the conflict is that not making *takfīr* is the opinion of the theologians and making it is the opinion of the jurists. And since the proponents of the two opinions are different, there is no conflict. If this explanation was accepted, then it can be said that the second opinion is based on exaggeration in countering the opponents and the first one is based on honoring the state of the people of the *qibla,* for they are in general in agreement with us. [427–430][158]

Cursing the One who Commits an Enormity

[Qārī] Qūnawī says in his commentary of *ʿUmdat al-Nasafī,* "It is not permissible to curse the one who commits an enormity because his actual faith is not lost to him and does not lessen due to his performance of the enormity. It is not permissible to curse a believer." [218]

Abū Ḥanīfa's Stance Regarding Those Who Commit Enormities

[Qārī] Qūnawī has mentioned that Abū Ḥanīfa has been labeled a Murji'ī because of his holding back from condemning the performer of an enormity, and his leaving the matter to be decided by the will of Allāh Most High; this is because *irjā'*[159] [literally] means to "postpone." Abū Ḥanīfa used to say, "I have hope for the one who commits a major or minor sin and I am afraid for both. I have hope for the one who commits a minor sin, and I am afraid for the one who commits an enormity." The true [technical] definition of a *murji'ī*

---

158 This entire section on reconciling the conflicting narrations regarding *takfīr* is from an appendix in Qārī's *Minaḥ al-Rawḍ al-Azhar* and is not from his commentary.

159 *Irjā'* means "to postpone" or "to defer," and it is of two types: (1) the *irjā'* as an innovation and deviance; this is the *irjā'* of those [antinomians] who claim that disobedience in matters of faith does not bring harm, but that Allāh forgives all sins if faith is established, and (2) the *irjā'* of Sunna, which is the *irjā'* of the Ahl al-Sunna who say if the believer leaves this world with sins for which he has not sought forgiveness, his affair is in the hands of Allāh Most High. If Allāh wills, He will forgive him and if He wills, He will punish him. The proof of this is in what Allāh says, "Allāh forgives not that partners should be ascribed to Him; but He forgives all but that to whom He pleases" (Qur'ān 4:48). Thus, the *irjā'* of Sunna is between two extremes: between the blameworthy *irjā'* [of the Murji'a] which is tantamount to unbelief and [the other extreme] of the Khawārij and Muʿtazila. The Khawārij considered the performance of a sin sufficient to remove one from Islam and to earn him a place in the Hellfire forever if one died without repentance. The Muʿtazila claimed that such a person is neither a true believer [nor an unbeliever but will be in a rank between the two ranks] (*Al-Taʿlīq al-Muyassar* 221–223).

is one who claims that there is no sin after belief, meaning a believer will not be held accountable for sins, just as there is no benefit with unbelief. So how does this type of *irjā'* relate to the figure of Abū Ḥanīfa?[160] [223]

The Beliefs of the Murji'a

[Qārī] The Murji'a hold that those who enter the Hellfire will dwell therein without punishment, just as a whale dwells in the ocean. According to them, the only difference between the inhabitants of Hell and the believers is that the believers will be able to eat and drink and enjoy Paradise, whereas the unbelievers will not be able to do so in Hellfire. This is a completely erroneous opinion according to the Qur'ān, Sunna, consensus of the Ahl al-Sunna wa 'l-Jamāᶜa, and all the sects. Many verses in the Qur'ān illustrate the contrary: "Therein will they cry aloud (for assistance)" (35:37); "As often as their skins are consumed" (4:56); "Nor shall its punishment be lightened for them" (35:36); and "So taste (the fruits of your deeds), for no increase shall We grant you, except in Punishment" (78:30).

In support of their opinion that Hellfire will one day come to an end, the Murji'a quote a fabricated narration in which the Prophet ﷺ is related to have said, "A day will come upon Hell when a wind will knock on its doors and there will be no one inside." This narration is fabricated, but even if we were to assume its veracity, its apparent conflict with other texts can be easily reconciled by it being interpreted as referring to the specific section of Hell in which the sinning believers shall dwell. After they have been punished and sent to Paradise, it will be left empty. [225–226]

160 The Great Imām wrote a letter to ᶜUthmān al-Battī, after the latter had written to him informing him that he had heard the Imām was a Murji'ī. In it, he said, "Know that I say, 'The people of the *qibla* are believers, and I do not remove them from belief due to their leaving something of what has been made obligatory upon them. Whoever obeys Allāh Most High in all that is obligatory with true faith is, according to us, of the inhabitants of Paradise. Whoever leaves faith and action is an unbeliever and an inhabitant of Hellfire. Whoever attains faith and leaves off something of the obligatory is a sinning believer, and Allāh Most High has the right to do with him as He wills; if He wills, He will punish him, and if He wills, He will forgive him. If He punishes him for what he abandoned, He punishes him for a sin, and if He forgives him, then the sin is forgiven. As to what has been mentioned regarding the label of Murji'ī [upon myself], what is the sin of a people who speak of justice? It is the people of innovation who have called them this name, whereas the truth is that they are the people of justice and the people of the Sunna. Verily this name [i.e., Murji'ī] has been applied to them by the people of dispute." (*Al-Taᶜlīq al-Muyassar* 222–223)

Wiping Leather Socks

Wiping over leather socks is a *sunna*.[161] That is, its permissibility has been established through well-known narrations (*sunna mashhūra*). It is feared that one who rejects it is an unbeliever, because the evidence is of a degree very close to that of an [indisputable] uninterrupted narration (*khabar mutawātir*).

Imām Abū Ḥanīfa says in *Al-Waṣiyya:*

> We declare that wiping over leather socks is permissible for one day and night for the resident and three days and three nights for the traveler, as the ḥadīth elucidates. Unbelief is feared for the one who denies this because its status is close to that of the uninterrupted narration (*mutawātir*). Shortening the prayers and forgoing the fasts [and making them up later] are discretions established through Qur'ānic text, as Allāh Most High says, "When you travel through the earth, there is no blame on you if you shorten your prayers" (Qur'ān 4:101), and regarding forgoing the fast, Allāh Most High says, "If any of you is ill, or on a journey, the prescribed number (should be made up) from days later" (2:184).

Tarāwīḥ Prayer

Tarāwīḥ prayer during the nights of the month of Ramaḍān is a *sunna*. This is a rebuttal of the Rawāfiḍ, since they reject the *tarāwīḥ* prayer and the wiping of leather socks. They wipe their bare feet, without socks. The author of *Al-Khulāṣa* writes, "It states in *Al-Muntaqā*[162] that Abū Ḥanīfa (may Allāh have mercy on him) was asked to explain the beliefs of the Ahl al-Sunna wa 'l-Jamāʿa. He explained, 'It is that you give preference to the *shaykhayn* (two elders) [Abū Bakr and ʿUmar], you love the two son-in-laws (*khatanayn*) [ʿUthmān and ʿAlī], you believe in wiping leather socks, and you pray behind any righteous or unrighteous person.'"[163] And Allāh is the one who guides.

---

161 This point and the next one regarding *tarāwīḥ*, though not of the articles of faith, are mentioned here as a rebuttal of the Rāfiḍī Shīʿa who deny the wiping over the leather socks and the *tarāwīḥ* prayer.

162 This is written by Muḥammad ibn Muḥammad ibn Aḥmad ibn ʿAbdillāh ibn Ismāʿīl al-Marwazī, more popularly known as Ḥākim al-Shahīd al-Balkhī. He wrote *Al-Muntaqā* and *Al-Kāfī*, both of which are considered to be foundational texts of the Ḥanafī school after the books of Imām Muḥammad. He died a martyr in 344/955, earning the title "shahīd" (martyr).

163 Jalāl al-Dīn al-Khawārizmī al-Kirlānī, the author of *Al-Kifāya*, writes that the Imām took this statement from the Companion Anas ibn Mālik 🙵 (see *Al-Kifāya* on the margin of Ibn al-Humām's *Fatḥ al-Qadīr* 1:127).

[Qārī] The Prophet ﷺ performed the *tarāwīḥ* prayer for a few days in Ramaḍān, then left it out of compassion for the people so that it not be made binding upon them, or so that the people would not take it as obligatory. As for ʿUmar's ﷺ statement regarding it: "What a good innovation,"[164] this was in reference either to its revival or to his being the means for its performance in congregation after it having previously been performed individually. This is along with the fact that the Messenger ﷺ said, "Hold on to my Sunna and the Sunna of the rightly-guided caliphs" (*Abū Dāwūd, Tirmidhī*), then specifically ordering the umma to emulate Abū Bakr and ʿUmar by saying, "Follow the two after me" (*Tirmidhī*). [226–227]

Prayer is permissible behind any righteous or unrighteous believer because of [the presence of] his faith, but it is undesirable (*makrūh*) because of his neglect of religious matters. The Messenger of Allāh ﷺ said, "Whoever prays behind a pious scholar (*ʿālim taqī*), it is as though he has prayed behind a prophet, and whoever prays behind a prophet, his past sins are forgiven,"[165] that is, his minor sins.

[Qārī] This is due to the saying of the Prophet ﷺ, "Pray behind the righteous

164 The word *bidʿa* (innovation) refers to any newly introduced matter that does not have a precedent. If it is in agreement with Islamic law, then it is considered a good innovation. An example of this is ʿUmar's ﷺ gathering the believers in *tarāwīḥ* prayer behind one *imām,* and Abū Bakr's ﷺ gathering the written verses of the Qur'ān in one place fearing for their loss, even though the Messenger of Allāh ﷺ did not do this during his lifetime; his not having compiled the Qur'ān can be explained by the fact that the revelations were ongoing and only ceased at his death. If, on the other hand, the newly introduced matter is in conflict with Islamic law, then it is a reprehensible innovation; this would include the deviant beliefs in contradiction to established Islamic beliefs such as the denial of predestination (*qadar*) or attributing infallibility to other than the prophets. Imām Shāfiʿī said, "Invented matters are two types. One is what is innovated in contradiction to the Book of Allāh, the Sunna of the Prophet ﷺ, his narrations, or the consensus; this is a misguided innovation. The other is what is innovated of good that does not conflict with any of the above; this is a non-blameworthy innovation" (Bayhaqī, *Manāqib al-Shāfiʿī* 1:499). (*Al-Taʿlīq al-Muyassar* 227)

165 This particular wording was not found by Sakhāwī, as mentioned in his *Maqāṣid al-Ḥasana* and quoted by ʿAjlūnī from him. There are, however, other narrations that are similar. Ḥākim and Ṭabarānī relate through a weak chain on the authority of Abū Farqad al-Ghanawī from the Messenger ﷺ that, "If it makes you happy to have your prayer accepted, then the best among you should lead you in prayer." In a version related by Ṭabarānī, the following is added: "[The best are] your scholars, for they are your delegation between you and your Lord." Similar is related by Dāraquṭnī. Daylamī related on the authority of Jābir ﷺ: "Advance your elect ones, and your prayers will be more pure" (*Kashf al-Khafāʾ* 2:26).

and the unrighteous" (*Dāraquṭnī, Bayhaqī*). In one version of this narration, he ﷺ added, "And pray upon the righteous and the unrighteous, and fight behind the righteous and the unrighteous [leader]." Whosoever abandons the Friday and other congregational prayers behind an unrighteous leader is an innovator (*mubtadiʿ*) according to most of the scholars. The correct position on this is that one pray behind him and is not required to repeat the prayer. As an illustration of this, Ibn Masʿūd ﷺ and others used to pray behind Walīd ibn ʿUqba ibn Abī Muʿayt [in Kūfa], who was given to drinking wine to the extent that once he led them in the Fajr (dawn) prayer by performing four *rakʿas* [instead of two]. Then he asked, "Should I add more for you?" Ibn Masʿūd replied, "From today we are in constant excess with you!"[166] It is related in *Al-Muntaqā* that Abū Ḥanīfa was asked about the path of the Ahl al-Sunna wa 'l-Jamāʿa, and he said, "That you prefer the *shaykhayn* (two elders) [Abū Bakr and ʿUmar], that you love the two sons-in-laws (*khatanayn*) [ʿUthmān and ʿAlī], that you believe in wiping upon leather socks, and that you pray behind the righteous and the unrighteous." [227–228]

We do not claim that a believer is unharmed by sin or that he will not enter Hellfire, as is the belief of the Murji'a. Imām Rāzī states in *Kitāb al-Arbaʿīn,* "There are three opinions regarding a sinner who is not an unbeliever but has committed an enormity. One is the opinion of those who are convinced he will not be punished. This is the opinion of Muqātil ibn Sulaymān (d. 150/767) and the Murji'a. The second is the opinion of those who are convinced he will be punished. This is the opinion of the Muʿtazila and Khawārij. The third is the opinion of those who are not convinced of either. This is the opinion of the majority of Imāms, and it is the preferred opinion." | nor do we claim that he will remain in the fire of Hell forever, even if he is unrighteous, after leaving the world a believer, as opposed to the Muʿtazila, who are convinced that the unrighteous (*fāsiq*) will remain forever in the punishment of Hellfire, like an unbeliever.

[Qārī] Allāh accepts repentance from His servants and forgives the sin of associating partners with Him [if one repents] and other sins according to

166 The Arabic text to this reads: *"mā zilnā maʿaka mundh al-yawma fī ziyādatin"* and was condemning sarcasm from Ibn Masʿūd ﷺ.

what He has promised and of that which He has informed us. This is not out of any obligation upon Him, as the Muʿtazila claim. They say it is binding upon Allāh to punish the disobedient one and to reward the obedient one and accept a person's repentance. [230]

There is no difference of opinion that there are certain sins that are deemed by evidence in Islamic law to be signs of unbelief. For example, prostration to an idol, placing the Qur'ān in the trash, uttering words of unbelief, and other such things that have been proven through sacred texts to constitute unbelief.[167] [231]

We do not claim that our good deeds are [surely] accepted and bad deeds [surely] forgiven, as the Murji'a do. But we state that whoever performs a good deed in conformity with all its conditions, such as intention, sincerity, etc., among those that are obligatory, and free from corruptive defects, like ostentation, seeking recognition (*sumʿa*), and vanity, and does not invalidate it by unbelief, apostasy/ Allāh Most High says, "Whoever denies the faith, his work is in vain" (Qur'ān 5:6). The belief of the Ahl al-Sunna wa 'l-Jamāʿa is that committing enormities does not corrupt good actions or invalidate their reward. | or bad character until he leaves the world a believer, then Allāh Most High will not disregard the deed, but will accept it from him and reward him for it—not because of any obligation [upon Allāh] or entitlement [of the servant], but purely out of His generosity and in fulfillment of His promise. Allāh Most High says, "Allāh has promised the believers, men and women, gardens" (9:72) and "That is Allāh's bounty; He gives it to whom He will" (5:54) and "Allāh breaks not a promise" (3:9).

For any sin lesser than partnering others with Allāh or unbelief altogether, whether a minor sin or enormity, in which the perpetrator did not repent, but died a believer, but as a transgressor persistent in his sins, he will be within the will of Allāh Most High—if Allāh wills He will punish him with the Fire out of His justice, and then will release him from it, out of His generosity, and if He wills He will forgive him and not punish him with the Fire at all out of His generosity and mercy, or by the intercession of the intercessors. In some editions [of *Al-Fiqh al-Akbar*], it states, "If He wills He will forgive him and

167 These would be expressions of unbelief even if a person did them while confessing belief in Islam with his tongue, except in the case of duress; hence, such actions are to be avoided at all costs.

will not punish him with the Fire ever." That is, any believer whom Allāh Most High punishes, will not be punished in Hellfire forever, because true faith prevents permanent residence in Hell.

If ostentation becomes part of any action, it eliminates its reward/ Allāh Most High says, "O you who believe! Render not vain your almsgiving by reproach and injury, like him who spends his wealth only to be seen by people" (Qur'ān 2:264); similarly, the Messenger of Allāh ﷺ said, "Allāh Most High will not accept any action containing an atom's measure of ostentation in it" (*Marāsīl Qāsim ibn Mukhaymir*). The author (may Allāh have mercy on him) spoke only of the invalidation of the reward, not the invalidation of the action, in regard of the great importance of merit and reward, since the ultimate aim and objective of actions is merit and reward. | similar is vanity, that is, if vanity becomes part of any action, it invalidates the reward and the action, just as ostentation does.[168] This is because a person with vanity considers himself secure from the planning of Allāh, and is not afraid of the destruction of his faith and [the reward of his] actions. To consider oneself secure from the punishment of Allāh is unbelief.

[Qārī] Imām Abū Ḥanīfa specifically mentions these two blameworthy traits and not others to indicate that other sins do not destroy one's good deeds as these do. [234]

---

168 Ostentation and vanity only invalidate an act of pure worship, like ritual prayer (*ṣalāt*) or fasting, and diminish its reward, if the opening intention is corrupt and not if the corruption creeps in after beginning it. Actions that are not objective acts of pure worship like ritual ablution (*wuḍū'*) or bath (*ghusl*) are not invalidated by ostentation and vanity, since intention is not a precondition in them (according to the Ḥanafī school). Therefore, the claim made by some that the worship of the unrighteous are never valid or accepted is incorrect. What Maghnīsāwī intends to say here is that any act of pure worship done for ostentation or vanity from the outset is invalidated and entails loss of reward (see *MS. 4405* for more details).

MUʿJIZĀT, KARĀMĀT, AND *ISTIDRĀJ*

وَالْآيَاتُ ثَابِتَةٌ لِلْأَنْبِيَاءِ. وَالْكَرَامَاتُ لِلْأَوْلِيَاءِ حَقٌّ. وَأَمَّا الَّتِيْ تَكُوْنُ لِأَعْدَائِهِ مِثْلِ إِبْلِيْسَ وَفِرْعَوْنَ وَالدَّجَّالِ فَمَا رُوِيَ فِي الْأَخْبَارِ أَنَّهُ كَانَ وَيَكُوْنُ لَهُمْ لَا نُسَمِّيْهَا آيَاتٍ وَلَا كَرَامَاتٍ، وَلٰكِنْ نُسَمِّيْهَا قَضَاءَ حَاجَاتِهِمْ، وَذٰلِكَ لِأَنَّ اللهَ تَعَالٰى يَقْضِيْ حَاجَاتِ أَعْدَائِهِ اسْتِدْرَاجًا لَهُمْ وَعُقُوْبَةً لَهُمْ، فَيَغْتَرُّوْنَ بِهِ وَيَزْدَادُوْنَ طُغْيَانًا وَكُفْرًا، وَذٰلِكَ كُلُّهُ جَائِزٌ مُمْكِنٌ. وَكَانَ اللهُ تَعَالٰى خَالِقًا قَبْلَ أَنْ يَخْلُقَ وَرَازِقًا قَبْلَ أَنْ يَرْزُقَ.

Signs of the prophets are real, and miracles of divine favor are true of the friends of Allāh. As for whatever is performed by the enemies of Allāh, such as Iblīs (Satan), Pharaoh, and the Antichrist—some of which, it is narrated, has already occurred and others of which are yet to occur—we do not call them established signs or miracles of divine favor, but will call them the fulfillment of their needs. This is because Allāh Most High fulfils the needs of His enemies to delude and punish them. Hence, they are deluded and they increase in their tyranny and unbelief. This is all conceivable and possible.

Allāh Most High was the Creator before He created and the Sustainer before He gave sustenance.

❁

Signs, that is, inimitable miracles (*muʿjizāt*), of the prophets (upon them be peace) are real. Signs signify extraordinary acts observed from prophets that defy what is customary, such as reviving the deceased, the gushing of water from between the fingers, and fire refusing to burn. These are called signs (*āyāt*), because by having them exhibited by the prophets, Allāh Most High intends them to be indications and proofs of their prophethood and their truthfulness.

and miracles of divine favor are true of the friends of Allāh, that is, the acts observed from the friends of Allāh (*awliyā*) that defy what is customary are called miracles of divine favor (*karāmāt*). By having the miracles performed by them, Allāh Most High intends to honor and strengthen them. *Walī* literally means "someone close"; hence, when a servant becomes close to Allāh Most High through abundant obedience and sincerity, the Lord Most High becomes close to him through His mercy, grace, and kindness.

[Qārī] The difference between a *karāma* (miracle of divine favor) and a *muʿjiza* (inimitable miracle) is that a *muʿjiza* is a matter that departs from the norm, such as bringing the dead back to life or destroying a mountain, as a result of a challenge (*taḥaddī*), that is, the claim to prophethood.[169] The *karāma* also represents a departure from the norm, but one that does not come out of a challenge. Rather, it is a miracle [performed] at the hand of the friend of Allāh (*walī*) and a proof of the truth of his prophet, because the miracle of the follower is a miracle of the followed.[170] A *walī* (friend of Allāh) is the

169 Essentially, the claim to prophecy is translated into a challenge for all those who are being called to witness his message.

170 Many miracles of divine favor (*karāmāt*) have been related in the Qur'ān and Sunna. Allāh says regarding those who possess the Knowledge of the Book, "Said one who had Knowledge of the Book, 'I will bring it to you within the twinkling of an eye!' Then when (Sulaymān) saw it placed firmly before him, he said, 'This is by the Grace of my Lord!'" (Qur'ān 27:40). Allāh Most High also speaks of the miracle of Maryam (Mary) (upon her be peace): "Every time that he (Zakariyya) entered (her) chamber to see her, he found her supplied with sustenance. He said, 'O Maryam! From where (comes) this to you?' She said, 'From Allāh, for Allāh provides sustenance to whom He pleases without measure'" (3:37).

In the Sunna, a narration speaks about Jurayj, the hermit for whom [in his defense against a slander] Allāh made an infant speak. The Messenger of Allāh ﷺ said, "No infants spoke in their cradle except three: ʿĪsā son of Maryam, an infant in the time of Jurayj the devotee, and another infant . . ." (*Bukhārī, Muslim*). The great ḥadīth master Ibn Ḥajar al-ʿAsqalānī also relates an account of the following miracle. The second caliph ʿUmar ؓ had sent an army to Nahāwand [a town today in the Hamadān province in Iran] with Sāriya ؓ as the commander. The enemy was hiding at the base of a nearby mountain, unknown to the Muslim army. ʿUmar while on the pulpit in Madīna was delivering the Friday sermon when he suddenly cried, "Sāriya, the mountain, the mountain!" His voice was heard by the Muslim army in Nahāwand. ʿAlī ؓ reports that the date of this incident was written down. Then a messenger from the front lines of the Muslim army returned and said, "Leader of the Faithful, we were engaged in battle on Friday during the time of the sermon, and the enemy was defeating us, when suddenly a person was heard shouting, "Sāriya, the mountain!" We immediately took support behind us with the mountain, and Allāh defeated the unbelievers by the blessing of that voice" (*Al-Iṣāba fī Maʿrifat al-Ṣaḥāba* 1:410).

Another miracle is reported regarding ʿUmar ؓ. ʿAmr ibn al-ʿĀṣ, after the conquest of Egypt, had written to ʿUmar ؓ in Madīna informing him of the custom of the Egyptians, who annually sacrificed a young girl to the Nile, believing the Nile flowed by this sacrifice. ʿUmar ؓ drafted

knower of Allāh and His attributes to the utmost degree possible for him. He is regular in his obedience and keen to avoid disobedience and engrossment in pleasures, desires, heedlessness, and play.

The Muʿtazila oppose the Ahl al-Sunna wa 'l-Jamāʿa with regard to *karāmāt* because none of them have witnessed this station [of friendship with Allāh]. Also, the Shīʿa have confined miracles to the twelve Imāms but lack any proof for this exclusivity. [237]

In conclusion, the scholars agree that any departure from the norm with respect to a prophet is a miracle whether it is exhibited at the hand of a prophet of Allāh or at the hand of one of his followers; in short, the only difference between the two is the inclusion of a challenge in the inimitable miracle (*muʿjiza*) of a prophet and [its exclusion in] a miracle of divine favor exhibited by the friend of Allāh (*karāma*).

Abū ʿAlī al-Jūzajānī (d. 352/964) advised, "Be a seeker of steadfastness, not a seeker of miracles. Verily your lower self is engaged in seeking miracles, but steadfastness is what your Lord is seeking from you." Shaykh Suhrawardī[171] says in his *ʿAwārif,*

> This is important advice on this matter, for a great number of diligent worshippers who hear of the pious predecessors and the miracles and extraordinary experiences they had, constantly pursue them and wish for something similar to happen to them. Consequently, some of them may be disheartened, reproaching themselves on the correctness of their worship when no miracle occurs to them. If they only knew the secret of this [path], the matter would have been much easier on them. They would then know that Allāh opens this door only to some of those who struggle in sincerity. The wisdom behind this is to increase such a person in certitude, by the miracles and signs they witness testifying to the power of Allāh; in turn, their resolve for asceticism in this world and escaping the pangs of desire becomes strengthened. Thus, the path of the truthful one demands the self to be steadfast, and this is the ultimate miracle. [238–239]

---

a letter to him and ordered it to be thrown into the Nile. It said: "If you flow by your own order, then do not flow. If Allāh is the one who makes you flow, then you will flow." ʿAmr ☙ threw the letter into the Nile [on Friday] as instructed, and when they awoke on Saturday morning, Allāh had caused the river to flow and rise sixteen cubits overnight (*Al-Bidāya wa 'l-Nihāya* 7:100). See *Al-Taʿlīq al-Muyassar* 235–237.

171 Shihāb al-Dīn ʿUmar ibn Muḥammad ibn ʿAbdillāh al-Suhrawardī al-Baghdādī, the great *ṣūfī* master and author of *ʿAwārif al-Maʿārif* and *Bahjat al-Abrār*. He passed away in 632/1234 (*Siyar Aʿlām al-Nubalāʾ* 22:239).

Firāsa (Spiritual Intuitiveness)

[Qārī] Know that the Prophet ﷺ said, "Beware of the deep insight (*firāsa*) of the believer, for he sees with the light of Allāh." Then he recited, "Lo! therein verily are portents for those who read the signs" (Qur'ān 15:75) (*Tirmidhī*). *Firāsa,* "deep insight" or "spiritual intuitiveness" is of three types: *firāsa īmāniyya, firāsa riyāḍiyya,* and *firāsa khilqiyya.*

Firāsa īmāniyya or "faith-based insight" is a light which Allāh Most High places in the heart of His servant. Its reality is that it is a thought that enters into the heart and pounces upon it like a lion pounces upon its prey. The word *firāsa* is actually derived from the same root word as the word *farīsa,* "prey." This type of insight is proportionate to the strength of one's faith, such that those with stronger faith will have deeper insight. Abū Sulaymān al-Dārānī (may Allāh have mercy on him) said, "Insight is the unveiling of the self (*mukāshafat al-nafs*) and the seeing of the unseen (*muʿāyanat al-ghuyūb*); it is from the stations of faith."

Firāsa riyāḍiyya or the "insight attained through exercise" is what is attained by disciplining the self through hunger, sleeplessness, and isolation. For when the self is shed of hindrances and ties with creation, it develops insight and unveilings according to its freedom from them. This type of insight is found among both believers and unbelievers, and it is not a sign of faith or nearness to Allāh (*wilāya*). It does not unveil any beneficial truth or the straight path. Rather, its manifestations are of the same type as the intuitive perceptions that administrators, interpreters of dreams, traditional healers, and others possess.

Firāsa khilqiyya or "physiognomy" is a study about which physicians and others have written, by which insight is gained into the inner character of someone from their outward appearance due to the relationship created by Allāh Most High between the two. This is similar to inferring the weakness of the intellect from an abnormally small head and the strength of the intellect from the large size of the head, and inferring a generous personality from the broadness of one's chest and a mean character by its narrowness, etc. [239–240]

As for whatever is performed by the enemies of Allāh, such as Iblīs (Satan), Pharaoh, and the Antichrist—some of which, it is narrated, has already occurred and others of which are yet to occur—we do not call them established signs [or inimitable miracles], because they are reserved for the prophets (upon them be peace), or miracles of divine favor, because they are reserved for the friends of Allāh Most High, as an honor and kindness to them, but will call them the fulfillment of their needs.

[Qārī] Extraordinary actions of Iblīs, for example, are similar to the contracting of the earth for him so that he is able to whisper to those in the East and the West, his flowing in the human [body] like the flow of blood, among other things. For Pharaoh, it was the Nile flowing upon his order as he is quoted in the Qur'ān as saying, "Is not mine the sovereignty of Egypt and these rivers flowing under me?" (43:51) and what has been related regarding the legs of his horse becoming longer or shorter based on whether he wanted to ascend or descend from his palace. For the Antichrist (Dajjāl), it will be that he will slay a person and then bring him back to life. [240]

Since there is a possibility that the concept of fulfilling the needs of one's enemies sounds unconvincing to some short-sighted intellects, the Great Imām repels the doubt and explains the wisdom behind the matter, saying, This is because Allāh Most High fulfils the needs of His enemies to delude and punish them. Hence, they are deluded by the fulfillment of their needs and they increase in their tyranny and unbelief. Thus, they become worthy of humiliating punishment. Allāh Most High says, "And let not the unbelievers suppose that the indulgence We grant them is good for them; We grant them indulgence only that they may increase in sin" (3:178). This is all conceivable and possible, that is, its occurrence is not inconceivable to the mind. Allāh Most High says, "We will draw them on little by little from whence they know not" (7:182). And the Messenger of Allāh ﷺ said, "If you ever see Allāh granting a servant whatever he pleases while the servant remains persistent in sin, then that is Allāh deluding him" (*Aḥmad, Ṭabarānī*).

[Qārī] This is all based on the will of the divine to lead them further astray. The plan of Allāh is to slowly draw the unbeliever near to his punishment by increasing his "blessings" in this world and leaving him to feel that he is close to Allāh Most High, while he is actually moving farther away from Him and is being forsaken. [241] Another type of extraordinary behavior is to bring humiliation to one desiring the opposite of it. It is related that Musaylama the

Liar prayed to cure a man's blindness in one eye; instead, the man lost sight in his healthy eye too.[172] [243]

Allāh Most High was the Creator before He created and the Sustainer before He gave sustenance. The Great Imām repeats this statement for emphasis. It means that Allāh Most High was the Creator (Khāliq) before the existence of anything created, the Sustainer (Rāziq) before the existence of anything to be sustained, the Omnipotent (Qādir) before the existence of anything over which to wield power, the Vanquisher (Qāhir) before the existence of anything to be vanquished, the Merciful (Raḥīm) before the existence of anything upon which to be shown mercy, the Worshipped (Maʿbūd) before the existence of anyone to worship, the Answerer (Mujīb) before the existence of anyone to ask, the Wealthy (Ghanī) before the existence of the heavens and earth, the Possessor (Mālik) before the existence of the kingdom and anyone [in it] to be possessed, and the Everlasting (Bāqī) after the annihilation of all created beings.

172 This incident is also related by Ibn Kathīr in his *Al-Bidāya wa 'l-Nihāya* (6:359) but with a slight variation.

THE BEATIFIC VISION OF ALLĀH

وَاللهُ تَعَالَىٰ يُرَىٰ فِي الْآخِرَةِ وَيَرَاهُ الْمُؤْمِنُوْنَ وَهُمْ فِي الْجَنَّةِ بِأَعْيُنِ رُؤُوْسِهِمْ بِلَا تَشْبِيْهٍ وَلَا كَيْفِيَّةٍ وَلَا يَكُوْنُ بَيْنَهُ وَبَيْنَ خَلْقِهِ مَسَافَةٌ.

Allāh Most High will be seen in the Hereafter. The believers will see Him, while in Paradise, with their own eyes, without any comparison or modality. There will not be any distance between Him and His creation.

❁

Allāh Most High will be seen in the Hereafter. [In the Arabic text,] *ākhira* (Hereafter, lit., last) is the adjective of *dār* (abode), as in the words of Allāh, "That is the Final Abode" (Qur'ān 28:83). It is called *ākhira* (last) because it succeeds this world, and it is derived from those adjectives that have become nouns because of frequent use. [One can make] a similar case with the world *dunyā* (closer); it is called *dunyā* because of its proximity and closeness to the Hereafter. The believers will see Him, while in Paradise, with their own eyes/ The Messenger of Allāh ﷺ said, "When the inhabitants of Paradise will enter Paradise, Allāh, the Blessed and Exalted, will ask them, 'Is there anything more you need that I may bestow upon you.' They will say, 'Have you not brightened our faces? Have you not entered us into Paradise and delivered us from the Hellfire?' Allāh will say, 'Certainly.'" The Messenger of Allāh ﷺ said, "Then the veils will be removed and they will see the Countenance of Allāh Most High. They will not have been bestowed anything more beloved to them than the sight of their Lord." The Messenger of Allāh ﷺ then recited, "For those who do good is the best (reward) and more" (Qur'ān 10:26) (*Muslim*, "al-Īmān," 266). | without any comparison or modality, as opposed to the Comparers (*mushabbiha*) and the Anthropomorphists (*mujassima*). There will not be any distance between Him and His creation when they will see Him. The word *masāfa* literally means "distance." Here it means location, place, and direction (*muqābala*).

Know that seeing Allāh with one's own eyes in the Hereafter is true, known, and established through sacred texts, not through reason, but it is from the matters of ambiguous description. Fakhr al-Islam ʿAlī al-Bazdawī (may Allāh have mercy on him) states in his *Uṣūl al-fiqh,* "An example of a matter ambiguous in description is proving with a Qur'ānic text that Allāh Most High will truly be seen with the eyes in a direct encounter in the Hereafter; the said text is where Allāh Most High says, "That day will faces be resplendent, looking toward their Lord" (75:22–23). And although He exists with the attributes of perfection (to be visible to Himself and to others is among the attributes of perfection) and the believer, in his honored position, is qualified to see Him, it is impossible to determine a direction [for Him]. Hence seeing Him becomes ambiguous in its description. And yet, it is obligatory to accept the ambiguity while believing in the reality [of the vision].

[Qārī] "Seeing" something does not necessitate encompassing or grasping (*idrāk*) it completely, and thus there is no contradiction with the verse: "No vision can grasp Him" (Qur'ān 6:103) since encompassment (*idrāk*) is a capacity beyond just sight. Hence, the Lord Most High will be seen but knowledge cannot completely encompass him. One may be able to see the sun but not encompass it completely in its full reality.

The commentator on *Al-ʿAqīda al-Ṭaḥāwiyya,* [Ibn Abi 'l-ʿIzz al-Ḥanafī] erred on this issue when he said, "Is it logically possible to see something without being face to face with it? In this is the proof that He is 'above' His creation. [Whoever says that Allāh will be seen without any direction should consult with his intellect" (*Sharḥ al-Ṭaḥāwiyya* 1:219)]. It is as though the commentator holds the opinion of Allāh [physically] being in the above direction.[173]

173 If the commentator had merely recalled the verse "And nothing is like unto Him, and He is the one who hears and sees (all things)" (Qur'ān 42:11) and the fact that Allāh is not described by what created beings are described by in terms of possessing a direction or place, he would have restricted himself to what has been transmitted—the vision itself, without attributing any place or direction to it. Allāh existed before there was direction or place and He remains as He always has been, glorified is He. Abstaining from delving into this matter more deeply is wiser. As for attributing to Him a direction, it is inconceivable with respect to Allāh Most High (*Al-Taʿlīq al-Muyassar* 249–250).

The way of the Ahl al-Sunna wa 'l-Jamāʿa is that Allāh Most High is not seen in a direction. The saying of the Prophet ﷺ: "You will see your Lord as you see the full moon" (*Bukhārī, Muslim*), is just to show general resemblance between the sighting of the one and the other, and not to show a resemblance in every aspect between what is actually seen. [249–250]

Imām Abū Ḥanīfa says in *Al-Waṣiyya:* "The meeting of Allāh with the people of Paradise is a reality [and is to occur] without modality, corporealism, or direction."

ĪMĀN, ISLĀM, AND *DĪN*

وَالْإِيْمَانُ هُوَ الْإِقْرَارُ وَالتَّصْدِيْقُ. وَإِيْمَانُ أَهْلِ السَّمَاءِ وَالْأَرْضِ لَا يَزِيْدُ وَلَا يَنْقُصُ مِنْ جِهَةِ الْمُؤْمَنِ بِهِ وَيَزِيْدُ وَيَنْقُصُ مِنْ جِهَةِ الْيَقِيْنِ وَالتَّصْدِيْقِ. وَالْمُؤْمِنُوْنَ مُسْتَوُوْنَ فِي الْإِيْمَانِ وَالتَّوْحِيْدِ، مُتَفَاضِلُوْنَ فِي الْأَعْمَالِ. وَالْإِسْلَامُ هُوَ التَّسْلِيْمُ وَالْانْقِيَادُ لِأَوَامِرِ اللهِ تَعَالٰى، فَمِنْ طَرِيْقِ اللُّغَةِ فَرْقٌ بَيْنَ الْإِيْمَانِ وَالْإِسْلَامِ وَلٰكِنْ لَا يَكُوْنُ إِيْمَانٌ بِلَا إِسْلَامٍ وَلَا يُوْجَدُ إِسْلَامٌ بِلَا إِيْمَانٍ، وَهُمَا كَالظَّهْرِ مَعَ الْبَطْنِ. وَالدِّيْنُ اسْمٌ وَاقِعٌ عَلَى الْإِيْمَانِ وَالْإِسْلَامِ وَالشَّرَائِعِ كُلِّهَا.

Īmān means to affirm and be convinced. The faith of the inhabitants of the heavens and earth neither increases nor decreases in terms of the articles of faith; it increases and decreases in certainty and conviction. Believers are equal in faith and divine oneness, dissimilar in actions.

Islām is to surrender and to submit to the commands of Allāh Most High. Hence, there is a literal difference between *īmān* and *islām.* However, *īmān* (faith) does not exist without *islām* nor *islām* without *īmān:* they are as the back with the stomach. *Dīn* (religion) is a noun that encompasses *īmān, islām,* and all sacred laws.

❀

Īmān literally means to be convinced, which is to accept in the heart the information of an informer. Its meaning in Turkish is *inanmak.* In sacred law (Sharīʿa), it means to affirm with the tongue and to be convinced with the inner heart that Allāh Most High is One, that He has no partner, that He possesses His essential and active attributes, and that Muḥammad ﷺ is His Messenger, that is, His Prophet whom He sent with His scripture and sacred law (Sharīʿa). Therefore, affirmation alone cannot be true faith, because if it were, then all the hypocrites would be believers. Likewise, being aware [of Allāh] alone cannot be true faith, because if it were, then all the People of the Book would be believers. But Allāh Most High says regarding the hypocrites, "And Allāh bears witness that the hypocrites are indeed liars" (Qur'ān 63:1). And He says regarding the People of the Book, "Those whom We gave the Book recognize it as they recognize their sons" (2:146). Hence, whoever intends to be among the umma of Muḥammad ﷺ and says with his tongue, "There is no Lord but Allāh and Muḥammad is His Messenger," and his heart confirms its meaning, then he is a believer, even if he is not aware of the obligations and prohibitions [of faith]. Thereafter, if he is told that five prayers (*ṣalawāt*) are obligatory upon him each day and night, and he acknowledges and accepts their obligation, then he remains on his faith. If he rejects and does not accept the obligation, then he is a disbeliever of Allāh. Similar is the case with all the obligations and prohibitions that are established through absolute proof, i.e., from the Qur'ān, Sunna, consensus (*ijmāᶜ*) of the umma, and the analogy (*qiyās*) of the jurists.[174]

[Qārī] Affirmation (*iqrār*) is mentioned before conviction (*taṣdīq*) here, because it is what is normally observed first in expression and because the law has sufficed with confession [in many matters], though conviction (*taṣdīq*) is what is really taken into consideration [in terms of real faith]. Abū Ḥanīfa writes in his book *Al-Waṣiyya,* "True faith consists of affirmation with the tongue and conviction in the heart. Affirmation alone cannot be faith, for if it were, the hypocrites would all be considered believers. Likewise, conviction alone cannot be faith, for if it were, the People of the Book would have all been considered believers. Allāh says regarding the hypocrites, 'And Allāh bears witness that the hypocrites are indeed liars' (Qur'ān 63:1), [that is, He bears witness to the invalidity of the hypocrites' claim to belief, because of an absence of conviction in their hearts]. And Allāh Most High also says regarding the People of the Book, 'The People of the Book know this [Allāh and His Messenger] as they know their own sons' (2:146), yet this is not taken as a sign of their belief, for [some of them] believed that Muḥammad ﷺ was sent specifically for the Arabs."[175] [250–251]

---

174 This final part, "And the analogy of the jurists," is not to be found in any of the manuscripts.

175 Both groups are shown to have a lack of coherence between what is in their hearts and what is on their tongues, and thus, both are taken to have not entered into true belief.

Verbal Affirmation (Iqrār): An Integral or Condition?

[Qārī] Furthermore, conviction (*taṣdīq*) is an integral pillar (*rukn*) [of faith] whose excellence is intrinsic (*ḥasan li ʿaynihī*) so that it cannot be dispensed with under any circumstance [for one to remain within the fold of Islam]. Affirmation (*iqrār*) by tongue, on the other hand, is either a condition (*sharṭ*) or an integral pillar (*rukn*) whose excellence is extrinsic (*ḥasan li ghayrihī*) and can be dispensed with in cases of duress or need [without rendering one an unbeliever]. This is because the tongue is the interpreter of the heart, and thus will be the proof for or against the conviction [that lies] in it. Hence, if one is to alter one's affirmation at a time when one has no legal dispensation, then one is an unbeliever. However, when one's ability is taken away by duress, then one will not become an unbeliever, since the obvious fear for one's life is a clear proof of the conviction in one's heart, and that one is only altering the affirmation to repel harm from oneself. Allāh says, "Anyone who, after accepting faith in Allāh, utters unbelief—except under compulsion, his heart remaining firm in faith—but those who open their breast to unbelief, upon them shall be wrath from Allāh, and theirs will be a dreadful penalty" (Qur'ān 16:106). Shams al-A'imma al-Sarakhsī therefore mentions that if one were to refuse affirmation with the tongue while in a state of safety, then it would be an indication that one has changed the state of one's belief. In this case, the presence or absence of affirmation becomes an integral pillar of belief. In fact, the opinion that affirmation (*iqrār*) by the tongue is an integral pillar (*rukn*) of belief, is only that of some scholars. It is the opinion of Imām Shams al-A'imma al-Ḥalwānī and Fakhr al-Islām as well as Shams al-A'imma al-Sarakhsī.

Conversely, Abu 'l-Barakāt ʿAbdullāh Aḥmad ibn Maḥmūd al-Nasafī,[176] the author of *Al-ʿUmda,* explains that affirmation with the tongue is only a condition (*sharṭ*) for carrying out the sacred laws [and to validate treating such a person as a Muslim], and not an integral pillar (*rukn*) of his faith. This is the favored opinion of the Ashʿarīs, and is also the opinion of Abū Manṣūr al-Māturīdī.

Thus the majority of theological specialists (*muḥaqqiqīn*) have established that *īmān* is only conviction (*taṣdīq*) in the heart, and that the affirmation

176 ʿAbdullāh ibn Aḥmad ibn Maḥmūd, Abu 'l-Barakāt Ḥāfiẓ al-Dīn al-Nasafī (d. 701/1301) the great Ḥanafī jurist and Qur'ānic exegete who wrote *Al-Wāfī,* its commentary *Al-Kāfī, Kanz al-Daqā'iq, Al-ʿUmda, Madārik al-Tanzīl,* and many other works (*Al-Fawā'id al-Bahiyya* 101–102, *Muʿjam al-Mu'allifīn* 6:32).

(*iqrār*) of the tongue is a requirement for the application of Islamic laws [on the person] in this world only [and is not an integral pillar of faith]. This is because conviction of the heart is an inward matter that is in need of an outward manifestation. So whoever believes in his heart and does not affirm with his tongue is considered a believer by Allāh Most High, even if he is not considered a believer by others in their dealings with him in the world. Conversely, the opposite applies for whoever affirms with the tongue but does not have conviction in the heart, such as the hypocrite; [he is considered a believer in the world, but is considered an unbeliever by Allāh]. This is the preferred position of Abū Manṣūr al-Māturīdī.[177] Many sacred texts affirm this position. For instance, Allāh says [regarding the desert Arabs who had not completely internalized their faith], "For not yet has faith entered your hearts" (49:14) and the Messenger of Allāh ﷺ said to Usāma ibn Zayd ؓ when he killed a warrior who had said, "There is no god except Allāh," "Why did you not tear open his heart to see if he was speaking the truth or lying?" (*Muslim, Abū Dāwūd*).

Furthermore, it states in *Sharḥ al-Maqāṣid,*[178]

> If affirmation is taken as being necessary for the application of worldly laws, then it is necessary that it be done openly in front of the Muslim leader and the Muslim public so that it becomes known. If it is taken as an integral pillar of faith, then it would be sufficient for one to say it to oneself only, and not to others. It is also clear that merely adhering to the requirements of Islamic law [in public] should take the place of professing it in words [as is the requirement of the first opinion]. [251–254]

General and Specific Knowledge of the Tenets of Faith

[Qārī] It is important to note that the absence of the mention of the actual tenets of faith [in detail] in Abū Ḥanīfa's statements is an indication that [an] undetailed [acknowledgement of] faith (*īmān ijmālī*) is acceptable. Therefore, as mentioned in the *Sharḥ al-ʿAqāʾid*, *īmān* is to confirm with the heart everything known by necessity (*bi 'l-ḍarūra*) to have been brought by

---

177 This is also the opinion of Abū Ḥanīfa as quoted by the great Ḥanafī ḥadīth master Imām Badr al-Dīn al-ʿAynī in his *ʿUmdat al-Qārī* (*Al-Taʿlīq al-Muyassar* 254).

178 Saʿd al-Dīn Masʿūd ibn ʿUmar al-Taftāzānī's (d. 791/1388) commentary on his *Al-Maqāṣid fī ʿIlm al-Kalām*.

the Messenger of Allāh ﷺ from Allāh, and that such belief is sufficient to fulfill the responsibility of being "a believer" and is not inferior to the status of knowing belief in detail. However, it is more preferable to say that the type of affirmation required needs to be in accordance to the circumstance—if one is questioned about belief in general, general affirmation is sufficient, whereas if the question is about specific aspects or tenets of belief, specific affirmation of those is necessary. Therefore, if one does not confirm the obligation of ritual prayer (*ṣalāt*) or the prohibition of intoxicants when asked about them, then one is not a believer. [252]

What is Known by Necessity to be Part of Faith

[Qārī] What is meant by "everything known by necessity to be part of the faith" is that which is known [about the religion] by the general laity without the need to employ syllogistic speculations (*naẓar*) [from major premises that are either sense perceptions or rational perceptions] or know proof-texts. This includes such things as the oneness of the Creator, the obligation of prayer, and the prohibition of wine. This condition is necessary since the denial of rulings derived through *ijtihād* (scholarly endeavor) is not considered unbelief by consensus. As for the one who adopts a non-literal interpretation of the transmitted texts regarding the resurrection of bodies, the originated nature (*ḥudūth*) of the world, or of the knowledge of Allāh encompassing the particulars (*juz'iyyāt*) of things, he is considered an unbeliever on account of such aspects being definitively known to be accepted in their literal meaning. This is different from what has been transmitted regarding those guilty of enormities not remaining in the Fire for eternity due to the conflicting narrations regarding such people.

Also, that general faith is not inferior to knowing belief in detail, only applies to the [legal] validity of attributing faith to people who have such faith, where both are equally deserving of the title "believer." There is no doubt though that possessing general belief is nowhere close to having detailed knowledge of faith and its tenets in the attainment of spiritual knowledge of Allāh and the perfection of one's faith (*iḥsān*). [252–253]

The faith of the inhabitants of the heavens and earth neither increases nor decreases in terms of the articles of faith; it increases and decreases in certainty and conviction. This means that the faith of the angels, humans, and jinn does not increase in the world or the Hereafter in terms of the articles of faith (*mu'man bihī*). Because whoever says, "I believe in Allāh and whatever has come from Allāh, and I believe in the Messenger of Allāh and whatever has come from the Messenger of Allāh," then he has believed in all that is obligatory [for him] to believe in and is thus a believer. However, a person who believes in only part of what is obligatory to believe (e.g., he believes in Allāh, His angels, His scriptures, and His messengers, and he does not believe in the Last Day), then he is an unbeliever. Whoever believes in Allāh and His Messenger and does not believe in anything else is also an unbeliever. Therefore, there is no difference between the one who believes in only some of the articles of faith and the one who disbelieves in all of them, in terms of them both being absolute unbelievers.[179]

Imām Abū Ḥanīfa says in *Al-Waṣiyya:*

> True faith does not increase or decrease for its decrease cannot be conceived of except in connection with the increase of unbelief, and its increase cannot be conceived of except in connection with the decrease of unbelief. How is it possible for a single person to be a believer and an unbeliever at the same time, when the believer is in truth a believer and an unbeliever is in truth an unbeliever? There is no doubt in belief just as there is no doubt in unbelief, as Allāh says, "They are in truth believers" (Qur'ān 8:4) and "Such are unbelievers in truth" (4:151). And the disobedient ones from the umma of Muḥammad ﷺ are all true believers and are not unbelievers.[180]

---

179 Imām Nawawī said in his *Fatāwā,* "The opinion of the majority of our theologians and others is that the essence (*nafs*) of belief itself does not increase or decrease. This is because if it allowed for increase [or decrease], it would become doubt and disbelief. Another group of our theologians said that the essence itself does not increase or decrease, but it increases with respect to its attributes and effects; this is according to what they have interpreted the verses of the Qur'ān, ḥadīths, and sayings of the predecessors" (*Al-Taʿlīq al-Muyassar* 256).

180 It states in *Al-Musāyara,* "Abū Ḥanīfa and his companions say 'faith does not increase or decrease.' From the Ashʿarīs, Imām al-Ḥaramayn and many others also adopted this view; however, the majority of the Ashʿarīs are of the opinion that it does increase and decrease. It has been said that the difference of opinion is based on the inclusion or exclusion of acts of obedience in the understanding of faith. According to the first position [of inclusion], faith increases with an increase in acts of obedience and decreases with a decrease in them. According to the second position, it does not increase, because faith is the name of firm conviction (*taṣdīq jāzim*) coupled with submission (*idhʿān*), and this does not change by an accretion in obedience or sin. However, this explanation is problematic, since even many of those who define faith as conviction only, say that it increases and decreases because of many clear texts. For example, Allāh Most High says,

Believers are equal in faith, in terms of the articles of faith, as has been mentioned, and divine oneness, which is to negate partnership in godhood (*ulūhiyya*), lordship (*rubūbiyya*), creation (*khāliqiyya*), preeternality (*qadīmiyya*), everlastingness (*azaliyya*), self-subsistence (*qayyūmiyya*), and sovereignty (*ṣamadiyya*). Whoever negates partnership in some of these aspects and not in the others is a polytheist (*mushrik*) and is not a monotheist (*muwaḥḥid*). In this sense, belief in divine oneness neither increases nor decreases in these terms. But in the sense of following (*taqlīd*) [certain evidences] and inferring (*istidlāl*) [certain proofs], it does increase and decrease [according to the amount of proofs one possesses or according to one's strength]. The belief in divine oneness of a person who infers using intellectual proofs, however, is not like the belief of a knower of Allāh (*ʿārif*) who has achieved spiritual unveilings (*mukāshafāt*), contemplative spiritual visions (*mushāhadāt*), divine gnosis (*maʿārif ilāhiyya*), and religious knowledge. Likewise, their faith will also be unequal in these terms.

dissimilar in actions, that is, physical and spiritual acts of obedience. This indicates that righteous actions are not [an integral] part of *īmān* (true

---

'It increased them in faith' (Qur'ān 8:2), and it is related that Ibn ʿUmar ﷺ said, 'We asked, "O Messenger of Allāh, does faith increase and decrease?" He said, "Yes, it increases until it brings its possessor into Paradise and decreases until it brings its possessor into Hellfire"' (Abū Isḥāq al-Thaʿlabī in his *Tafsīr;* and supported by a narration in *Bukhārī* and *Ibn Māja*). The theologians say that there is no rational reason to deny this, since the certainty (*yaqīn*) that is constituted from the conviction (*taṣdīq*) vacillates in strength between the clearest of immediate perceptions (*badīhiyyāt*) to the vaguest of syllogistic speculations (*naẓriyyāt*). Therefore, Ibrāhīm ﷺ, when addressed by Allāh 'Do you not believe?' answered, 'Yes, but to satisfy my heart' (Qur'ān 2:260). The Ḥanafīs, Imām al-Ḥaramayn, and others do not deny the increase and decrease with regard to outside aspects that are not the essence itself, and agree that by such fluctuation, the believers differ. It is reported that Abū Ḥanīfa said, 'I say that my faith is "like" (*ka*) the faith of Jibrīl but I do not say that it is "equal" (*mithl*) to the faith of Jibrīl,' because equality (*mithliyya*) dictates equality in every trait, whereas "likeness" (*tashbīh*) does not generate that equality. There is no one who equates the faith of individual people with the faith of the angels and the messengers. Rather, the faith of human beings differs from the latter, which begs the question, is the difference in the actual essence of faith or in aspects supplementary to it? The Ḥanafīs and those who agree with them deny the first possibility." Shaykh ʿUlwān al-Ḥamawī concludes that the difference is a semantic one. Therefore, whoever said there is increase and decrease in faith, they looked at the increase and decrease of its characteristics, such as its strength and weakness, and whoever denied the increase and decrease looked at its essence, that is, purely the conviction (*taṣdīq*) itself. This is the best way to view this issue according to the people of insight (Maydānī, *Sharḥ al-ʿAqīda al-Ṭaḥāwiyya* 100, 103). It is related that the faith of the angels does not increase or decrease, the faith of the prophets (upon them be peace) increases and does not decrease, the faith of regular humans or jinn increases and decreases, and the faith of the unrighteous (*fussāq*) decreases and does not increase (*Tuḥfat al-Murīd* 31).

faith), because actions increase and decrease. Some people perform all the five prayers (*ṣalawāt*) and others perform only a few. The prayer of the one who performs only a few is valid, not invalid; the fast of a person who fasts the full month of Ramaḍān is valid, and the fast of the one who fasts half of the month of Ramaḍān is also valid, not invalid. And so goes with all actions, whether obligatory or supererogatory. Faith (*īmān)* is different, because the faith of a person who believes in only some of the articles of faith is not valid, but invalid, as is the fast of a person who fasts only part of the day and then breaks his fast [prematurely].

Imām Abū Ḥanīfa says in *Al-Waṣiyya:*

> Actions are other than belief and belief is other than actions, the evidence of which is that in many instances, believers can be excused from certain actions, but it cannot be said that faith is also excused. For example, Allāh Most High lifts [the obligation of] ritual prayer (*ṣalāt*) from a menstruating woman, but it is not permitted to say that her faith is likewise excused or that she is commanded to abandon faith. The legislator [Muḥammad ﷺ] said [to the menstruating woman], "Leave fasting and make it up later" but it is not permitted to say, "Leave belief and make it up later." [Similarly,] it is permitted to say, "*Zakāt* is not obligatory on the impoverished," but it is not permitted to say, "Belief is not obligatory on the impoverished."

Islām is to surrender and to submit to the commands of Allāh Most High. It is stated in *Al-Ṣiḥāḥ*[181] that *taslīm* [in the Arabic text] means to express [complete] satisfaction with the command [of Allāh]; and *inqiyād* (compliance) means humility, fearfulness, satisfaction, and humbleness. Therefore, the meaning of *islām* is to be satisfied with the laws of Allāh—the obligations and prohibitions. To elaborate further, it means satisfaction with the commands of Allāh Most High that some things are obligatory, some are lawful, and some are unlawful, without any objection or disapproval. Hence, there is a literal difference between *īmān* and *islām,* because *īmān* literally means conviction as Allāh Most High says, "And you believe not what we say even when we speak the truth" (Qur'ān 12:17), whereas *islām* is defined as surrender. Conviction comes from a specific place, which is the heart, and the tongue

181 *Tāj al-Lugha wa Ṣiḥāḥ al-ʿArabiyya* by Abū Naṣr Ismāʿīl ibn Ḥammād al-Jawharī (393/1002).

is its interpreter. As for surrender, it is [an act] shared by the heart, tongue, and limbs. What indicates that *islām* is more general in the literal sense, is that hypocrites can be classified as *muslimīn* (surrenderers) literally, but not in terms of sacred law; whereas they cannot be classified as *mu'minīn* (true believers), neither literally nor in terms of sacred law. Allāh Most High says, "The desert Arabs say, 'We believe.' Say, 'You do not believe'; rather say, 'We submit'" (49:14). This is because of [their] affirmation of the tongue, which is *islām* in the literal sense, but not *īmān* in the literal sense, because of the absence of conviction in the heart.

However, *īmān* (faith) does not exist without *islām*, in terms of sacred law, because *īmān* is affirmation and conviction in the godhood (*ulūhiyya*) of Allāh Most High as He is with all His attributes and names. Therefore, whoever affirms and bears conviction, then the acceptance of the obligation of Allāh's commands and acceptance of the truthfulness of His commands and sacred laws is present within him. | nor *islām* without *īmān*, because *islām* is surrender and submission to the commands of Allāh, and they cannot be found except after conviction and affirmation. Thus, in terms of sacred law, a believer who is not a *muslim* or a *muslim* who is not a believer cannot be conceived. This is the understanding of the scholars regarding the interchangeability of the two words, and the oneness of their meaning. | they are as the back with the stomach, that is, *īmān* and *islām* are inseparable and do not become detached from one another, just as the back does not become detached from the stomach or the stomach from the back.

Dīn (religion) is a noun that encompasses *īmān, islām,* and all sacred laws. The word *dīn* is sometimes used and *īmān* is intended; sometimes it is used and *islām* is intended; sometimes it is used and the sacred law of Muḥammad ﷺ is intended; sometimes it is used and the sacred law of Mūsā عليه السلام is intended; and sometimes it is used and the sacred law of ʿĪsā عليه السلام or of some other messenger عليه السلام is intended.

KNOWING ALLĀH MOST HIGH

نَعْرِفُ اللهَ تَعَالٰى حَقَّ مَعْرِفَتِهِ كَمَا وَصَفَ اللهُ تَعَالٰى نَفْسَهُ فِيْ كِتَابِهِ بِجَمِيْعِ صِفَاتِهِ. وَلَيْسَ يَقْدِرُ أَحَدٌ أَنْ يَعْبُدَ اللهَ تَعَالٰى حَقَّ عِبَادَتِهِ كَمَا هُوَ أَهْلٌ لَهُ وَلٰكِنَّهُ يَعْبُدُهُ بِأَمْرِهِ كَمَا أَمَرَهُ بِكِتَابِهِ وَسُنَّةِ رَسُوْلِهِ. وَيَسْتَوِي الْمُؤْمِنُوْنَ كُلُّهُمْ فِي الْمَعْرِفَةِ وَالْيَقِيْنِ وَالتَّوَكُّلِ وَالْمَحَبَّةِ وَالرِّضَاءِ وَالْخَوْفِ وَالرَّجَاءِ وَالْإِيْمَانِ فِيْ ذٰلِكَ، وَيَتَفَاوَتُوْنَ فِيْمَا دُوْنَ الْأَيْمَانِ فِيْ ذٰلِكَ كُلِّهِ.

We know Allāh Most High as much as is His right to be known, as He has described His essence in His Book with all of His attributes. Nobody is able to worship Allāh Most High as much as is His right to be worshipped, to the extent He is worthy. However, a person worships Him at His command as He has commanded through His Book and the Sunna of His Messenger.

All believers are equal in knowledge, certainty, trust, love, satisfaction, fear, hope, and belief therein. However, they are dissimilar in everything other than in the belief in them all.

❀

We know Allāh Most High as much as is His right to be known, that is, we know Him to the extent He has made us responsible [to know Him], as He has described His essence in His Book with all of His attributes, that is, we know Allāh Most High as much as is His right to be known, through all His attributes with which He has described Himself in His great book, His pre-eternal speech [the Holy Qur'ān], and by all His Beautiful Names, which are found in the Qur'ān and Sunna. This means that we are capable of knowing Allāh by His attributes and names in detail, but we are not able to understand the nature of His essence. This is the meaning of the statement, "We do not know You as much as is the right of knowing You."

Nobody is able to worship Allāh Most High as much as is His right to be worshipped, to the extent He is worthy because worship is to exalt and glorify the Lord, and there is no limit to His exaltedness, glory, and grandeur. Therefore, it is not possible for a servant to produce any worship that befits the exaltedness, glory, and grandeur of Allāh. And nobody is able to worship Allāh Most High with worship that can be equal to [the amount of] His reward, because His reward and merit are beyond any limit or end, whereas the actions of servants have a limit and end. Likewise, a servant is not able to express gratitude to Allāh as much as is His right, because the servant's gratitude can be counted and enumerated, whereas the bounties of Allāh Most High are uncountable. Allāh Most High says, "If you count the bounty of Allāh you cannot enumerate it" (Qur'ān 14:34). However, a person worships Him at His command as He has commanded through His Book and the Sunna of His Messenger.

All believers are equal in knowledge/ [In the Arabic text,] *maʿrifa* literally means "to know," and technically, it means to know the names and attributes of Allāh Most High with sincerity in all conduct with Him. This means that all believers are equal, whether boy or girl, old man or woman, freeman or slave, in knowing; that is, in the obligation of knowing Allāh first, and then knowing the actions—the obligatory, required, lawful, and unlawful. | certainty/ *Yaqīn* literally means an awareness that is without doubt, and technically it means to see clearly through the strength of true faith, and not through proofs and evidences. Allāh Most High has mentioned *yaqīn* in the Qur'ān in three different ways: *ʿilm al-yaqīn*, *ʿayn al-yaqīn*, and *ḥaqq al-yaqīn*. *ʿIlm al-yaqīn* (knowledge or science of certainty) is that which is gained through hearing or contemplation; *ʿayn al-yaqīn* (eye or vision of certainty) is that which is gained through personally witnessing; and *ḥaqq al-yaqīn* (reality or truth of certainty) is [that which is gained] when they both come together.[182] The first [category] applies to the ordinary scholars (*ʿawāmm al-ʿulamā'*), the second for the elect scholars (*khawāṣṣ al-ʿulamā'*) and friends of Allāh (*awliyā'*), and the third for the prophets (upon them be peace). | trust/ *Tawakkul* is reliance in what Allāh Most High possesses and despair of what people possess. | love/ *Maḥabba* literally means love. Technically, love of a servant for Allāh Most

182 These have been compared respectively to hearing about the description of fire, seeing fire, and being consumed by fire.

High is a state a servant finds in his heart that cannot be described or defined by anything more accurate and easy to understand than the word *maḥabba* (love). Some learned scholars are of the opinion that the love of a servant for Allāh Most High is his glorifying Him, giving preference to satisfaction [with His commands], feeling restlessness in being away from Him, and always receiving abundant pleasure in His remembrance. | satisfaction/ *Riḍā'* means the happiness of the heart at the bitter ordainment of calamities and afflictions. | fear/ *Khawf* means to expect the undesirable to happen or something beloved to be lost. | hope/ *Rajā'* literally means hope, and technically means the attachment of the heart to the future acquisition of something cherished. Know that hope cannot exist without fear just as fear cannot exist without hope. They are inseparable, because hope without fear is false security and delusion, and fear without hope is hopelessness and despair of the mercy of Allāh Most High.

Fear and Hope

[Qārī] True and praiseworthy fear (*khawf*) is that which comes between its possessor and what Allāh Most High has prohibited. If it transcends beyond this, it could become hopelessness and despair. Praiseworthy hope is when a person performs acts of obedience through a light from Allāh and anticipates His reward, or when one commits a sin and then repents to Allāh hoping for forgiveness. As for one who is constantly indulging in excesses and wrongdoings and is entertaining hopes of mercy from Allāh Most High without doing good deeds, then this is a delusion, empty wishing, and false hope.

Abū ʿAlī al-Rawdhbārī (may Allāh have mercy on him) says, "Fear and hope are like the two wings of a bird, if they are both balanced, then the bird is stable in flight, and if there is an imbalance, then it could lead the bird to its death. This is similar in essence to what has been related of ʿUmar ﷺ. He said, "If it is announced in the assembly (*maḥshar*) [on the Day of Judgment] that only one person is to enter Paradise, I would hope that [that person] is me, and if it is announced that only one person will enter Hellfire, I would fear that that is me." Some have related that generally hope should dominate in a person because of the ḥadīth qudsī: "I am as My servant thinks of Me, so he should think of Me as he wishes" (*Bukhārī, Muslim*). However, others have said that it is better to let fear be dominant during one's youth and healthy times, and hope be dominant during old age and illness, based on what the

Messenger of Allāh ﷺ said, "None of you should die except while holding good opinions about his Lord" (*Muslim*). [270–271]

and belief therein. This means that all believers are equal in the belief that they are all equal on the basis (*aṣl*) of knowledge, conviction, trust, etc. However, they are dissimilar in everything other than in the belief in them all, that is, believers are dissimilar as regards the conditions mentioned [i.e., knowledge, certainty, trust, etc.], in their presence and absence and their increase and decrease. They are not dissimilar in their belief with respect to what has to be believed, but they are with respect to their conviction and certainty [in them].

[Qārī] Imām Ṭaḥāwī (may Allāh have mercy on him) said, "Faith is one; its people are equal in its foundation and the differential comes from fear (*khawf*), God-consciousness (*tuqā*), opposing the lower self, and upholding the worthier [actions]." [273]

ALLĀH
THE GENEROUS AND JUST

وَاللهُ تَعَالَى مُتَفَضِّلٌ عَلَى عِبَادِهِ، عَادِلٌ قَدْ يُعْطِي مِنَ الثَّوَابِ أَضْعَافَ مَا يَسْتَوْجِبُهُ الْعَبْدُ تَفَضُّلًا مِنْهُ، وَقَدْ يُعَاقِبُ عَلَى الذَّنْبِ عَدْلًا مِّنْهُ، وَقَدْ يَعْفُو فَضْلًا مِّنْهُ.

Allāh Most High is kind and just to His servants: He may give many times more reward to a servant than he is entitled to out of His kindness, He may punish for a sin out of His justice, and He may forgive out of His generosity.

❁

Allāh Most High is kind and just to His servants: He may give many times more reward to a servant than he is entitled to, that is, [He gives] whatever the servant is entitled to according to the promise of Allāh and His command. Allāh Most High says, "Whoever brings a good deed will receive tenfold the like thereof" (Qur'ān 6:161). The Messenger of Allāh ﷺ said, "All the actions of the son of Ādam are multiplied—good deeds are multiplied tenfold to seven hundred" (*Muslim,* "al-Ṣiyām," 1945). | out of His kindness. This is to negate any self-entitlement [on the part of the servant], because the promise and command of reward is not obligatory on Allāh Most High, but rather, it is out of His generosity and choice [to fulfill]. He may punish for a sin out of His justice because that is administration in His own dominion, whereas oppression (*ẓulm*) is administration in somebody else's dominion without consent. | and He may forgive out of His generosity. He sometimes forgives sins, whether they are minor sins or enormities and whether they have been repented from or not. His forgiveness of whomever He wills is generosity and kindness, not a right of the servant. *'Afw* (forgiveness) means the cancellation of punishment from a person who should have been punished. Allāh Most High says, "It is He who accepts repentance from His servants and pardons evil deeds" (Qur'ān 42:25).

The Right of Allāh to Recompense One Servant More than Another

[Qārī] As for the saying of one commentator, "It is not for Allāh to give more reward to one of two people who are equal in worship and certitude than what He gives to the other, nor to forgive one of two people who are equal in sin and not the other, since there is no discrepancy in His favor and justice," it is a grave error and in opposition to the Qur'ān and the Sunna. Moreover, it constitutes a judgment on Allāh Most High in the realm of His predestination (*qadar*) and will (*irāda*), [which is wholly inconsistent] with His statement: "All bounties are in the hand of Allāh; He grants them to whom He pleases" (Qur'ān 3:73). [275]

INTERCESSION AND SOME OTHER ESCHATOLOGICAL REALITIES

وَشَفَاعَةُ الْأَنْبِيَاءِ عَلَيْهِمُ الصَّلَاةُ وَالسَّلَامُ حَقٌّ، وَشَفَاعَةُ النَّبِيِّ عَلَيْهِ الصَّلَاةُ وَالسَّلَامُ لِلْمُؤْمِنِيْنَ الْمُذْنِبِيْنَ وَلِأَهْلِ الْكَبَائِرِ مِنْهُمْ الْمُسْتَوْجِبِيْنَ الْعِقَابَ حَقٌّ ثَابِتٌ. وَوَزْنُ الْأَعْمَالِ بِالْمِيْزَانِ يَوْمَ الْقِيَامَةِ حَقٌّ. وَحَوْضُ النَّبِيِّ عَلَيْهِ الصَّلَاةُ وَالسَّلَامُ حَقٌّ. وَالْقِصَاصُ فِيْمَا بَيْنَ الْخُصُوْمِ بِالْحَسَنَاتِ يَوْمَ الْقِيَامَةِ حَقٌّ، وَإِنْ لَمْ تَكُنْ لَهُمُ الْحَسَنَاتُ فَطُرِحَ السَّيِّئَاتُ عَلَيْهِمْ حَقٌّ جَائِزٌ. وَالْجَنَّةُ وَالنَّارُ مَخْلُوْقَتَانِ الْيَوْمَ لَا تَفْنَيَانِ أَبَدًا، وَلَا تَمُوْتُ الْحُوْرُ الْعِيْنُ أَبَدًا، وَلَا يَفْنٰى عِقَابُ اللهِ تَعَالٰى وَثَوَابُهُ سَرْمَدًا.

Intercession by the prophets (upon them be peace) is a reality; and intercession by the Prophet ﷺ for sinful believers and for believers guilty of enormities who deserve to be punished is an established reality. The weighing of deeds on the Scale on the Day of Judgment is a reality. The Watering Pool of the Prophet ﷺ is a reality. Settling of accounts with good deeds between litigants on the Day of Judgment is a reality; if they do not possess good deeds, then bad deeds being cast on them is true and possible. Paradise and Hellfire have already been created and will never cease to exist, the wide-eyed maidens will never die, and the punishment and reward of Allāh will never end.

❁

Intercession by the prophets (upon them be peace) is a reality; and intercession by the Prophet ﷺ for sinful believers and for believers guilty of enormities who deserve to be punished is an established reality through the Qur'ān, Sunna, and the consensus of the umma. Allāh Most High says, "Who is there that will intercede with Him save by His leave" (Qur'ān 2:255). This verse establishes the right of intercession for those who have been permitted to intercede. The Messenger of Allāh ﷺ said, "My intercession will be for those guilty of enormities from my umma. Whoever rejects it will not receive it."[183] The Messenger of Allāh ﷺ also said, "Three types of people will intercede on the Day of Judgment: the prophets, then the scholars, and then the martyrs (*Ibn Māja,* "al-Zuhd," 4304).

The Intercession of the Prophet ﷺ

[Qārī] Further proof for this is in what Allāh says: "Then will no intercession of (any) intercessors profit them" (Qur'ān 74:48), the implied meaning (*mafhūm*) of which is that it will benefit the believers, and "The Day that the Spirit and the angels will stand forth in ranks, none shall speak except those who are permitted by (Allāh) Most Gracious, and He will say what is right" (78:38). Likewise, the scholars (*ʿulamā'*), the friends of Allāh (*awliyā'*), the martyrs, the destitute, the children of believers, and those patient throughout hardships will also be permitted to intercede there. [277]

Imām Abū Ḥanīfa says in *Al-Waṣiyya:* "The intercession of our Prophet Muḥammad ﷺ is a reality for all those who are believers from among the people of Paradise, even if it is one guilty of enormities."[184]

The Weighing of Deeds

The weighing of deeds on the Scale on the Day of Judgment is a reality. Allāh Most High says, "The weighing on that day is true" (Qur'ān 7:8). To affirm the weighing (*wazn*) on the Day of Judgment is from among the beliefs of the Ahl al-Sunna wa 'l-Jamāʿa, and Allāh Most High knows best its description. The Great Imām states in *Kitāb al-Waṣiyya,* "The Scale is a reality, as He Most High says, 'We shall set up Scales of Justice for the Day of Judgment' (21:47),

183 *Tirmidhī,* "Ṣifat al-Qiyāma wa 'l-Raqā'iq wa 'l-Waraʿ," 2360. This version does not contain the second sentence "Whoever rejects it . . . ."

184 There will be many types of intercession: (1) intercession by the Messenger ﷺ for the whole of mankind [on the Day of Assembly] in hastening the reckoning and bringing about relief from the lengthy standing and anxiety of waiting on that day, (2) bringing a group of believers into Paradise without reckoning; this type of intercession is specific to the Messenger ﷺ too as Nawawī has said, though Ibn Ḥajar al-ʿAsqalānī and Ibn Daqīq al-ʿId have reservations about that, (3) intercession for people who are deserving of Hellfire whereupon they do not enter it, (4) intercession for the believers who are in Hellfire; this one is not specific to the Messenger ﷺ), (5) and intercession for the elevation of a person's status in Paradise. Not even the Muʿtazila deny this intercession just as they do not deny the first one (see Maydānī, *Sharḥ al-Ṭaḥāwiyya* 80 and Sakhāwī, *Al-Qawl al-Badīʿ* 374).

and the reading of the Books [of deeds] is a reality, as Allāh Most High says, 'Read your book! Your soul suffices you this day as a reckoner against you'" (17:14).

The Watering Pool

The Watering Pool of the Prophet ﷺ is a reality. The Messenger of Allāh ﷺ said, "The size of my watering pool (*ḥawḍ*) is a month's journey, and its sides are all equal. Its water is whiter than milk, its fragrance superior to that of musk, and its drinking vessels number like the stars in the sky. Whoever drinks from it will never experience thirst again."[185]

[Qārī] Imām Qurṭubī[186] says, "They are two pools. One is before the Bridge (*ṣirāṭ*) and the Scale, according to the more reliable opinion. People will come out thirsty from their graves and will come to the pool before the Scale and Bridge. The other pool is in Paradise and both are called *Al-Kawthar.*" [283]

Settling of Accounts

Settling of accounts with good deeds between litigants on the Day of Judgment is a reality; if they do not possess good deeds, then bad deeds being cast on them is true and possible. The Messenger of Allāh ﷺ said, "Whoever is guilty of a wrong against his brother, regarding an issue of honor or something else, then he should expiate for it today, before [the time comes] when there will be no *dīnārs* or *dirhams.* If one possesses good deeds, they will be taken from him in proportion to his wrongdoings. If he does not possess any good deeds, then the sins of the other person will be taken and cast on him."[187] The Messenger of Allāh ﷺ once asked, "Do you know who is bankrupt?" The Companions replied, "The bankrupt is one who has neither *dirhams* nor any property." The Messenger of Allāh ﷺ said, "The bankrupt one from my umma is one who will appear on the Day of Judgment with prayer (*ṣalāt*), fasts, and *zakāt* [as his deeds], but he will come having sworn at somebody, slandered somebody,

---

185 *Bukhārī,* "al-Riqāq," 6093 without the words, "Its sides are all equal"; *Muslim,* "al-Faḍā'il," 4244 with "whiter than silver" in place of "whiter than milk."

186 Muḥammad ibn Aḥmad ibn Abī Bakr ibn Faraḥ, Abū ʿAbdillāh al-Anṣārī al-Khazrajī the great Mālikī scholar (d. 671/1272) and author of the famous exegetic work *Al-Jāmiʿ li Aḥkām al-Qur'ān;* this work established him as one of the greatest imāms of *tafsīr.*

187 *Bukhārī,* "al-Riqāq," 6053 without the words, "Either regarding an issue of honor or something else."

consumed somebody's wealth, shed the blood of somebody, and beaten up somebody. Each one of those people will be given [their share] from his good deeds. If his good deeds are exhausted before his burdens are paid off, then sins from those people will be taken and cast on him, after which he will be cast in Hellfire" (*Aḥmad,* "Bāqī musnad al-mukthirīn," 8487).

The Use of the Terms "True" and "Possible"

[Qārī] "True and possible," these expressions are used [here in *Al-Fiqh al-Akbar*] for emphasis and their meaning is clear: "possible by reason and transmitted by narration." [282]

Paradise and Hellfire

Paradise, abode of everlasting reward, and Hellfire, abode of everlasting punishment, have already been created/ Allāh Most High says, "And vie with one another for forgiveness from your Lord, and for a garden whose breadth is as the heavens and earth, prepared for the God-fearing" (Qur'ān 3:133), and He says, "And fear the Fire that has been prepared for the unbelievers" (3:131). A past tense verb is one that indicates the occurrence of an action in a time that precedes the time the information is given to you. Hence, Paradise and Hellfire were created before Jibrīl ﷺ conveyed to Muḥammad ﷺ that "[Paradise] has been prepared for the believers" and "[Hellfire] has been prepared for the unbelievers" [where the past tense *uʿiddat* has been used]. Similarly, "We appoint" in the verse "That is the abode of the Hereafter; We appoint it for those who desire not high-handedness in the earth, nor corruption. The good end is for the God-fearing" (28:83) means "We give" just as in the verse "And I appoint for him ample wealth" (74:12), i.e., "I give him." | and will never cease to exist. This means that destruction will befall them, but not permanently; it will be temporary, because Allāh Most High says, "Everything will perish save His countenance" (28:88).[188] Or it means that destruction will not befall

188 The Muslims considered Jahm ibn Ṣafwān to have committed unbelief when he claimed that Paradise and Hellfire would come to an end. Ibn Taymiya (may Allāh have mercy on him) also claimed that Hell would come to an end, using unestablished narrations as proof. He was considered to have erred or even to have committed unbelief by some of his contemporaries like Ibn al-Subkī, who wrote a rebuttal of his views in *Al-Iʿtibār bi Baqā' al-Janna wa 'l-Nār* (In Consideration of the Endurance of Paradise and Hell) among other works. Likewise, Muḥammad ibn Ismāʿīl al-Ṣanʿānī al-Yamānī wrote *Rafʿ al-Astār li Ibṭāl Adillat al-Qā'ilīn bi Fanā' al-Nār* (Lifting the Veils to Invalidate the Proofs of the Proponents of the Extinction of Hellfire). Nāṣir al-Dīn

them at all, in which case the words of Allāh "Everything will perish save His countenance" (28:88) means that every possible thing is destructible in itself, in the sense that possible existence (*al-wujūd al-imkānī*) in contrast to necessary existence (*al-wujūd al-wājibī*) is like non-existence, and non-essential continuity (*al-baqā' al-ʿāriḍī*) in contrast to essential continuity (*al-baqā' al-dhātī*) is like destruction (*fanā'*).

Where is Paradise and Hellfire?

[Qārī] Among other opinions, the most reliable one is that Paradise is in the Heavens. This is indicated by the words of Allāh: "By the lote-tree of the utmost boundary, nigh unto which is the Garden of Abode" (Qur'ān 53:14–15), and the words of His Messenger: "The ceiling of Paradise is the Throne of the Merciful" (*Tirmidhī, Aḥmad*). Other weaker opinions exist which state that it is on the earth, or that one should refrain from making a judgment since only Allāh knows. As for the Hellfire, it is said to be under the earth, or above it, or that one should refrain from making a judgment since only Allāh knows. [285]

Imām Abū Ḥanīfa says in *Al-Waṣiyya:* "Paradise and Hellfire are a reality, and they have already been created for their inhabitants, as Allāh Most High says regarding the believers, '[Paradise] that has been prepared for the God-fearing' (Qur'ān 3:133) and regarding the unbelievers, '[Hellfire] that has been prepared for the unbelievers' (3:131). Allāh created them for reward and punishment." Imām Abū Ḥanīfa also says in *Al-Waṣiyya,* "The people of Paradise will be forever in Paradise and the people of Hellfire will be forever in Hellfire, as Allāh Most High says regarding the believers, 'Such are rightful owners of the Garden. They will abide therein forever' (2:82) and regarding the unbelievers, He says, 'Such are rightful owners of the Fire. They will abide therein forever'" (2:81).

---

al-Albānī published this work and did not negate the attribution of this opinion to Ibn Taymiya. It is possible, though, that Ibn Taymiya may have repented from this opinion toward the end of his life, by the will of Allāh (*Al-Taʿlīq al-Muyassar* 289). Ibn Abi 'l-ʿIzz in his commentary on the *Ṭaḥāwiyya* wrongly presents it as an alternative view of a "group" of the *salaf* and *khalaf* without stating that it is Ibn Taymiya or Ibn al-Qayyim al-Jawziyya from whom it originated, though Albānī rejects it by stating that the view has not been reported from any of the *salaf*" (see *Sharḥ al-ʿAqīda al-Ṭaḥāwiyya* 424).

The Bridge

[Qārī] The Prophet ﷺ said, "Verily the Bridge is a causeway laid out on the back of Hellfire (*jahannam*), thinner than a hair and sharper than a sword." In another report, it states, "The believers pass over it like the blink of an eye, or like a flash of lightning, or like a bird, or like a high-pedigree horse, or a camel, so there will be one passing over it safe and sound, and one crossing it after being poked and grazed, and one gathered up in Hellfire" (*Bukhārī, Muslim*). [286]

The Wide-Eyed Maidens of Paradise and Allāh's Reward and Punishment

The wide-eyed maidens will never die/ that is, they will never become non-existent. It is reported from ʿAlī ؓ that the Messenger of Allāh ﷺ said, "There will be a gathering of wide-eyed maidens in Paradise. They will raise their voices with a sound unlike anything the creation would have ever heard. They will say, 'We are the ever remaining ones; we will never perish. We are the tender ones; we will never become wretched. We are the satisfied ones; we will never become angry. Glad tidings to the one who is for us and we for them'" (*Tirmidhī*, "Ṣifat al-Janna," 2488). | and the punishment and reward of Allāh will never end. Allāh Most High says, "And in the chastisement they shall dwell forever" (Qur'ān 5:80), and He says, "And those who believe and do deeds of righteousness, We shall admit them to gardens underneath which rivers flow, therein dwelling forever and ever; the promise of Allāh in truth" (4:122). The verses and ḥadīths regarding the inhabitants of Paradise and the inhabitants of Hellfire living forever and ever are numerous.

ALLĀH GUIDES AND LEAVES ASTRAY

وَاللهُ تَعَالٰى يَهْدِيْ مَنْ يَشَاءُ فَضْلًا مِّنْهُ وَيُضِلُّ مَنْ يَشَاءُ عَدْلًا مِنْهُ: وَإِضْلَالُهُ خِذْلَانُهُ. وَتَفْسِيْرُ الْخِذْلَانِ أَنْ لَا يُوَفِّقَ الْعَبْدَ إِلٰى مَا يَرْضَاهُ عَنْهُ، وَهُوَ عَدْلٌ مِّنْهُ، وَكَذَا عُقُوْبَةُ الْمَخْذُوْلِ عَلَى الْمَعْصِيَةِ. وَلَا يَجُوْزُ أَنْ نَقُوْلَ: إِنَّ الشَّيْطَانَ يَسْلُبُ الْإِيْمَانَ مِنَ الْعَبْدِ الْمُؤْمِنِ قَهْرًا وَجَبْرًا، وَلٰكِنْ نَقُوْلُ: الْعَبْدُ يَدَعُ الْأَيْمَانَ فَحِيْنَئِذٍ يَسْلُبُهُ مِنْهُ الشَّيْطَانُ.

Allāh Most High guides aright whom He wills, out of His generosity; and leaves to stray whom He wills, with justice. His leaving a person to stray is His forsaking him, and the explanation of *khidhlān* (forsaking) is that He not grant a servant divine guidance toward what pleases Him: this is justice on His part. Likewise is [His] punishing the forsaken for disobedience.

It is not permissible for us to state that Satan takes away faith from a faithful servant by force or compulsion. We state instead that the servant abandons his faith, and then Satan takes it away from him.

❁

Allāh Most High guides aright whom He wills, out of His generosity; and leaves to stray whom He wills, with justice. His leaving a person to stray is His forsaking him, and the explanation of *khidhlān* (forsaking) is that He not grant a servant divine guidance toward what pleases Him: this is justice on His part. Likewise is [His] punishing the forsaken for disobedience; that is, this is just. There is no oppression in it, because Allāh Most High is not an oppressor by forsaking [a person] or by punishing the forsaken one for [his] sin, because oppression (*ẓulm*) means to place something out of its rightful place, whereas Allāh Most High administers in His own dominion, not in another's dominion. The Great Imām has defined Allāh's *iḍlāl* (leaving somebody to stray) as *khidhlān,* and has explained *khidhlān* as His not granting a servant *tawfiq* (divine guidance) toward that which pleases Him. Therefore, *hidāya* (guidance) here means *tawfiq,* i.e., to make the means in accordance with bliss and virtue.

[Qārī] Allāh says, "The one whom Allāh (in His plan) wills to guide, He opens his breast to Islam" (Qur'ān 6:125); that is, He expands his breast and illuminates it for divine oneness. The sign of this is the servant's turning toward the eternal abode, withdrawing from the deceptive abode, and achieving a readiness for death before its arrival (*ʿAbd al-Razzāq, Ibn Abī Ḥātim*). [291]

It is not permissible for us to state that Satan takes away faith, the affirmation and conviction, from a faithful servant by force or compulsion, because the aim of Satan by taking away the faith of a person is to have him punished. Hence, employing force or compulsion would not fulfill this aim, because a believer is not punishable if he is forced into having his faith taken away. Satan, therefore, does not take it by force. We state instead that the servant abandons his faith, and then Satan takes it away from him, because if Satan takes it away before the servant abandons it [himself], it would mean that Allāh Most High forces the servant into unbelief. And we have learned that Allāh Most High does not create unbelief in a servant's heart without the servant's own preference and liking for it.

ESCHATOLOGICAL REALITIES OF THE GRAVE

وَسُؤَالُ مُنْكَرٍ وَنَكِيْرٍ حَقٌّ كَائِنٌ فِي الْقَبْرِ. وَإِعَادَةُ الرُّوْحِ إِلَى الْجَسَدِ فِيْ قَبْرِهِ حَقٌّ. وَضَغْطَةُ الْقَبْرِ وَعَذَابُهُ حَقٌّ كَائِنٌ لِلْكُفَّارِ كُلِّهِمْ، وَلِبَعْضِ عُصَاةِ الْمُؤْمِنِيْنَ حَقٌّ جَائِزٌ.

Questioning by Munkar and Nakīr is a reality and occurs in the grave. The returning of the soul to the body in one's grave is a reality. The constricting of the grave and punishment therein is a reality befalling all unbelievers, and a reality and possibility in the case of some disobedient believers.

❁

The Intermediate Realm and the Hereafter

[Qārī] The shaykh of our shaykhs, Imām Suyūṭī, has compiled the narrations regarding the affairs of the intermediate realm (*barzakh*) and the Hereafter in his two works, *Sharḥ al-Ṣudūr fī Aḥwāl al-Qubūr* (The Expanding of the Breasts on the States of the Grave) and *Al-Budūr al-Sāfira fī Aḥwāl al-Ākhira* (The Unveiled Moons on the States of the Hereafter). You should refer to these books if you wish to understand these matters and remove all conflict from your mind.

Among the general proofs [dealing with punishment in the intermediate realm] is, "In front of the Fire will they be brought, morning and evening" (Qur'ān 40:46); that is, morning and night prior to the Resurrection, and this will be in the grave as is said, "And on the day that judgment will be established: 'Cast the people of Pharaoh into the severest penalty!'" (40:46). The meaning of their being brought in front of the Fire is that they will be burned in it until the Day of Judgment and this [punishment] will afflict their souls (*arwāḥ*). Likewise, another verse says, "And verily We make them taste the lower punishment before the greater" (32:21). [293]

Questioning by Munkar and Nakīr is a reality and occurs in the grave. The returning of the soul to the body in one's grave is a reality. The constricting of the grave and punishment therein is a reality befalling all unbelievers, and a reality and possibility in the case of some disobedient believers. *Munkar* is a passive participle (*mafʿūl*), and *Nakīr* on the pattern of *faʿīl* conveys the meaning of the passive participle. These angels have been given these names because the deceased will not recognize them and will not have seen their forms [before]. In *Al-Ṣiḥāḥ* it states that Munkar and Nakīr are the names of two angels. It is related in *Al-Maṣābīḥ* from Abū Hurayra ؓ that the Messenger of Allāh ﷺ said, "When the deceased is buried, two blue [eyed] dark angels approach him. One of them is called Munkar and the other Nakīr. They ask him, 'What did you used to say about this man?' [i.e., the Messenger of Allāh ﷺ]. If the deceased is a believer, he will reply, 'He is the servant of Allāh and His Messenger. I testify that there is no one worthy of worship but Allah and Muḥammad is His Messenger.' They will then say, 'We knew you would say that.' His grave is then expanded seventy-by-seventy cubits and lit up for him, and he is told to sleep. He asks them to go back to his household and inform them [of his state]. They instruct him to sleep—sleep like a bridegroom who is not awakened but by the most beloved person to him of his household—until Allāh Most High will raise him from his sleeping place. And if the deceased is a hypocrite or an unbeliever, he will answer, 'I used to hear people saying something, and I said the same. I do not know.' The angels say to him, 'We knew you would say that.' The ground is ordered to contract so that it contracts upon him. His ribs become interlocked, and he remains in the grave in punishment, until Allāh Most High raises him from this resting place" (*Tirmidhī,* "al-Janā'iz," 991).

[Qārī] This tightening in the grave is a reality and occurs even to the complete believer. However, [for the believer] the earth is initially tight, and then Allāh Most High causes it to expand and widen as far as the person's eye can see. Some have said that for the believer, it will feel like a compassionate mother's embrace when her son returns from a long journey. [293]

Imām Abū Ḥanīfa says in *Al-Waṣiyya:* "We declare that the punishment in the grave is certain to occur, and the questioning by Munkar and Nakīr is a reality because of ḥadīths that have been transmitted."

Life in the Grave

[Qārī] The scholars of the truth are in agreement that Allāh Most High creates in the dead person a small component of life in the grave by which he can experience pain or pleasure. However, they have disagreed as to whether or not the spirit (*rūḥ*) is actually returned to the body. The position transmitted from Abū Ḥanīfa is of refraining from making a judgment, except that here, his statement indicates that it is returned, because answering the angels is a purposeful action and cannot be imagined without the spirit. Some have said it is imaginable: do you not see that the spirit of a sleeping person leaves the body and remains associated with it such that a person still experiences pain and pleasure? [294]

The Spirit (Rūḥ)

[Qārī] There is difference of opinion as to the reality of the spirit (*rūḥ*). It has been said that it is a subtle body that is intricately infused with the flesh just as water permeates a fresh stick, and Allāh has established a system by which life continues as long as the spirit resides within the body. [Conversely,] death takes over when it separates from the body. A group from among the Ahl al-Sunna wa 'l-Jamāʿa have described it as a substance flowing through the body just as rose water flows within the rose. This does not necessarily contradict what Allāh says, "Say, the spirit is by command of my Lord, and you are not given anything of knowledge but a little" (Qur'ān 17:85), for all commands belong to Allāh; or that speaking of the genus of the spirit in general terms is part of the little knowledge given, although the stronger and superior position is that its knowledge be completely consigned to Allāh. This is the opinion of the majority of the Ahl al-Sunna wa 'l-Jamāʿa. [298]

Imām Abū Ḥanīfa says in *Al-Waṣiyya:* "We declare that Allāh Most High will revive these souls after death and resurrect them on a Day whose length is fifty thousand years for repayment and reward and to pay off the rights owed, as He Most High says, 'Allāh will raise up all who are in the graves'" (Qur'ān 22:7).

EXPRESSING THE ATTRIBUTES OF ALLĀH IN OTHER THAN ARABIC

وَكُلُّ شَيْءٍ ذَكَرَهُ الْعُلَمَاءُ بِالْفَارِسِيَّةِ مِنْ صِفَاتِ اللهِ تَعَالٰى عَزَّ اسْمُهُ فَجَائِزٌ الْقَوْلُ بِهِ، سِوَى الْيَدِ بِالْفَارِسِيَّةِ.
وَيَجُوْزُ أَنْ يُقَالَ بروئ خدااىٔ عَزَّ وَجَلَّ بِلَا تَشْبِيْهٍ وَلَا كَيْفِيَّةٍ.

It is permissible to express all the attributes of Allāh Most High that the scholars have expressed in Persian, with the exception of hand in Persian. It is permissible to say *rūe khudā* (the Countenance of God) Most Mighty and Majestic without any comparison or modality.

❁

It is permissible to express all the attributes of Allāh Most High that the scholars have expressed in Persian, that is, in any language other than Arabic. Likewise, it is permissible to express all other terms the scholars have expressed in other languages concerning the names of Allāh Most High. Hence, it is permissible to say *khudāy taʿālā tawānast* (God Most High is the All-powerful). | with the exception of hand in Persian, that is, in non-Arabic. Hence, it is not permissible to say *daste khudā* (the Hand of God) [in Persian]. It is permissible to say *rūe khudā* (the Countenance of God) Most Mighty and Majestic without any comparison or modality.[189]

---

189 It seems as if there were negative or problematic connotations with using the translated term for hand in Persian, *"dast,"* and thus the prohibition of the term in that language. Shahrastānī writes that it was out of greater scrupulousness on the part of some of the predecessors that they would avoid translating such terms into Persian (*Al-Milal wa 'l-Niḥal* 1:105). This is not necessarily the case with the English language. Employing translations of such terms in any language will be governed by the usage of scholars fluent in that language as Imām Abū Ḥanīfa has indicated. See also Bayāḍī's *Ishārat al-Marām* 190–191. The phrase "with the exception of hand in Persian" and

[Qārī] What is understood from this is that it is permissible for the scholars [of other languages] and others to express the attributes of Allāh [in those languages] by mentioning, for instance, the hand (*yad*) according to the way they have been revealed [in the texts, while specifically avoiding anthropomorphic interpretation or insinuation]. [301]

---

the next sentence above is found in the manuscripts of *Al-Fiqh al-Akbar* we consulted with the exception of MS Azhar 2756-133.

THE CLOSENESS AND DISTANCE OF A PERSON TO ALLĀH MOST HIGH

وَلَيْسَ قُرْبُ اللهِ تَعَالٰى وَلَا بُعْدُهُ مِنْ طَرِيْقِ طُوْلِ الْمَسَافَةِ وَقِصَرِهَا وَلٰكِنْ عَلٰى مَعْنَى الْكَرَامَةِ وَالْهَوَانِ.
وَالْمُطِيْعُ قَرِيْبٌ مِّنْهُ بِلَا كَيْفٍ، وَالْعَاصِيْ بَعِيْدٌ مِّنْهُ بِلَا كَيْفٍ، وَالْقُرْبُ وَالْبُعْدُ وَالْإِقْبَالُ يَقَعُ عَلٰى الْمُنَاجِيْ.
وَكَذٰلِكَ جِوَارُهُ فِي الْجَنَّةِ وَالْوُقُوْفُ بَيْنَ يَدَيْهِ بِلَا كَيْفِيَّةٍ.

The closeness and distance of Allāh is not in terms of long and short distances; rather, it is in terms of honor and humiliation. The obedient is close to Him without description, and the disobedient is far from Him without description. Closeness, distance, and turning toward are applied to a servant who converses intimately with Allāh. Likewise without modality are the servant's closeness to Allāh in Paradise and his standing before Him.

❀

The closeness and distance of Allāh, that is, the closeness of a servant to Allāh Most High and his distance from Allāh Most High, is not in terms of long and short distances: because closeness and distance in those terms can only be imagined in a possible [or created] thing (*mumkin*) and in something which is spatial (*mutaḥayyiz*) in a particular place or direction, but Allāh Most High is transcendent of place, confines, and direction, because He is neither substance (*jawhar*) nor accident (*ʿaraḍ*). | rather, it is in terms of honor and humiliation,[190] that is, the closeness of a servant to Allāh Most High signifies

190 This part of the text appears such in *Al-Fiqh al-Akbar,* in all the printed editions and manuscripts of *Al-Fiqh al-Akbar,* and Maghnīsāwī's commentary. However, there are slight differences in all editions and manuscripts of Qārī's commentary, which read "And *neither (wa lā)* in terms of honor and humiliation, *but* (*walākin*) the obedient is close to Him without description. . ." in place

his having honor and perfection, and the distance of a servant from Allāh signifies his being humiliated and imperfect. Using closeness for honor and distance for humiliation is a metaphor that employs cause in place of the effect [since being close to Allāh is a cause for honor and farness from Him is a cause for humiliation]. The obedient is close to Him without description/ His closeness to Allāh Most High is not in terms of the [physical] shortness of distance or direction. | and the disobedient is far from Him without description. His distance from Allāh Most High is not in terms of the [physical] length of distance or direction. Closeness, distance, and turning toward are applied to a servant who converses intimately with Allāh, that is, applied to a servant who is submissive to Allāh and who earnestly entreats Him; they are not applied to Allāh Most High. Do you not see that closeness and farness is defined as honor and humiliation, whereas Allāh Most High is closer to a servant than his jugular vein? Likewise without modality are the servant's closeness to Allāh in Paradise and his standing before Him, that is, this does not carry its apparent meaning, but is one of the ambiguities (*mutashābihāt*). Imām Ghazālī states, "Closeness to and distance from Allāh Most High are attributes of animals and beasts. To imbue oneself with noble character, which is the divine character, is in fact closeness in description, not place [i.e., physical closeness]. One who is not close but then becomes close is transformed from a state of wretchedness to bliss, by virtue of his good deeds."[191]

---

of "*Rather,* it is in terms of honor and humiliation. *The* obedient is close to Him without..." as it is here. Qārī's comments on this text are: "And neither in terms of honor and humiliation, that is, they cannot be interpreted in the meaning of honor and favor and humiliation and degradation, for this is an interpretation in the realm of the people of knowledge (*ahl al-ʿirfān*), whereas the Great Imām has kept it with certainty of the ambiguous matters (*mutashābihāt*). This is why he says, "but the obedient is close to Him without description..." (*Minaḥ al-Rawḍ al-Azhar* 303).

It is difficult to say which is the more authentic rendering, since one cannot be dismissed over the other as being incorrect; they both express sound positions. Furthermore, both negate the literal meaning of closeness and distance. However, where one goes on to negate a possible metaphorical interpretation, the other seeks to establish it. Based on Qārī's commentary of the passage and the general methodology of the Imām when dealing with the attributes of Allāh being that of complete consignment (*tafwīḍ*), it could be said that the rendering in Qārī's edition may be closer to accuracy. This however is not supported by the rendering in the independent manuscripts of *Al-Fiqh al-Akbar.* And Allāh knows best.

191 This final part, "Is transformed from a state of wretchedness to bliss through the virtue of his good deeds," is only found in the published edition and not in any of the manuscripts.

MORE CONCERNING THE QUR'ĀN

وَالْقُرْآنُ مُنَزَّلٌ عَلٰى رَسُوْلِ اللهِ صَلَّى اللهُ عَلَيْهِ وَسَلَّمَ وَهُوَ فِي الْمَصَاحِفِ مَكْتُوْبٌ. وَآيَاتُ الْقُرْآنِ فِيْ مَعْنَى الْكَلَامِ كُلُّهَا مُسْتَوِيَةٌ فِي الْفَضِيْلَةِ وَالْعَظَمَةِ، إِلَّا أَنَّ لِبَعْضِهَا فَضِيْلَةَ الذِّكْرِ وَفَضِيْلَةَ الْمَذْكُوْرِ مِثْلُ آيَةِ الْكُرْسِيِّ، لِأَنَّ الْمَذْكُوْرَ فِيْهَا جَلَالُ اللهِ تَعَالٰى وَعَظَمَتُهُ وَصِفَاتُهُ فَاجْتَمَعَتْ فِيْهَا فَضِيْلَتَانِ: فَضِيْلَةُ الذِّكْرِ وَفَضِيْلَةُ الْمَذْكُوْرِ، وَلِبَعْضِهَا فَضِيْلَةُ الذِّكْرِ فَحَسْبُ مِثْلُ قِصَّةِ الْكُفَّارِ، وَلَيْسَ لِلْمَذْكُوْرِ فِيْهَا فَضْلٌ وَهُمُ الْكُفَّارُ. وَكَذٰلِكَ الْأَسْمَاءُ وَالصِّفَاتُ كُلُّهَا مُسْتَوِيَةٌ فِي الْعَظَمَةِ وَالْفَضْلِ لَا تَفَاوُتَ بَيْنَهَا.

The Qur'ān has been revealed upon the Messenger of Allāh ﷺ and written in texts. The verses of the Qur'ān, in that they are the speech of Allāh Most High, are all equal in virtue and exaltedness, except that some possess [both] the virtue of [their] mention along with the virtue of what is mentioned [in them, i.e., their subject matter], such as the Throne Verse, which deals with the exaltedness, sublimity, and attributes of Allāh Most High; therefore, the two virtues are combined in it—that of being mentioned and that of its content. Some verses possess only virtue of being mentioned, such as the stories of the unbelievers, which have no virtue in their content (namely the unbelievers). Similarly, the names and attributes [of Allāh Most High] are all equal in exaltedness and virtue, without any difference between them.

❁

The Qur'ān has been revealed upon the Messenger of Allāh ﷺ and written in texts. The verses of the Qur'ān, in that they are the speech of Allāh Most High, are all equal in virtue and exaltedness/ The Messenger of Allāh ﷺ said, "The superiority of the speech of Allāh Most High over all other speech is like the superiority of Allāh Most High over His creation" (*Tirmidhī,* "Faḍā'il al-

Qur'ān," 2850). All the verses of the Qur'ān are equal in their virtue. Hence, the superiority of the speech of Allāh Most High over all other speech is like the superiority of Allāh Most High over His creation. | except that some possess [both] the virtue of [their] mention along with the virtue of what is mentioned [in them, i.e., their subject matter], such as the Throne Verse, which deals with the exaltedness, sublimity, and attributes of Allāh Most High; therefore, the two virtues are combined in it—that of being mentioned and that of its content, which is about Allāh Most High, His attributes and names. The verses in which the prophets and the friends of Allāh (*awliyā'*) are mentioned are similar in that they also possess two virtues. Some verses possess only virtue of being mentioned, such as the stories of the unbelievers, which have no virtue in their content (namely the unbelievers). They possess the virtue of being in the Qur'ān, because it is the speech of Allāh and not their speech.

Similarly, the names and attributes [of Allāh Most High] are all equal in exaltedness and virtue, without any difference between them, that is, there are no differences between the [various] names of Allāh and there are no differences between the [various] attributes of Allāh. They are all equal in their exaltedness and virtue, which they possess by merit of their being the names and attributes of Allāh, and their being neither Him Himself nor anything extraneous to Him. Imām Ghazālī (may Allāh have mercy on him) states, "Know that this name—Allāh—is the greatest of the ninety-nine names, because it is indicative of His essence, inclusive of the divine attributes. Also, it is the most specific name, since it cannot be attributed to anybody else neither in its real meaning nor metaphorically. In contrast, all the other names are sometimes attributed to others, e.g., the Powerful (*al-qādir*), the Knowledgeable (*al-ʿālim*), and the Merciful (*al-raḥīm*), and the rest."[192]

[Qārī] This does not negate the fact that some of the names and attributes

192 The complete statement of Ghazālī from his *Al-Maqṣad al-Asnā fī Maʿānī Asmā' Allāh al-Ḥusnā* is as follows: "As for his saying 'Allāh,' it is the name for the True Existent, the One who unites the divine attributes, is characterized by the attributes of Lordship, and is unique in true existence. . . . Know that this name is the greatest of the ninety-nine names, because it is indicative of the essence that unifies all the divine attributes, so that none of them are left out. Conversely, each of the remaining names only refer to a single attribute: knowledge, power, agency, and the rest. 'Allāh' is the most specific of the names as no one uses it for anyone other than Him, neither literally nor metaphorically; the rest of the names may be used to designate other than He, as in, 'the powerful,' 'the knowing,' 'the merciful,' and the rest. So because of these two reasons, it seems that this name is the greatest of these names." See Ghazālī, *The Ninety Nine Beautiful Names of God* 51.

are greater than others, based upon what has been firmly established in the ḥadīth regarding the superiority of the Greatest Name of Allāh (*ism al-aʿẓam*). And Allāh knows best. [306]

Understanding Good and Evil Through Reason

[Qārī] Ḥākim al-Shahīd relates in his *Muntaqā* that Abū Ḥanīfa said, "There is no excuse for anyone to be ignorant of his Creator because of what he sees of the creation of the heavens and earth and his own self." He also said, "If Allāh Most High had not sent a messenger, it would still have been obligatory for created beings to recognize Him through their intellect and reason (*ʿaql*)."

The difference between us and the Muʿtazila who hold that good and ugliness is known through reason is what Ustādh Abū Manṣūr al-Māturīdī and the general consensus of Samarqandī scholars (may Allāh have mercy on them) have explained. They say that, according to the Muʿtazilīs, if reason perceives some goodness or ugliness, then that in itself obligates Allāh and His servants to judge accordingly. However, according to us, the one who necessitates servants to judge something as good or ugly is Allāh Most High, and according to the agreement of the Ahl al-Sunna wa 'l-Jamāʿa, nothing is made binding upon Allāh. For us, reason (*ʿaql*) is a means by which these judgments are made known to us, that is, by Allāh revealing to it the good and ugliness found in an action.

Then the difference between us [the Māturīdīs] and the Ashʿarīs [in this matter] is that they say that none of the rulings of Allāh can be known except through the coming of a prophet. We say that some rulings can be known without the aid of a prophet. This is done by Allāh Most High creating knowledge of them in His servants, sometimes not even requiring that they strive to acquire (*kasb*) [this knowledge]. Such rulings would include the obligation to believe in a prophet and the prohibition of harmful lying; at other times, He requires acquisition through contemplation and thought. We say, however, that most rulings cannot be known except through the Book [of Allāh] or a prophet.

The Imāms of Bukhārā, on the other hand, held that belief does not become obligatory, nor does disbelief become prohibited until Allāh has sent a prophet; this is similar to what the Ashʿārīs believe. They interpret the narration from Abū Ḥanīfa above as indicating the lack of excuse for unbelief *after* the sending of a prophet.

Ibn al-Humām says that one may take Abū Ḥanīfa's use of the term "obligatory" (*wājib*) in the above quote as "recommended" (*yanbaghī*) and not to mean that one would be punished if one did not recognize Allāh in the absence of a prophet. If one takes it in this sense, the Imām's statement does not conflict with the statement of Allāh in the Qur'ān: "And We will not punish until We send a prophet." (17:15), nor is there a need then to interpret the punishment mentioned in the verse as a punishment of this world, or subscribe to another interpretation.

Ibn al-Humām also says that the end result of the difference between these opinions is seen clearly in how a person who does not receive the message of any prophet and does not believe in Allāh before he dies is judged. The Muᶜtazila and the first group of the Ḥanafīs hold that he dwells in Hellfire for eternity, as opposed to the Ashᶜarīs and the second group of Ḥanafīs [the Imāms of Bukhārā]. Subsequently, the latter group question the validity of a person's faith: if he is not responsible for faith but happens to believe in the oneness of Allāh, is his faith valid? Meaning, is he rewarded for it in the Hereafter? According to the Ḥanafīs [in this group], he is, just as the belief of a child who comprehends the meaning of Islam and accountability (*taklīf*) is valid. An opinion related from the Shāfiᶜī scholar Abu 'l-Khaṭṭāb is that this type of belief is not accepted, just as the belief of a child who has not reached maturity is not accepted. This is according to the preponderant opinion in their school [i.e., Shāfiᶜī school], which is different from the opinion of the other three schools, since the Prophet ﷺ invited ᶜAlī ؓ to Islam [when he was still a child] and he accepted; it is also contrary to the consensus that his devotions like prayer, fasting, etc., were valid. [306–308]

Making One Responsible Over What One Has no Power

[Qārī] Imām Ghazālī says, "It is conceivable for Allāh Most High to hold His servants responsible over that which they have no power, contrary to the position of the Muᶜtazila. If it were not permissible, it would have been impossible [and meaningless] to ask for protection from it as in the Holy Qur'ān: 'Our Lord! Lay not on us a burden greater than we have strength to bear' (2:286). Also, Allāh Most High declared that Abū Jahl would never believe in the Prophet ﷺ, while at the same time, he is commanded to believe in everything that the Prophet ﷺ teaches, including that he [Abū Jahl] will never believe in him. So how is he to believe in the fact that he will never believe? This is a paradox."[193] Others have also mentioned this point, but concerning Abū Lahab.[194] [309] This is the Ashᶜarī opinion.

The Māturīdī opinion is that it is not permissible to hold one responsible for what one does not have the ability to do, because Allāh says, "On no soul does Allāh place a burden greater than it can bear" (2:286). Though Imām Ashᶜarī allowed it [hypothetically], there is a difference of opinion among the Ashᶜarīs as to whether it ever occurred. The most correct opinion is that it did not. The meaning of holding someone responsible for that over which he has no ability is to make one responsible for what is beyond human ability, like holding a blind person responsible for sight, or a chronically disabled person for walking, in such a way that he is rewarded for doing it and punished for not doing it. As far as accountability for what is impossible due to other reasons [and not intrinsically impossible] like the belief of those whom Allāh knows [in His eternal knowledge] will not become believers like Pharaoh, Abū Jahl, Abū Lahab, and all other unbelievers who die on unbelief, all scholars agree that it is possible for it to legally occur. So as far as the verse: "Our Lord! Lay not on us a burden greater than we have strength to bear" (2:286) is concerned, it is [according to the Māturīdīs] a prayer of refuge from being [physically] burdened with what one cannot bear, and not from its [legal] accountability; according to us [Māturīdīs], it is permissible for Allāh to burden someone to lift a mountain that one cannot, such that it be placed on one, causing one to be killed, but it is not permissible to make one accountable for lifting it, such that if he did so he would be rewarded and if not, then he would be punished. Therefore, there is no doubt on the validity of seeking refuge from it through the words of Allāh: "Our Lord! Lay not on us a burden . . . ." [400]

193 And thus it is asking Abū Jahl for more than he is able to do. Of course, since Allāh has eternal knowledge, He was foretelling the fact that Abū Jahl would never become a Muslim, not that He compelled him not to believe.

194 This is more appropriate since chapter 111 of the Qur'ān (Sūrat al-Masad) announced his and his wife's condemnation.

ABŪ ṬĀLIB, THE PARENTS OF ALLĀH'S MESSENGER ﷺ, AND HIS CHILDREN

[وَأَبُوْ طَالِبٍ عَمُّهُ وَأَبُوْ عَلِيٍّ مَاتَ كَافِرًا.] وَقَاسِمٌ وَطَاهِرٌ وَإِبْرَاهِيْمُ كَانُوْا بَنِيَّ رَسُوْلِ اللهِ صَلَّى اللهُ عَلَيْهِ وَسَلَّمَ، وَفَاطِمَةُ وَرُقَيَّةُ وَزَيْنَبُ وَأُمُّ كُلْثُوْمٍ كُنَّ جَمِيْعًا بَنَاتِ رَسُوْلِ اللهِ صَلَّى اللهُ عَلَيْهِ وَسَلَّمَ.

[The Prophet's uncle and ʿAlī's father, Abū Ṭālib, died an unbeliever.][195] Qāsim,

195 There is some confusion regarding the text of *Al-Fiqh al-Akbar* at this point. There are three separate statements found, some of which are mentioned in some editions but not in others. They are as follows: (1) "The Messenger of Allāh ﷺ died on faith," (2) "The Prophet's uncle and ʿAlī's father, Abū Ṭālib, died an unbeliever," and (3) "The parents of the Messenger of Allāh died on unbelief (*al-kufr*)." As far as the first statement is concerned, it is found in all the published versions of *Minaḥ al-Rawḍ al-Azhar* to which I had access, and also in all six of the manuscripts from Al-Maktaba al-Azhariyya. In most of the manuscripts, it is not placed or highlighted as part of *Al-Fiqh al-Akbar* itself as it is in the published editions, but mentioned by Qārī in his commentary with the words: "In one edition, [it states . . .]," after which, he goes on to explain that this statement is not found in the original of any commentary since the point is clear in terms of its purport, and there is no need to mention it because of the lofty position of the Messenger of Allāh ﷺ. He then provides some possible reasons for its inclusion if one assumes that it is a part of *Al-Fiqh al-Akbar.* Furthermore, it is not found in any of the nine manuscripts of Maghnīsāwī's commentary in my possession, nor in its published versions, nor in any of the three manuscripts of *Al-Fiqh al-Akbar* itself. For this reason, it has been left out in this edition, too.

As far as the second statement is concerned, it is found in all published editions and manuscripts of *Al-Fiqh al-Akbar* and its commentaries, with the exception of the two published editions of Maghnīsāwī's commentary. This statement has been included in this edition along with Maghnīsāwī's brief comment.

The third statement is very problematic. Although, it has not been included in any of the published editions of *Al-Fiqh al-Akbar* and its commentaries, with the exception of *Al-Qawl al-Faṣl,* it is found in some form or the other in nearly all the manuscripts available to me. Shaykh Ghāwjī's published edition does include it as part of Qārī's commentary in brackets. One of the manuscripts of this commentary (*MS. 2743*) adds, "or they died on *fiṭra* (primordial nature)" after it, and one of the manuscripts of *Al-Fiqh al-Akbar* (*MS. 5844*) has the word *"al-jāhiliyya"* (ignorance) in place of *"al-kufr."* Another manuscript of Maghnīsāwī's commentary (*MS. 41174*) has what seems like *"al-kufr"* crossed out and *"al-fiṭra"* (natural disposition) written after it. No doubt since Qārī commented on it and also initially took the path that he did of considering the

Ṭāhir, and Ibrāhīm were the sons of the Messenger of Allāh ﷺ, and Fāṭima, Ruqayya, Zaynab, and Umm Kulthūm were all his daughters.

❁

The Prophet's uncle and ʿAlī's father, Abū Ṭālib, died an unbeliever.[196] This is a rebuttal of those who say he died on faith, and they are the Rawāfiḍ.

---

parents of the Messenger ﷺ to be unbelievers (he reverted from this opinion later as highlighted in his commentary of Qāḍī ʿIyāḍ's *Al-Shifā'* 1:601), he considered it part of the original. Shaykh Zāhid al-Kawtharī strongly denies the authenticity of this statement being from Abū Ḥanīfa and expresses hope that someone would republish the work after comparing the manuscripts of the Library of Egypt with those at the Library of ʿĀrif Ḥikmat in Madīna Munawwara, which he considers to be the most authentic and reliable.

In his introduction to the five books of the Imām, Kawtharī writes, "In some of those manuscripts, it states, 'The parents of the Prophet ﷺ died on the *fiṭra*,' and the word *al-fiṭra* is easily altered to *al-kufr* in the Kūfic script. However, in the majority of the manuscripts, it is *mā mātā ʿala 'l-kufr*, 'They did *not* die on unbelief.'... Ḥāfiẓ Muḥammad al-Murtaḍā al-Zabīdī, the commentator of the *Iḥyā'* and *Qāmūs* says in his treatise *Al-Intiṣār li Wāliday al-Nabiyy al-Mukhtār* (Support for the Parents of the Chosen Prophet), "When the copyist saw a repetition of the word *mā* in *mā mātā* (ما ماتا) he took one of them to be superfluous and removed it, after which this incorrect rendering became widespread. The proof for this is the context itself, for if the parents and Abū Ṭālib had both been in the same state, then the Imām would have placed all three of them together in one sentence with a single judgment and not in two separate sentences [as is the case here].' This is a well-founded opinion from Ḥāfiẓ al-Zabīdī, except that he had not seen the edition that contained the words *mā mātā* but had quoted it from someone who had." Kawtharī then says, "I, with all praise to Allāh, have seen it with the words *mā mātā* in two manuscripts in the Library of Egypt just as a friend of mine has seen the words *mā mātā* and *ʿala 'l-fiṭra* in two old manuscripts in the library of Shaykh al-Islām ʿĀrif Ḥikmat. ʿAlī al-Qārī based his commentary on the incorrect version and acted unethically (may Allāh forgive him)" (Kawtharī 7–8).

Among the manuscripts I have, *MS. 74634*, written in 1150/1737, contains some comments and notes in its margins written by an ʿUmar ibn Muṣṭafā al-Āmidī al-Diyārbakrī, who happens to be one of the main students of Zabīdī. He writes that toward the end of the ʿAbbāsid era in 600/1203, the issue regarding the parents of Allāh's Messenger ﷺ came up, which led to a great difference of opinion. Some said the same as what Qārī said and others opposed the position. This controversy over the words of the Imām perturbed the Caliph greatly and so he sent people to research every edition of the work they could find in libraries and in private collections. They came across a manuscript written by the third [Ḥanafī] Imām [Muḥammad al-Shaybānī] which had been read in front of the Imām [Abū Ḥanīfa] in the presence of the rest of the class. It contained the following statement: "The parents of the Messenger of Allāh ﷺ did not die (*mā mātā*) on unbelief (*al-kufr*)." The Caliph also sent someone to Kūfa, where he found another edition also containing the same words; they deemed the Kūfan work to be the correct version and rectified their copies." Diyārbakrī mentions the same point that Zabīdī made regarding the likelihood of a copyist error given that many copyists were unlearned (in religious sciences) and could have thought the *mā* was a stray word and removed it. He then says, "What I have written is correct, I have shown it to my shaykh, liegelord, and master Abu 'l-Fayḍ Muḥammad al-Murtaḍā." And Allāh knows best. I have left this statement out in this edition following the majority of the published editions of this work.

196 Regarding the belief of the parents of the Messenger of Allāh ﷺ, Mullā ʿAlī al-Qārī (may

[Qārī] It is related that when Abū Ṭālib was near to death, the Messenger of Allāh ﷺ went to him and found Abū Jahl and his ilk by him. The Messenger ﷺ said, "Uncle, say a formula (*kalima*) by which I can argue for you in the court of Allāh." Abū Jahl said to him, "Are you turning away from the religion of ʿAbd al-Muṭṭalib?" This went on until Abū Ṭālib declared as a final statement, "I am on the religion of ʿAbd al-Muṭṭalib," and refused to say, "There is

---

Allāh have mercy on him) for a period held that they were in the Hellfire. He wrote a booklet on this issue and also expressed the same opinion in his commentary on *Al-Fiqh al-Akbar.* However, he later changed his position, as can be seen from his statement in his commentary of Qāḍī ʿIyāḍ's *Al-Shifā'* which he completed in 1011/1602, three years before his death. There, he says, "As for the religion of the parents of Allāh's Messenger ﷺ, there are many opinions. The most correct one is that they were believers according to the consensus of the greatest of the scholars, mentioned by Suyūṭī (d. 911/1505) in his three books." He goes on to say, "As far as what they have mentioned regarding his bringing them back to life [and their testifying to his prophethood], the most correct opinion according to the majority of trustworthy scholars and as also mentioned by Suyūṭī in his three works, is that it did happen (*Sharḥ al-Shifā'* 1:601). (*Al-Taʿlīq al-Muyassar* 18)

There are actually a few opinions on this issue, based on the various ḥadīths that have been related about it. According to some ḥadīths, the Messenger of Allāh ﷺ said that they will be in the Hellfire, or that he was prohibited from seeking forgiveness for them. Yet there are other ḥadīths which say that his ancestry was always through the honorable institution of marriage and never out of wedlock through immorality; some weaker narrations say that he ﷺ brought them back to life, and they declared their belief in him. Given these various reports, there is quite a bit of confusion on this matter. Since they died during the time of the cessation of prophethood (*zaman al-fatra*), the judgment regarding the people of that time according to the Ashʿarīs is that they are considered excused and are not accountable for faith because no prophet was sent to them. Accordingly, they will be saved. However, it is a more difficult issue with the Māturīdīs, as Ibn ʿĀbidīn al-Shāmī relates by saying, "If they died before having the time to reflect [on what is around them and the universe] and they did not make a [conscious] decision to believe or to disbelieve, then there is no punishment upon them, as opposed to a scenario where they did disbelieve during this time or did not make any decision to believe or disbelieve after having had the time to reflect. The scholars of Bukhārā among the Māturīdīs have agreed with the Ashʿarīs on this matter. They have essentially interpreted the opinion of Abū Ḥanīfa (see "Understanding Good and Evil Through Reason" above) as pertaining to a person remaining unaware of Allāh even after the coming of a prophet. Ibn al-Humām also adopted this opinion in his *Taḥrīr.* However, this applies to the one who did not die having conscious disbelief, for Nawawī and Fakhr al-Rāzī [both Ashʿarīs] have clarified that those who died as polytheists before the coming of the Prophet ﷺ, will be in the Hellfire." Ibn ʿĀbidīn then says that the difference of opinion is therefore regarding those who were not polytheists but remained indifferent (*ghafla*) to such beliefs, or those who gained guidance through their intellect and took up monotheism, like Quss ibn Sāʿida and Zayd ibn ʿAmr ibn Ṭufayl. In the end, he says that "it is our good thought in Allāh that the parents of the Prophet ﷺ were from among these two groups" and thus saved. Ibn ʿĀbidīn then concludes with a very important point: "To summarize, as some of the specialists have said, it is not appropriate to discuss this issue except with the utmost respect and due decorum. Moreover, it is not from among those matters ignorance from which would be harmful or that one will be questioned about in the grave or on the Day of Judgment. Therefore, guarding one's tongue from speaking about the issue in any way except favorably is the best and safest course" (*Radd al-Muḥtār* 2:386). In sum, it is best to avoid making any judgment on the issue and consign the matter to Allāh.

no god except Allāh." Upon [hearing] this, the Messenger ﷺ said, "By Allāh, I will certainly seek forgiveness for you until I am prohibited." After this Allāh revealed, "It is not fitting, for the Prophet and those who believe, that they should pray for forgiveness for pagans, even though they be of kin, after it is clear to them that they are companions of the Fire" (Qur'ān 9:113).[197] Allāh also revealed the following verse after Abū Ṭālib's refusal to say the formula of faith: "It is true you will not be able to guide everyone whom you love; but Allāh guides those whom He will" (28:56). (*Bukhārī, Muslim*)

Attesting to a Believer's Place in Paradise or Hellfire after his Death

[Qārī] Know that the pious predecessors had three opinions with regard to attesting to a believer's place in Paradise after death. The first is that one cannot make such an attestation except for the prophets (upon them be peace). This is narrated from Muḥammad ibn al-Ḥanafiyya[198] and Awzāʿī.[199] This would be a definitive judgment, and there is no disagreement about it. The second opinion is that one can attest to Paradise for any believer for whom there is some transmitted proof [e.g., the Companions]. This is the opinion of a great number of scholars, but this would be a speculative (*ẓannī*) judgment. The third opinion is that one may attest for whomever the believers attest, as is found in the two *Ṣaḥīḥs* that a funeral procession passed by the Messenger ﷺ and some of the Companions praised the deceased. The Messenger ﷺ said, "It has been made obligatory." Then another funeral passed by and they criticized him for his evil, whereupon the Messenger ﷺ said, "It has been made obligatory." At this, ʿUmar ﷺ asked, "Messenger of Allāh, what has been made obligatory?" The Messenger ﷺ said, "Paradise has been made obligatory for the one you praised for his goodness, and Hellfire has been made obligatory for the one you criticized for his evil. You are the witnesses of Allāh upon the earth"

---

197 Ibn ʿAṭiyya has considered it unlikely that this verse was revealed in relation to this incident, for Sūrat al-Tawba was from among the last verses to be revealed (see his commentary). (*Al-Taʿlīq al-Muyassar* 313)

198 Muḥammad ibn al-Ḥanafiyya was the son of ʿAlī ibn Abī Ṭālib, the fourth caliph. He was called Ibn al-Ḥanafiyya after his mother who was named Khawla bint Jaʿfar but known as Ḥanafiyya after her tribe Banū Ḥanīfa. He died during the reign of ʿAbd al-Malik ibn Marwān at the age of 65 in 80/699 or 81/700 in Madīna, Ayla, or Ṭā'if.

199 ʿAbd al-Raḥmān ibn ʿAmr ibn Yuḥmid, Abū ʿAmr al-Awzāʿī, Shaykh al-Islam and the Wise Scholar of the People of Shām. He was considered one of the *mujtahid* imāms during the time of the *salaf* along with the four Imāms. He died in 157/773.

(*Muslim, Abū Dāwūd, Tirmidhī*). This type of judgment is a [non-binding] statement of what is likely to occur. And Allāh knows best. [312]

Qāsim, Ṭāhir, and Ibrāhīm were the sons of the Messenger of Allāh ﷺ, and Fāṭima, Ruqayya, Zaynab, and Umm Kulthūm were all his daughters. This is a rebuttal of those who have related that the children of the Messenger of Allāh ﷺ were either more or fewer than the number mentioned in this narration, which is the authentic narration. The Messenger of Allāh ﷺ married Khadīja when he was twenty-five years old, and had six children from her. He had Ibrāhīm from Māriya, the Coptic slave girl. Ibrāhīm was born in Madīna and passed away while still being nursed. Barā' ؓ reports that when Ibrāhīm passed away, the Messenger of Allāh ﷺ said, "He has a wet nurse in Paradise" (*Bukhārī*, "al-Janā'iz," 1293).

[Qārī] Qāsim is the first son born to the Messenger ﷺ before prophethood, and this is from where he ﷺ took his agnomen (*kunya*) Abu 'l-Qāsim. Qāsim lived long enough to walk, and some relate that he lived for two years, while others said he lived until he was able to ride a beast. The most correct report is that he lived for seventeen months and passed away before the message (*risāla*) was conferred upon the Prophet Muḥammad ﷺ. As for Ṭāhir, Al-Zubayr ibn Bakkār reports that aside from Qāsim and Ibrāhīm, the Messenger ﷺ had another son, ʿAbdullāh, who died at a young age in Makka. He was also called Ṭayyib (pleasant) and Ṭāhir (pure)—three names. This is also the opinion of most of the genealogists. ʿAbdullāh was given those names because he was born after prophethood [and thus the connotations of purity]. However, it is also said that Ṭayyib and Ṭāhir are other than ʿAbdullāh, as Imām Dāraquṭnī has related. Another opinion is that there were two sets of twins born to the Messenger ﷺ, Ṭayyib and Muṭayyib and Ṭāhir and Muṭahhir,[200] as mentioned by the author of *Al-Ṣafwa*.[201] [As for the daughters of Allāh's Messenger ﷺ, they lived to adulthood, married, and bore children.]

Ibrāhīm was the son of the Messenger ﷺ through Māriya the Copt, and

200 These were all the children of Khadīja ؓ. According to Dāraquṭnī, the most accepted order of birth for the Messenger's ﷺ children from her is Qāsim, Zaynab, ʿAbdullāh, Umm Kulthūm, Fāṭima, and Ruqayya. It is also said that Ruqayya was born before Fāṭima and this is more likely (*Al-Taʿlīq al-Muyassar* 313).

201 This is the work of Abu 'l-Faraj ʿAbd al-Raḥmān ibn al-Jawzī (d. 597/1200) called *Ṣifat al-Ṣafwa*.

he passed away when he was seventy or so days old. The Messenger ﷺ prayed upon him in the Baqīʿ Cemetery. [313–314]

The Wives of the Prophet ﷺ

[Qārī] The Great Imām did not mention the wives of the Messenger ﷺ. I will mention them here briefly for completeness. The mothers of the believers are Khadīja, Sawda, ʿĀ'isha, Ḥafṣa, Umm Salama, Umm Ḥabība, Zaynab bint Jaḥsh, Zaynab bint Khuzayma, Maymūna, Juwayriyya, and Ṣafiyya (may Allāh be pleased with them all). They are eleven, with all of whom he ﷺ consummated marriage. There is no disagreement among the scholars regarding them. However, it has been related that he also married women other than these. [318]

Imām Abū Ḥanīfa says in his *Kitāb al-Waṣiyya,* "After Khadīja, ʿĀ'isha is the most excellent of the women of the world. She is the Mother of the Believers, pure from fornication, and free from the allegations of the Rawāfiḍ; whoever charges her with immorality (*zinā*) is himself the offspring of immorality (*walad al-zinā*)." This is no doubt a very strange statement from the Imām as is not lost on those knowledgeable of rulings. It is possible that he has employed a profound allegory here in order to indicate that such a person is like the illegitimate offspring being the worst of the three: this statement is in reference to a ḥadīth that has been related [from the Messenger of Allāh ﷺ, "The illegitimate offspring is the worst of the three" (*Abū Dāwūd*), i.e., if he indulges in the same action as his biological parents].[202] Whoever slanders ʿĀ'isha ﵂ with immorality is a disbeliever of the verses in the Qur'ān revealed about her exoneration from the slander brought against her person (see Qur'ān 24:11–17). As for one who curses ʿĀ'isha ﵂ because of her fighting against and opposing ʿAlī ﵁, that person is a misguided obscene unrighteous innovator. [318–319]

202 The Imām's statement may be explained in an even simpler way, namely that since ʿĀ'isha ﵂ is one of the mothers of the believers (*ummahāt al-mu'minīn*), any believer accusing her of immorality has effectively rendered himself an illegitimate offspring.

WHEN DOUBT ARISES ABOUT ANY OF THE SUBTLETIES OF *TAWḤĪD*

وَإِذَا أَشْكَلَ عَلَى الْإِنْسَانِ شَيْءٌ مِنْ دَقَائِقِ عِلْمِ التَّوْحِيْدِ فَإِنَّهُ يَنْبَغِي لَهُ أَنْ يَعْتَقِدَ فِي الْحَالِ مَا هُوَ الصَّوَابُ عِنْدَ اللهِ تَعَالٰى إِلٰى أَنْ يَجِدَ عَالِمًا فَيَسْأَلُهُ، وَلَا يَسَعُهُ تَأْخِيْرُ الطَّلَبِ، وَلَا يُعْذَرُ بِالْوَقْفِ فِيْهِ، وَيَكْفُرُ إِنْ وَقَفَ.

Whenever any issue from the subtleties of the science of divine oneness pose problems for a person, it is obligatory that he believe immediately whatever is correct according to Allāh, until he finds a learned person and inquires from him. It is not permissible for him to delay in his inquiry, and he will not be excused for abstaining from it. He will be committing unbelief, if he hesitates.

❀

Whenever any issue from the subtleties of the science of divine oneness and [the science of the] attributes [of Allāh] pose problems for a person—a believer—it is obligatory that he believe immediately whatever is correct according to Allāh, e.g., by saying, "Whatever Allāh intends by it is the existent reality," or by saying, "I believe in whatever is correct according to Allāh Most High." This much will be sufficient until he finds a learned person who is knowledgeable about the issues of divine oneness and attributes and inquires from him regarding what is causing him doubt. It is not permissible for him to delay in his inquiry of what is causing him doubt from the subtleties of the science of divine oneness, and to delay in seeking the knowledge that is obligatory upon him, which is the knowledge of true faith, the knowledge of that which eliminates true faith and brings about unbelief, and the knowledge of the beliefs of the Ahl al-Sunna wa 'l-Jamāʿa. Allāh Most High says, "Know therefore that there is no god save Allāh" (Qur'ān 47:19) and "Question the people of the Remembrance, if it should be that you do not know" (16:43). The Messenger of Allāh ﷺ said, "To seek knowledge is obligatory upon every believing man and woman."[203] The Messenger of Allāh ﷺ [is also reported to have] said, "Seek knowledge even if in China."[204] | and he will not be excused for abstaining from it, that is from inquiring about what is causing him doubt. He will be committing unbelief if he hesitates regarding what is causing him doubt, if it is from the articles of the faith, because hesitancy regarding the tenets of belief is unbelief. This is because hesitancy prevents conviction. If the person said, "I believe in Allāh and hold belief in whatever is the truth according to Allāh," then his faith in general (*īmān ijmālī*) is established.

Differences of Opinion: A Mercy in Law not in Fundamentals

[Qārī] What is meant by the subtleties of the science of divine oneness is that which, if doubted, would negate faith and annul the conviction regarding the essence of Allāh, His attributes, and the knowledge of the descriptions of the tenets of faith relating to the Hereafter. There is no conflict with the fact that the Imām abstained from making judgments on certain matters since they were from the sacred laws (*sharāʾiʿ*) of Islam. Differences regarding the science of juridical laws (*aḥkām*) is a mercy, whereas difference regarding the science of divine oneness (*tawḥīd*) and Islam is a deviance and innovation. Mistakes committed in the science of juridical laws (*aḥkām*) are forgiven—in fact the scholar is rewarded—as opposed to mistakes in the *kalām* (theology), for such mistakes are unbelief and fabrication, and the one committing them is sinful.[205] [321–322]

---

203 *Ibn Māja,* "al-Muqaddima," 220 without the addition "and woman."

204 Bayhaqī, Khaṭīb, Ibn ʿAbd al-Barr, and Daylamī have related it from Anas, and it is weak; in fact Ibn Ḥibbān has said it is baseless (*bāṭil*) and Ibn al-Jawzī has mentioned it among the fabrications (*mawḍūʿāt*). This can be contrasted with the comments of the ḥadīth master Mizzī who says that it has many versions which accumulatively could reach the status of an "acceptable" (*ḥasan*) narration. Dhahabī says in *Talkhīṣ al-Wāhiyāt,* "It has been related through many weak chains (*ṭuruq wāhiya*) and some sound (*ṣāliḥ*) ones." Abū Yaʿlā has related it and Ibn ʿAbd al-Barr has related from Anas with a chain that contains a liar . . . (*Kashf al-Khafāʾ* 1:124).

205 Differences in divine oneness and belief [are not permissible and] are cause for deviance and innovation, but differences regarding jurisprudence [are valid] and a source of mercy. It is enough of a proof that the Messenger ﷺ said, "If the judge rules on an issue exercising scholarly endeavor (*ijtahada*) and hits the mark, he receives two rewards. If he rules exercising his scholarly endeavor and misses the mark, he receives one reward [for the endeavor]" (*Bukhārī*). One of the seven renowned scholars of Madīna, Qāsim ibn Muḥammad said, "Differences among the Companions of Muḥammad ﷺ are a mercy for the servants of Allāh Most High" (Bayhaqī, *Al-Madkhal*).

CONCERNING THE ASCENSION AND SOME SIGNS OF THE LAST DAY

وَخَبَرُ الْمِعْرَاجِ حَقٌّ، وَمَنْ رَدَّهُ فَهُوَ مُبْتَدِعٌ ضَالٌّ. وَخُرُوْجُ الدَّجَّالِ، وَيَأْجُوْجَ مَأْجُوْجَ، وَطُلُوْعُ الشَّمْسِ مِنْ مَغْرِبِهَا، وَنُزُوْلُ عِيْسَى عَلَيْهِ السَّلَامُ مِنَ السَّمَاءِ، وَسَائِرُ عَلَامَاتِ يَوْمِ الْقِيَامَةِ عَلَى مَا وَرَدَتْ بِهِ الْأَخْبَارُ الصَّحِيْحَةُ حَقٌّ كَائِنٌ. وَاللهُ تَعَالَى يَهْدِيْ مَنْ يَّشَاءُ إِلَى صِرَاطٍ مُّسْتَقِيْمٍ.

The report regarding the Ascension is a reality. Whoever rejects it is a misguided innovator. The emergence of the Antichrist, Gog and Magog, the rising of the sun from its place of setting, the descent of ʿĪsā ﷺ from the heaven, and all the signs of the Day of Judgment according to what has been related in the authentic narrations, are a reality and destined to occur. Allāh Most High guides whom He wills to the straight path.

❁

The report regarding the ascension is a reality. Whoever rejects it is a misguided innovator, that is, whoever rejects the ascension to the heavens is a misguided innovator, because the physical ascension of the Messenger of Allāh ﷺ in a state of wakefulness is established through well-known narrations (*khabar mashhūr*) which are close to uninterrupted narrations (*mutawātir*) in evidentiary strength. It is stated in *Kitāb al-Khulāṣa,* "One who rejects

---

Ibn Saʿd has related it in his *Ṭabaqāt* as follows: "The differing of the Companions of Muḥammad is a mercy for the people." The caliph ʿUmar ibn ʿAbd al-ʿAzīz (may Allāh have mercy on him) said, "It would not have made me happy had the Companions of Muḥammad ﷺ not differed; for had they not differed, there would not have been any concessions" (*Al-Madkhal*). Imām Khaṭṭābī said, "There are two people who have criticized this ḥadīth; one is an insolent person and the other a heretic; they are Isḥāq al-Mawṣilī and ʿAmr ibn Baḥr al-Jāḥiẓ. Both said, 'If difference were a mercy, then agreement would be a punishment.'" (*Al-Taʿlīq al-Muyassar* 321)

the ascension (*miʿrāj*) will be considered an unbeliever if he also rejects the night journey (*isrā'*) from Makka to Jerusalem but not an unbeliever if he rejects the ascension from Jerusalem alone. This is because the night journey has been established through definitive proof (*dalīl qāṭiʿ*) from the Qur'ān. Allāh Most High says, "Glorified is He who took His servant by night from the Masjid al-Ḥarām (Sacred Masjid) to Masjid al-Aqṣā, whose precincts We have blessed, that We might show him some of Our signs. He is the All-hearing, the All-seeing" (17:1). However, the ascension from Jerusalem has not been established through definitive proof from the Qur'ān, so one who rejects it is classified as a misguided innovator. Muqātil states in the elucidation of the verse "Glorified is He who took His servant by night" (17:1) that the night journey occurred one year prior to the Emigration (*hijra*). The Messenger of Allāh ﷺ reported, "While I was in Masjid al-Ḥarām in the *ḥijr*[206] by the House [of Allāh] between sleep and wakefulness, Jibrīl ﷺ came to me with a Burāq. It was a white riding animal, tall, larger than a donkey, smaller than a mule, and its hooves would land where its sight reached. I mounted it until I reached Jerusalem and there, I fastened it to the ring to which the prophets fastened [their conveyances]. Then I entered the Masjid, performed two *rakʿas* (units) of prayer inside, and then emerged. Jibrīl ﷺ came to me with a container of wine and a container of milk. I chose the milk, upon which Jibrīl ﷺ remarked, "You have selected the natural disposition." Then the animal ascended with us to the skies . . ." (*Muslim,* "al-Īmān," 234).

The emergence of the Antichrist, Gog and Magog, the rising of the sun from its place of setting, the descent of ʿĪsā ﷺ from the heaven, and all the signs of the Day of Judgment according to what has been related in the authentic narrations, are a reality and destined to occur. It is related from Hudhayfa ibn Asīd al-Ghifārī ﷺ: "Once the Messenger of Allāh ﷺ approached us while we were engrossed in discussion. He asked what we were discussing, so we told him that we were discussing the Hour. The Messenger of Allāh ﷺ said, 'It will not occur until you witness ten signs before it.' He then mentioned the Antichrist, the Smoke, the Beast, the rising of the sun from its place of setting, the descent of ʿĪsā son of Maryam (Mary) ﷺ, Gog and Magog, and the three swallowings of the earth (*khusūf*): one in the east, one in the west, and one in the Arabian Peninsula. The last of the signs is a fire that will erupt from

206 See note 156 above.

Yemen and drive the people to their assembling place." Thus transmitted in *Al-Maṣābīḥ*.[207]

The Order of Events Leading to the Last Hour

[Qārī] The Mahdī will first appear in the two Noble Sanctuaries [Makka and Madīna], then he will go to Bayt al-Maqdis (Jerusalem). While there, the Antichrist (Dajjāl) will besiege him, and ʿĪsā ﷺ will descend from the eastern minaret in Damascus, Syria and begin to fight with the Antichrist. He will kill the Antichrist; for he will melt away at ʿĪsā's ﷺ descent from the heavens as salt does in water. ʿĪsā will meet with the Mahdī when the call for commencement (*iqāma*) of the prayer will have been made and the Mahdī will gesture for ʿĪsā ﷺ to lead the prayer, but he will refuse, saying that the call to commence was made for the Mahdī, and thus he is more rightful for the position.

It has been related that ʿĪsā ﷺ will remain on earth for forty years, after which he will pass away, and the Muslims will pray over him and bury him between the Prophet ﷺ and Abū Bakr. According to another narration, they will bury him between Abū Bakr and ʿUmar ؓ. The duration of his stay has also been narrated to be only seven years, which is said to be the more correct opinion. Therefore, the forty years mentioned in the first narration comprises of the total length of his life on earth before and after being raised to the heavens, for he was raised at the age of thirty-three. During ʿĪsā's ﷺ time on earth, Gog and Magog will appear and will eventually be destroyed by the blessing of his supplication against them. Then the believers will all die and the sun will rise from the west and the Qur'ān will be lifted from the face of the earth. Qurṭubī mentions that this will occur after the death of ʿĪsā ﷺ and after the Abyssinians (Ḥabasha) destroy the Kaʿba. [326–327]

Allāh Most High guides whom He wills to the Straight Path, that is, He bestows divine guidance (*tawfīq*) and keeps whom He wills steadfast upon correct beliefs and virtuous deeds, through the connection of His preeternal will with His guidance. The statement of the Great Imām (may Allāh have mercy on him) "Allāh guides whom He wills . . ." is as though He is saying, "Our responsibility is only to convey the message, and Allāh guides whom He wills to the Straight Path."

207 *Muslim,* "al-Fitan wa ashrāṭ al-sāʿa," 5162.

O Allāh, O Guider of the guided ones, guide us to the straight path through Your generosity and immense kindness, O Clement One. May peace be upon our master Muḥammad and his family, Companions, and upon all the prophets and messengers; and all praises to Allāh, the Lord of the worlds. This blessed commentary has been completed with praise to Allāh and through His assistance and His excellent divine success.

Bibliography

Abed, Shukri B. *Aristotelian Logic and the Arabic Language in Alfarabi.* New York: State University of New York Press, 1411/1991.

Abū Ḥanīfa, Nuʿmān ibn Thābit al-Kūfī. *Al-ʿĀlim wa 'l-Mutaʿallim, Al-Fiqh al-Absaṭ, Al-Fiqh al-Akbar, Risāla Abī Ḥanīfa, Al-Waṣiyya* [a collection of the five books of Abū Ḥanīfa]. Ed. Muḥammad Zāhid al-Kawtharī. First Edition. Cairo: Al-Maktaba al-Azhariyya li 'l-Turāth, 1421/2001.

Abū Zahra, Muḥammad. *Ḥayāt Imām Abī Ḥanīfa* [an Urdu translation with notes by Ghulām Aḥmad Ḥarīrī]. Faisalabad, 1403/1983.

al-ʿAjlūnī, Ismāʿīl ibn Muḥammad ibn ʿAbd al-Hādī al-Jarrāḥī al-Shāfiʿī. *Kashf al-Khafāʾ wa Muzīl al-Ilbās ʿamma 'Shtuhira min al-Aḥādīth ʿalā Alsinat al-Nās.* Ed. Muḥammad ʿAbd al-ʿAzīz al-Khālidī. 2 vols. First Edition. Beirut: Dār al-Kutub al-ʿIlmiyya, 1418/1997.

al-Baghdādī, Abū Bakr Aḥmad ibn ʿAlī ibn Thābit al-Khaṭīb. *Tārīkh Madīnat al-Salām wa Akhbār Muḥaddithīhā wa Dhikru Quṭṭānihā 'l-ʿUlamāʾ min Ghayri Ahlihā wa Wāridihā.* Ed. Bashshār ʿAwwād Maʿrūf. 17 vols and 3 supplementary vols. First Edition. Beirut: Dār al-Gharb al-Islāmī, 1422/2001.

al-Bājūrī, Ibrāhīm ibn Muḥammad ibn Aḥmad, and Ibrāhīm ibn Ḥasan Laqānī. *Tuḥfat al-Murīd ʿalā Jawharat al-Tawḥīd* [Bājūrī's commentary on Laqānī's poem]. Cairo: Maṭbaʿat al-Istiqāma, n.d.

———. *Ḥāshiyat al-Bājūrī ʿalā Matn al-Sanūsiyya fī 'l-ʿAqīda* [Muḥammad ibn Yūsuf al-Sanūsī's *Matn* printed above Bājūrī's interlineal commentary]. Ed. ʿAbd al-Salām Shannār. First Edition. Damascus: Dār al-Bayrūtī, 1415/1994.

al-Bayāḍī, Kamāl al-Dīn Aḥmad al-Ḥanafī. *Ishārāt al-Marām min ʿIbārāt al-Imām.* Ed. Yūsuf ʿAbd al-Razzāq al-Shāfiʿī and introduction by Muḥammad Zāhid al-Kawtharī. Reprint. Karachi: Zam Zam Publishers, 1425/2004.

Brockelmann, Carl. *Geschichte der Arabischen Litterature.* Second Edition. Leiden: Brille, 1361/1943.

al-Bukhārī, Abū ʿAbdillāh Muḥammad ibn Ismāʿīl. *Al-Jāmiʿ al-Musnad al-Ṣaḥīḥ al-Mukhtaṣar min Umūri Rasūlillāh wa Sunanihī wa Ayyāmihī* [the Arabic text of Bukhārī's *Al-Ṣaḥīḥ* with Aḥmad ʿAlī Sahāranpūrī and Abu 'l-Ḥasan al-Sindhī's marginalia, and Shāh Walī Allāh's work on the chapters and explanations (*Al-*

Abwāb wa 'l-Tarājim) of Bukhārī's book appended at the beginning of volume one]. 2 vols. 1305/1886. Reprint. Karachi: Qadīmī Kutub Khāna, n.d.

al-Bukhārī, Muḥammad Akbar Shāh. *Akābir ʿUlamā'e Deoband.* Lahore: Idāra Islāmiyyāt, 1419/1999.

The Concise Oxford Dictionary of Current English. Ed. R.E. Allen. Eighth Edition. England: Oxford University Press, 1411/1991.

Daiber, Hans. *The Islamic Concept of Belief in the 4th/10th Century: Abū l-Lait as-Samarqandī's Commentary on Abū Ḥanīfa (died 150/767) al-Fiqh al-absaṭ. Introduction, Text and Commentary.* Tokyo, 1995.

Doi, ʿAbd al-Raḥmān, I. *Sharī'ah: The Islamic Law.* London, Ta-Ha Publishers, 1404/1984.

———. *The Sciences of the Qur'ān: A Study in Methodology and Approach.* First Edition. Pretoria: Al-Madīnah Publishers, 1417/1997.

Elder, Earl Edger. *A Commentary on The Creed of Islam* [An English translation with Introduction and Notes on Taftāzānī's commentary on Nasafī's *ʿAqā'id*]. New York: Columbia University Press, 1400/1980.

Fawda, Saʿīd ʿAbd al-Laṭīf. *Al-Farq al-ʿAẓīm Bayn al-Tanzīh wa 'l-Tajsīm.* First Edition. Amman: Dār al-Rāzī, 1425/2004.

al-Ghazālī, Abū Ḥāmid. *Al-Ghazali: The Ninety Nine Beautiful Names of God* [An English translation with notes of Ghazālī's *Al-Maqṣad al-Asnā fī Sharḥ Asmā' Allāh al-Ḥusnā* by David B. Burrell and Nazih Dahler]. Reprint. Cambridge: Islamic Text Society, 1415/1995.

———. *Iljām al-ʿAwāmm ʿan ʿIlm al-Kalām.* Beirut: Dār al-Fikr, 1413/1993

Hughes, Thomas Patrick. *A Dictionary of Islam.* Lahore: Premier Book House, 1383/1964.

Iblāgh, ʿInāyatullāh. *Al-Imām al-Aʿẓam Abū Ḥanīfa al-Mutakallim.* Second Edition. Cairo: Wizārat al-Awqāf—Al-Majlis al-Aʿlā li 'l-Shu'ūn al-Islāmiyya, 1407/1987.

Ibn ʿĀbidīn, Muḥammad Amīn al-Shāmī, Muḥammad ibn ʿAlī al-Ḥaskafī, and Muḥammad ibn ʿAbdillāh al-Tumurtāshī. *Ḥāshiya Radd al-Muḥtār ʿala 'l-Durr al-Mukhtār Sharḥ Tanwīr al-Abṣār* [Ibn ʿĀbidīn's commentary on Ḥaskafī's *Al-Durr al-Mukhtār,* an interlineal exegesis of Tumurtāshī's *Tanwīr al-Abṣār*]. 7 vols. 1272/1855. Reprint. Beirut: Dār Iḥyā al-Turāth al-ʿArabī, n.d.

Ibn Abī 'l-ʿIzz, Muḥammad ibn ʿAlā' al-Dīn al-Ḥanafī. *Sharḥ al-ʿAqīda al-Ṭaḥāwiyya.* Ed. Muḥammad Nāṣir al-Dīn al-Albānī. Reprint. Karachi: Qadīmī Kutub Khāna, n.d.

Ibn Kathīr, Ismāʿīl ibn ʿUmar al-Qurashī al-Dimashqī. *Tafsīr al-Qur'ān al-ʿAẓīm.* 1 vol. Second Edition. Beirut: Dār Ibn Ḥazm, 1420/2000.

Ibn Nadīm, Muḥammad ibn Isḥāq. *Kitāb al-Fihrist.* Ed. Gustav Flügel. Beirut, 1385/1966.

Kaḥḥāla, ʿUmar Raḍā. *Muʿjam al-Mu'allifīn.* First Edition. Beirut: Mu'assasat al-Risāla, 1413/1993.

———. *Al-Mustadrak ʿalā Muʿjam al-Muʾallifīn.* Beirut: Muʾassasat al-Risāla, 1408/1988.

Kawtharī, Muḥammad Zāhid. *Muqaddimāt al-Imām al-Kawtharī.* Karachi: H. M. Saʿīd Company, n.d.

Keller, Nuh Ha Mim. *The Reliance of the Traveller. A Classic Manual of Sacred Law. In Arabic with Facing English Text, Commentary, and Appendices Edited and Translated. A Translation of Ibn Naqīb al-Miṣrī's ʿUmdat al-Sālik wa ʿUddat al-Manāsik.* Revised Edition. Evanston, Sunna Books, 1414/1994.

Khalīfa, Ḥājī (Kātib Çelebi). *Kashf al-Ẓunūn ʿan Asāmi 'l-Kutub wa 'l-Funūn.* Istanbul, 1360/1941.

al-Khuḍarī Bak, Muḥammad. *Itmām al-Wafāʾ fī Sīrat al-Khulafāʾ.* Ed. Maḥmūd al-Qaṭṭān. First Edition. Beirut: Dār Iḥyāʾ al-Turāth al-ʿArabī and Halab: Maktaba Usāma ibn Zayd, 1415/1995.

al-Kirlānī, Jalāl al-Dīn al-Khwārizmī. *Al-Kifāya fī Sharḥ al-Hidāya* [Kirlānī's commentary on *Al-Hidāya* printed below Ibn al-Humām's commentary *Fatḥ al-Qadīr*]. 9 vols. 1319/1901. Reprint. Beirut: Dār Iḥyāʾ al-Turāth al-ʿArabī, n.d.

Lane, E. W. *Arabic-English Lexicon.* Cambridge: Islamic Text Society, 1404/1984.

al-Maghnīsāwī, Abu 'l-Muntahā Aḥmad ibn Muḥammad. *Sharḥ al-Fiqh al-Akbar.* Reprint. First Edition. Karachi: Qadīmī Kutub Khāna. 1971/1391. [This edition was used as the primary text for the translation of this work.]

———. Second Edition. Hyderabad Deccan: Jamʿiyya Dāʾirat al-Maʿārif al-ʿUthmāniyya, 1365/1945.

al-Maydānī, ʿAbd al-Ghanī al-Ghunaymī. *Sharḥ al-ʿAqīda al-Ṭaḥāwiyya al-Musammā bi Bayān al-Sunna wa 'l-Jamāʿa* [Maydānī's interlineal exegesis on Ṭaḥāwī's *ʿAqīda*]. Ed. Muḥammad Muṭīʿ al-Ḥāfiẓ and Muḥammad Riyāḍ al-Māliḥ. Second Edition. Damascus: Dār al-Fikr and Beirut: Dār al-Fikr al-Muʿāṣir, 1412/1970.

Mīrathī. Badre ʿĀlam. *Tarjumān al-Sunna.* 4 vols. Lahore: Idāra Islamiyyāt, n.d.

Muḥammad, Muḥy al-Dīn ibn Bahāʾ al-Dīn. *Al-Qawl al-Faṣl Sharḥ al-Fiqh al-Akbar.* Istanbul: Waqf al-Ikhlāṣ, 1994/1414.

al-Muttaqī, Abu 'l-Ḥasan ʿAlāʾ al-Dīn ʿAlī ibn Ḥusām al-Dīn al-Hindī. *Kanz al-ʿUmmāl fī Sunan al-Aqwāl wa 'l-Afʿāl.* Ed. Isḥāq al-Ṭībī. 2 vols. Second Edition. Amman: Bayt al-Afkār al-Duwaliyya, 1426/2005.

al-Naysābūrī, Muslim ibn al-Ḥajjāj, and Yaḥyā ibn Sharaf al-Nawawī. *Al-Musnad al-Ṣaḥīḥ al-Mukhtaṣar min al-Sunan bi Naql al-ʿAdl ʿan al-ʿAdl ʿan Rasūli 'Llāh* ﷺ [the Arabic text of Muslim's *Al-Ṣaḥīḥ* above Nawawī's commentary with Abu 'l-Ḥasan al-Sindhī's marginalia at the bottom of the page]. Second Edition. 1375/1956. Reprint. Karachi: Qadīmī Kutub Khāna, n.d.

Nuʿmānī, Shiblī. *Imām Abū Ḥanīfa: Life and Works* [an English translation of Nuʿmānī's *Sīrat al-Nuʿmān* by M. Hadi Hussein]. Reprint. Karachi: Darul Ishaat, 1421/2000.

al-Patnī, Muḥammad ibn Ṭāhir ibn ʿAlī al-Gujrātī al-Hindī. *Majmaʿ Biḥār al-Anwār.*

Hyderabad Deccan: Maṭbaᶜ al-ᶜUthmāniyya, and Third Edition. Madīna Munawwara: Maktaba Dār al-Īmān, 1415/1994.

———. *Al-Mughnī fī Ḍabt Asmāʾ al-Rijāl.* Lahore and Karachi: Idāra Islāmiyyāt, n.d., and *Kitāb al-Mughnī fī Ḍabt Asmāʾ al-Ruwāt wa 'l-Anbāʾ.* Ed. Zayn al-ᶜĀbidīn al-Aᶜẓamī. First Edition. Kashmir, India: Maktaba Dār al-ᶜUlūm al-Raḥīmiyya Bāndīpūra, 1426/2006.

al-Qārī, Mullā ᶜAlī ibn Sulṭān Muḥammad. *Minaḥ al-Rawḍ al-Azhar* [Qārī's commentary on Abū Ḥanīfa's *Al-Fiqh al-Akbar* with marginalia by the editor Wahbī Sulaymān Ghāwjī al-Albānī named *Al-Taᶜlīq al-Muyassar ᶜalā Sharḥ al-Fiqh al-Akbar*]. Beirut: Dār al-Bashā'ir al-Islāmiyya. First Edition, 1998/1419.

———. *Sharḥ al-Kitāb al-Fiqh al-Akbar.* Ed. ᶜAlī Muḥammad Dandal. First Edition. Beirut: Dār al-Kutub al-ᶜIlmiyya, 1995/1416.

———. *Sharḥ Mullā ᶜAlī ibn Sulṭān Muḥammad al-Qārī al-Ḥanafī ᶜala 'l-Fiqh al-Akbar.* Second Edition. Cairo: Maktaba Muṣṭafā al-Bābī al-Ḥalabī wa Awlāduhū, 1375/1955.

———. *Ḍaw' al-Maᶜālī li Bad' al-Amālī* [Qārī's commentary on Abu 'l-Ḥasan Sirāj al-Dīn ᶜAlī ibn ᶜUthmān al-Ūshī's *Bad' al-Amālī*]. Dār al-Ṭibāᶜa al-ᶜĀmira, n.d.

al-Qazwīnī, ᶜAbū ᶜAbdillāh Muḥammad ibn Yazīd Ibn Māja. *Al-Sunan* [the Arabic text of Ibn Māja's *Sunan* with ᶜAbd al-Ghanī al-Dihlawī al-Madanī's marginalia *Injāḥ al-Ḥāja,* Jalāl al-Dīn al-Suyūṭī's *Miṣbāḥ al-Zujāja,* and other marginalia by Fakhr al-Ḥasan Gangōhī]. Reprint. Karachi: Qadīmī Kutub Khāna, n.d.

Ṣafdar, Muḥammad Sarfrāz Khān. *Maqāme Abū Ḥanīfa.* Gujrānwālā, 1416/1996.

al-Sakhāwī, Muḥammad ibn ᶜAbd al-Raḥmān. *Al-Qawl al-Badīᶜ fi 'l-Ṣalāt ᶜala 'l-Ḥabīb al-Shafīᶜ.* Ed. Muḥammad ᶜAwwāma. First Edition. Beirut: Mu'assasat al-Rayyān, 1422/2000.

al-Ṣāwī, Aḥmad ibn Muḥammad al-Mālikī, and Ibrāhīm ibn Ḥasan Laqānī. *Kitāb Sharḥ al-Ṣāwī ᶜalā Jawharat al-Tawḥīd* [Ṣāwī's commentary on Laqānī's poem]. Ed. ᶜAbd al-Fattāḥ al-Bizm. Third Edition. Damascus and Beirut: Dār Ibn Kathīr, 1424/2003.

Sezgin, Fuat. *Tārīkh al-Turāth al-ᶜArabī* [a translation of Sezgin's *Geschichte des Arabischen Schrifttums* in Arabic by Maḥmūd Fahmī Ḥijāzī]. Revised by ᶜArafa Muṣṭafā and Saᶜīd ᶜAbd al-Raḥīm. 10 vols. [Riyāḍ]: Idārat al-Thaqāfa wa 'l-Nashr bi 'l-Jāmiᶜa Imām Muḥammad ibn Ṣaᶜūd al-Islāmiyya. 1403/1983.

Shahrastānī, Muḥammad ibn ᶜAbd al-Karīm ibn Abī Bakr Aḥmad. *Al-Milal wa 'l-Niḥal.* Ed. Muḥammad Saᶜīd Kaylānī. 2 vols. Beirut: Dār al-Maᶜrifa, 1404/1983.

Sheikh, M. Saeed. *A Dictionary of Muslim Philosophy.* Second Edition. Lahore: Institute of Islamic Culture, 1401/1981.

al-Sijistānī, ᶜAbū Dāwūd Sulaymān ibn al-Ashᶜath. *Al-Sunan.* Ed. Maḥmūd al-Ḥasan Gangōhī Deobandī. 1316/1898. Reprint. Multan: Maktaba Ḥaqqāniyya, n.d.

al-Ṭabāṭabā'ī, Sayyid Muḥammad Ḥusayn. *Shi'ite Islam* [a translation of Ṭabāṭabā'īs

Shīʿah dar Islām into English with an introduction by Seyyed Hossein Nasr]. London: George Allen and Unwin Ltd, 1394/1975.

al-Taftāzānī, Saʿd al-Dīn Masʿūd ibn ʿUmar. *Sharḥ al-ʿAqāʾid al-Nasafiyya* [Taftāzānī's commentary on Nasafī's *ʿAqāʾid* along with referencing of the ḥadīths by Jalāl al-Dīn al-Suyūṭī]. Ed. Muḥammad ʿAdnān Darwīsh. Published by the editor, 1411/1990.

Ṭāhir, Barusehlī Muḥammad. *Osmanlı Müellifleri* [in Ottoman Arabic]. Istanbul, 1333/1914.

al-Tirmidhī, Abū ʿĪsā Muḥammad ibn ʿĪsā, and Anwar Shāh Kashmīrī. *Al-Jāmiʿ al-Mukhtaṣar min al-Sunan* [the Arabic text of Tirmidhī's *Sunan* above Kashmīrī's commentary *Al-ʿArf al-Shadhī,* with ʿAlī ibn al-Sayyid Sulaymān al-Dimnatī al-Mālikī's marginalia *Nafʿ Qūt al-Mughtadhī,* Maḥmūd al-Ḥasan Deobandī's lecture notes at the front of the edition, and Tirmidhī's *Kitāb al-ʿIlal* (*al-Ṣughrā*) and *Al-Shamāʾil* appended at the end]. Karachi: Saʿīd Company Limited, n.d.

Usmani, Muhammad Taqi. *ʿUlūm al-Qurʾān.* Deoband: Kutub Khāna Naʿīmiyya, n.d.

Webster's New World Pocket Geographical Dictionary based on Webster's New World Dictionary of American English. New York: Prentice Hall, 1414/1994.

Wehr, Hans. *A Dictionary of Modern Written Arabic.* Ed. J Milton Cowan. Reprint. Beirut: Librarie Du Liban. 1395/1976.

Wensinck, A. J. *The Muslim Creed: Its Genesis and Historical Development.* London: Frank Cass & Co. Ltd., 1384/1965.

al-Zabīdī, Muḥammad ibn Muḥammad al-Murtaḍā. *Itḥāf al-Sāda al-Muttaqīn bi Sharḥ Iḥyāʾ ʿUlūm al-Dīn* [Zabīdī's commentary on Ghazālī's *Iḥyāʾ ʿUlūm al-Dīn* with the *Iḥyāʾ* in the margins]. 10 vols. Reprint. Beirut: Dār al-Fikr, n.d.

al-Ziriklī, Khayr al-Dīn. *Al-Aʿlām: Qāmūs Tarājim li Ashhar al-Rijāl wa 'l-Nisāʾ min al-ʿArab wa 'l-Mustaʿrabīn wa 'l-Mustashriqīn.* 8 vols. Beirut: Dār al-ʿIlm li 'l-Malāyīn, 1399/1979.

Manuscripts of *Al-Fiqh al-Akbar* and its commentaries used in this work for verification and reference purposes.

Abū Ḥanīfa, Nuʿmān ibn Thābit al-Kūfī. *Al-Fiqh al-Akbar.*

———. *MS. 2756,* University of Al-Azhar Library

———. *MS. 5844,* University of Al-Azhar Library

———. *MS. 92443,* University of Al-Azhar Library

al-Qārī, Mullā ʿAlī ibn Sulṭān Muḥammad. *Minaḥ al-Rawḍ al-Azhar fī Sharḥ al-Fiqh al-Akbar*

———. *MS. 2368,* University of Al-Azhar Library

———. *MS. 17924,* University of Al-Azhar Library
———. *MS. 2743,* University of Al-Azhar Library
———. *MS. 20574,* University of Al-Azhar Library
———. *MS. 44726,* University of Al-Azhar Library
———. *MS. 74634,* University of Al-Azhar Library

al-Maghnīsāwī, Abu 'l-Muntahā Aḥmad ibn Muḥammad. *Sharḥ al-Fiqh al-Akbar*
———. *MS. 1198,* University of Al-Azhar Library
———. *MS. 42996* (1149 AH), University of Al-Azhar Library
———. *MS. 91438* (1104 AH), University of Al-Azhar Library
———. *MS. 4405,* University of Al-Azhar Library [This includes what seems to be either an extended commentary by Maghnīsāwī or a gloss on his commentary by someone else but without any separation between the two or mention of any other author.]
———. *MS. 41174,* University of Al-Azhar Library
———. *MS. 44723,* University of Al-Azhar Library
———. *MS. 33366,* (incomplete) University of Al-Azhar Library
———. *MS. 1062,* (Daibar collection 18) University of Tokyo Library
———. *MS. 145,* (Daibar collection 5) University of Tokyo Library
———. *MS. 2401,* (Daibar collection 18) University of Tokyo Library

Abū Ḥanīfa, Nuʿmān ibn Thābit al-Kūfī. *Kitāb al-Waṣiyya*
———. *MS. 5844,* University of Al-Azhar Library

Index

For definitions of terminology used and biographies of those authorities quoted in this work, please refer to the first page of their occurrence, which is indexed below.